THE MYSTICAL WAY

OTHER BOOKS BY
WILLIAM JOHNSTON

Being In Love
Lord, Teach Us To Pray
Silent Music
The Wounded Stag
The Mirror Mind
The Still Point
The Mysticism of *The Cloud of Unknowing*

TRANSLATIONS
From the Japanese
Silence (by Shusaku Endo)
The Bells of Nagasaki (by Takashi Nagai)

From the Middle English
The Cloud of Unknowing

THE MYSTICAL WAY

William Johnston

With a new Foreword

Originally published as *Silent Music* (1974)
and *The Wounded Stag* (1984)

Fount
An Imprint of HarperCollinsPublishers

Fount Paperbacks is an imprint of
HarperCollins*Religious*
Part of HarperCollins*Publishers*
77–85 Fulham Palace Road,
Hammersmith, London W6 8JB

First published in Great Britain
in 1993 by Fount Paperbacks

1 3 5 7 9 10 8 6 4 2

The material in this book was first published as follows:
Silent Music © William Johnston 1974, published in London in 1974 by
William Collins Sons & Co. Ltd, and in New York by Harper & Row, Inc.
The Wounded Stag © William Johnston 1984, published in London by
William Collins Sons & Co. Ltd, and in New York
(under the title *Christian Mysticism Today*) by Harper & Row, Inc.

William Johnston asserts the moral right to
be identified as the author of this work

A catalogue record for this book is
available from the British Library

ISBN 0 00 627665 2

Printed and bound in Great Britain by
HarperCollinsManufacturing Glasgow

FOREWORD

The twentieth century, which has seen so many revolutions, is now witnessing the rise of a new mysticism within Christianity. Built on total commitment to Jesus Christ and the Gospel, this mysticism is in continuity with what went before. Augustine and Bonaventure would recognize it as their own; the author of *The Cloud of Unknowing* and John of the Cross would greet it with a smile. And yet it has its own peculiar characteristics that make it different from the mysticism of the past. It is a unique product of our turbulent twentieth century.

For the new mysticism has learned much from the great religions of Asia. It has felt the impact of yoga and Zen and the monasticism of Tibet. It pays attention to posture and breathing; it knows about the music of the mantra and the silence of *samadhi*; it puts value on health and longevity and the development of human potential. Furthermore, it dialogues with modern science where contemplation of limitless space and the wonders of the subatomic world have forced bewildered scientists to look again at the paradoxes of the mystics. Such a mysticism could only come to birth in the twentieth century.

Needless to say, all Christian mysticism, old or new, has its roots in the New Testament, particularly in the writings of John and Paul. It flourished in the lives and writings of the Greek fathers, and it formed the very core of the great religious orders that came to birth in the Middle Ages. And then in the twentieth century Christian spirituality, like Christian theology, seemed to break down. The old ways did not suit the new people. This was the time of crisis, confusion, frustration.

Then it was that enterprising people went in search of new ways. Liturgical renewal opened up paths to deep prayer. Biblical studies brought many to the living word of God. The charismatic renewal opened minds and hearts to the action of the Holy Spirit. And at that time some imaginative people looked to the wisdom of Asia, asking if there also the Spirit was working and saying something to the world.

The two books published as *The Mystical Way* speak of the new mysticism, though at that time I did not use this terminology. To *Silent Music* I originally gave the subtitle "The science of mysticism" but the publisher, thinking that mysticism would not sell, asked me to change to "The science of meditation". The book was written in the context of dialogue with Asia and with modern science. It discusses not only meditation but also healing and the interpersonal relations that preoccupy modern men and women. The second book is *The Wounded Stag*. Written after a six-month stay in Israel, it emphasizes that while the new mysticism is in dialogue with other religions it is thoroughly Christian. Based on the Eucharist it opens one to a love for justice and peace.

Since these books were written, new forms of prayer have spread throughout the Christian world. Whereas the old mysticism was the monopoly of priests and monks and nuns, the new mysticism flourishes among the laity. Everywhere we find men and women sitting quietly and reciting a mantra; or they breathe silently before eucharist or ikon; or they wrestle with a biblical *koan*; or they pray musically in tongues. Now we see Christian forms of oga and Zen and vipassana. Assuredly we cannot immediately call these prayer-forms mystical; but they are gateways to mysticism. Those who persevere will find that God's grace quickly leads them to Teresa's prayer of quiet, where the important thing is not to think much but to love much. And from there they may pass to the higher mansions of a contemporary interior castle.

Karl Rahner once observed that the fervent Christian of the future will be a mystic. He did not say that the fervent Christian of the future will be a saint. He knew that Chrsitains will always be sinners. But in the midst of sin God's grace rises up mightily (Did not Paul say, "When I am weak, then I am strong"?) and spreads to the entire world.

And so, when future generations look back on the twentieth century they will see that the turmoil and crisis which seemed to herald disaster were really signs of growth. Painfully, very painfully, as the mother writhed in agony, a new child was born.

God has not abandoned his people. He will be with them all days, even to the consummation of the world.

Sophia University,
Tokyo,
1 January, 1993

SILENT MUSIC

THE SCIENCE OF MEDITATION

*For
all my friends
in Reno*

My Beloved is the mountains, the solitary wooded valleys, strange islands . . . silent music.

St John of the Cross

CONTENTS

Preface   *page* 9

PART I: MEDITATION   13

  1 The meditation movement   15
  2 The new science   23
  3 Brainwave and biofeedback   34
  4 The science of mysticism   48

PART II: CONSCIOUSNESS   57

  5 Initiation   59
  6 The road to ecstasy   73
  7 Return to the market-place   86
  8 A perilous journey   99

PART III: HEALING   113

  9 Meditation, therapy and passive energy   115
 10 The healing of the mind   123
 11 The deeper healing   132
 12 Cosmic healing   142

PART IV: INTIMACY   151

 13 Meditation and intimacy   153
 14 Mystical friendship   162
 15 Friendship – the cosmic dimension   173

EPILOGUE   179

 16 Convergence   181

Glossary of words used in the text   187
Books and articles quoted in the text   191
Index   195

PREFACE

It has become a commonplace to say that the human race stands at a unique point in its turbulent history and that we are faced with a new age. Talk of travel in outer space and of adventures in inner space reminds us that things are not what they used to be – that the old order changes, yielding place to new. Perhaps we really are on the brink of a brave new world. What kind of world this will be no one is quite sure. We just feel that something is stirring in the consciousness of modern man.

Among the many fascinating characteristics of the incipient, new age is the contemporary longing for dialogue. Already Hindu and Jew, Christian and Buddhist are coming together in sincerity and harmony to exchange experiences and to explore common goals. And as interfaith dialogue gets under way, it finds itself extending a hand of welcome to an unexpected newcomer on the scene; namely, the scientist. For now we find a group of serious-minded scientists, students of consciousness, who express a desire to learn more about the great religious traditions which have accumulated such wealth of experiential knowledge about the human mind. These are scholars who feel that their research will be incomplete unless it takes into consideration the experiences of the mystic and the discoveries of the man who meditates.

The religious activity that interests these scientists is not speculative theology but meditation. And this is indeed fortunate. Because meditation is precisely the area in which the great religions find themselves most united. I myself have discovered this in discussion with Buddhists in Japan. We found that dialogue based on theology and philosophy did not achieve much; but when we talked from experience we suddenly discovered how closely united we really were. So it is refreshing to see that the religio-scientific dialogue, like the inter-religious dialogue, will begin with meditation.

This book, then, is about meditation. Let me say, however, that the choice of this word has caused me some anguish. I use it in the widest possible sense to include discursive thinking and reasoning about ultimate matters as well as what Christians call *contemplation* and Hindus call *samadhi*[1] and Buddhists call *Zen*. In it I also include mysticism – which, in my opinion, is no more than a very deep form of meditation. It was difficult to find an all-embracing word that would include these disparate things, and it seemed to me that "meditation" was the best. For me meditation, in the last analysis, is the search for wisdom or the relishing of wisdom when it has been found. As such it is a word and a practice that unites us all. Religionists, scientists, businessmen and states-men can claim that they are looking for, and feel the need of, wisdom. And how beautiful and attractive this lady is! I am reminded of the Hebrew sage who loved her passionately and sang:

> I loved her and sought her from my youth,
> and I desired to take her for my bride,
> and I became enamoured of her beauty.

> (Wisdom 8:2)

This is the lady who enthralls both scientist and mystic. "My beloved is the mountains, the solitary wooded valleys, strange islands . . . silent music."

I sincerely hope that what I here write will be of interest and value to anyone who loves wisdom, whatever his religious affiliations or whatever his lack of them. While I myself am firmly entrenched in the Hebrew-Christian tradition, which I love more deeply than I can say, I have had the inestimable privilege of entering into dialogue with men and women of other faiths and other religious traditions. This has helped me a lot; and I would like this book to be an expression of gratitude to people who have greatly inspired me, even when they did not always share my convictions.

While writing, I have been somewhat fascinated by the word *tao*, meaning *way*. We ordinarily associate this word with oriental thought; and rightly so. But it is also interesting to recall that it is a profoundly biblical word. Its Greek equivalent, (*hodos*), is found no less than 880 times in the Septuagint, to say nothing of its frequent

---

[1] Explanations of this and other words which may be unfamiliar to the reader are given in the glossary at the end of the book.

use in the Synoptic Gospels, St John and the writings of St Paul. And in many cases its use is figurative, resembling closely that of the Orient. So *way*, like meditation, is a word that brings us together.

There are, I believe, many ways to wisdom. Each religion is a way and within each religion many smaller ways open up. In this book I try to outline some of the ways of meditation such as the repetition of a word or *mantra*, attention to the breathing, the use of the *mandala* and other methods of deepening consciousness. These are ways that are the same, and yet different, according to the faith of the meditator. But I also contend that friendship is a way, as also is purification or healing. And again I believe that the scientist has his way. All these ways influence one another. Knowledge of other ways can help the wanderer to find his own path and it can guide the traveller or pilgrim as he journeys towards wisdom, sometimes in anguish and dismay and temptation.

Dialogue between travellers of the various ways is surely one of the most significant events in our day. As the human race comes together with unprecedented rapidity, anyone with common sense knows that we must get together, form a single family and build the earth. For it is another commonplace that there is no longer any alternative to peace. Can it be that the Lady Wisdom will show us the way to union and harmony?

Finally, let me say that I am greatly indebted to a number of people for the experiences, insights and ideas they shared with me. First, I would like to express my deep gratitude to the Reno Carmelites, and especially to Laureen Grady, who worked with me in the writing of this book. Then I must thank my cousin, Dr Kevin Clearkin, who gave me so many stimulating ideas and so much encouragement – and also his wife, Flora, who looked after our material needs as we talked. Finally, there is Dr Tomio Hirai, of Tokyo University, with whom I spent many pleasant hours sipping green tea while talking about brainwave and biofeedback. His enlightening conversation and his meticulous research have let me see how sincerely the modern scientist searches for wisdom.

Sophia University,
Tokyo,
1974

PART I

MEDITATION

1

The meditation movement

The last decade has witnessed the rise of a great meditation movement which gathers momentum and appeals to men and women in all walks of life. Zen and Yoga, no longer a monopoly of the East, have become part of world culture and are practised not only by Buddhists and Hindus but also by Westerners – many of whom find in this methodology a way of deepening their traditional faith. Even more widespread than these, however, is transcendental meditation, popularly known as TM. Introduced to the West by the Maharishi Mahesh Yogi, this form of Yoga is now practised by tens of thousands of people in Europe and America. No doubt one reason for its popularity and wide appeal is the very simplicity and ease with which it can be practised by the ordinary person. Though religious in origin, going back for several millennia, the transcendental meditation introduced to the West is not attached to any one religion. Rather is it a means for developing human potential, thus enabling people to devote themselves with greater totality to the job on hand or to commit themselves more fully to their vocation.

Transcendental meditation has had its greatest success with students and young professors, but it is not without impact on the world of business. For, yes, the world of economics, too, casts an eye in the direction of meditation. We now hear the interesting news that business tycoons discover the value of silence and of the quiet room to which bruised and harassed executives can retire to find peace and inner security. And here another kind of meditational exercise is speedily making headway – meditation associated with biofeedback and the use of machines. This has been called "electronic yoga" and I would like to say more about it later. For now, enough to quote the *New York Times* for 16 April 1972 on "the biofeedback revolution that some people say is flowing over the country, creating a multi-million dollar industry with broad implications for physicians, government officials, teachers, scientists and businessmen". I laughed when I read this because the only class omitted from the list of interested persons is the clergy. Have they lost their interest in meditation? Or will they too become part of the business that is fast becoming part of modern culture and is already entering the curriculum of our schools? Be that as it may, biofeedback machines, advertised as teachers of meditation, are already cheaply available (though admittedly good ones are not cheap) and with them most people can learn in some measure to regulate their internal states of consciousness. No doubt transistorized biofeedback machines will soon be exported in large quantities from Japan and introduced to the hungry West.

Again, meditation in the business world is frequently linked to the numerous mind-control courses that are everywhere springing up. These courses teach deep relaxation and claim to introduce people to profound and subtle layers of psychic life. I had an opportunity to attend one such course in downtown New York. We were taught to take up a comfortable position, relax and "get our level"; that is to say, to enter into a deeper and healthier level of mind beyond the consciousness concerned with discursive reasoning. For anyone who has practised a little meditation this is not new; but the mind-control course went on to speak, somewhat alarmingly, about thought-projection, about programming oneself and others, about the diagnosis of illness, about psychic healing and all kinds of parapsychological activities. This was more challenging. It was not only a course in the power of positive thinking but also in the development of psychic powers. One aspect of the thing that interested me personally was the emphasis placed on visualization. We were taught to visualize minutely the place in which we could best relax, or the person with whom we wished to communicate telepathically. Visualization, it was claimed, makes this exercise more effective; and this interested me in view of the stress placed on visualization in certain religious traditions of meditation. It is not my intention here to evaluate mind-control. Enough to say that, even if I could not accept everything and if, alas, my telepathic efforts got me nowhere, I had a pleasant four days with a charming group of people. I had been led to think that these courses make their appeal to grim-jawed stockbrokers, red-faced businessmen and hard-nosed politicians; but the one I attended was not like that. In our group the feminine and artistic element predominated. A delightful, if exhausting, time was had by all.

Within Christianity, too, meditation is in vogue. Traditionally, it is true, silent and wordless contemplation was mainly for an élite of monks and nuns; but in recent times the people at large have shown a desire for deeper meditation. One of its popular forms is the famous *Jesus Prayer* which originated in the early Greek Church and was associated with the Hesychast movement. Like transcendental meditation this is practised by the constant repetition of a *mantra* or sacred word, in this case the word "Jesus". Not only are the vibrations important, the meaning of the word is also of the greatest significance. Through it one becomes more and more committed to, and identified with, the Jesus whose name is invoked. In some Pentecostal groups, too, a meditational dimension seems to be taking shape. Perhaps people are beginning to feel the need of solitude and silence to complement the communal experience that characterizes this form of shared prayer. Not that contemplation is necessarily absent from group worship. Most people who have taken part in group prayer will have sensed the deep interior silence that sometimes enshrouds the whole gathering as though the Spirit were palpably present. This, I believe, is a type of communal contemplation, a form of meditation that is particularly marked in a community of love. Here it is not only the individual but also the group that relishes an obscure sense of enveloping presence. Such an experience can also be found in Quaker meetings. Indeed this is a dimension of prayer that the Friends have always preserved and now share with others in a spirit of ecumenical generosity.

Again within Christianity there is the arrival of Christian Zen. While it is true that Christianity is still groping experimentally with this form of meditation, things are beginning to happen. Not long ago, a Japanese Zen master in the USA donned the Cistercian habit and led a retreat or *sesshin* for Christian monks, giving them as their *koan* the paradoxical and enigmatic problem, "What do you mean when you make the sign of the cross?" This was interesting for me because it confirmed my conviction that the crucifix is the great Christian *koan*. Be that as it may, in the coming decade some form of Zen may well develop within Christianity, enriching it with a new and beautiful dimension.

Many more instances of meditation movements could be cited. I mention these few; and it will be noticed that the common factor uniting such disparate things is a tendency to go beyond the emotional and intellectual consciousness to the deeper, more unified, intuitive or mystical consciousness. That is why these forms of meditation have few words. And sometimes they have no words at all. One is simply held in intense silence and unification, only conscious of the breathing or the beating of the heart or an obscure sense of presence. Modern people, it seems, are less attracted by wordy prayer. "In praying do not heap up empty phrases as the Gentiles do; for they think that they will be heard for their many words" (Matthew 6:7). People are now looking for silence, for depth, for interiority, for what has traditionally been called contemplation. They want something that opens up deeper layers of consciousness, bringing into play the more subtle and mystical faculties of the mind. This is what elsewhere I have called "vertical meditation" because it spirals down into its own silent depths, to the core of the being. Perhaps it is because this kind of meditative silence is found in the Japanese tea-ceremony, flower arrangement, archery and the rest that these have greatly attracted Western interest in recent times.

No doubt one reason for this boom is the realization that meditation brings interior unity. This is stressed by a medieval English mystic who charmingly speaks of meditation as a "oneing exercise" because it makes us whole. And the modern denizen of technopolis, torn asunder by the intolerable pressures of the global village and by the total involvement demanded by TV and advertising, finds himself torn in pieces by anguish, guilt and anxiety. And so he longs for unity and strength to cope with future shock. McLuhan said well that man must learn to defend himself against the tyranny of mass media; but he did not say clearly how this can be done. Many people seem to have found that meditation is one answer. Businessmen, psychologists and religionists are beginning to feel that it may indeed be so.

Now, as I have pointed out, a fascinating aspect of this whole meditation boom is that it is by no means confined to the ostensibly or professionally religious. We find ourselves confronted with the paradoxical picture of people meditating night and morning while claiming that they believe in nothing – neither in God nor in Christ nor in Krishna nor in the Buddha. In short, there is abroad a secular or seemingly agnostic brand of mystical meditation that disclaims affiliation with any religion and is totally devoted to the development of human potential. One might ask if twentieth-century man, having secularized art, music, poetry, education and politics, has finally decided to do the job properly and secularize prayer. After all, he needs prayer no less than he needs air and water, so he might as well have it without the burdensome trappings and useless paraphernalia of Christianity, Buddhism or anything else. In short, it might look as if the man of the 1970s begins to opt for prayer without religion.

To the traditional Jew or Christian, educated to look on meditation as a cry to God, this may seem incredible and he may wonder why anyone should take the trouble to meditate if he has no faith. But this radically secular meditation is much less strange to the Japanese who have known of such practice for generations. Zen, which originated in China and was practised there for centuries as a religious exercise, was quickly used in Japan, first by *samurai*, then by suicide pilots, and finally by business tycoons. This is one more example of the eminent practicality of the Japanese, who could adapt an originally religious exercise to waging war, making efficient washing-machines, and curing the common cold. Who but the Japanese could have done such a thing? Yet this is precisely what they did. And today one can see groups of fresh young executives sitting assiduously in Zen temples to expand their consciousness and enhance their devotion to the world of economics. And now the West, which knows a good thing when it sees it, follows suit. What makes yen in Tokyo might make dollars on Wall Street or pounds in Piccadilly. So why not give it a try?

But let me not be cynical. Even as I write I am aware that much of the seemingly agnostic meditation is not agnostic at all. Frequently the self-styled agnostic who meditates is searching for something ultimate. And the person who searches believes, or hopes, that an answer exists somewhere. In this sense he is not agnostic. Many meditators are in quest of truth, wisdom, ultimate values – things they have failed to find within their own religious tradition. It could be plausibly argued that secular meditation has arisen partly because traditional and established religion has ceased to give people, particularly young people, the religious experience for which they are craving. So they look elsewhere. They are tired of dogmas and formulations and words – "Words, words, words!" said Hamlet. However necessary these formulations may be (and some formulation is, I believe, necessary), they can sometimes erect barriers between man and reality. And contemporary man wants reality; he wants experience; he wants practice; he wants a "way". Way or *tao*, the great Eastern word used to describe religious experience, appears frequently in the Old Testament; and Christians were called "followers of the way", just as their founder called himself the Way. Anyhow, experience of meditation gives people the sense of being on a way that goes somewhere; and that is what they want.

So the religious dimension is not absent from the meditation movement. To say this, however, intimates that I know the meaning of this enigmatic word "religious". Much time and effort and energy have been expended in attempts to say what the word means, and as yet there seems to be little unanimity of opinion. So perhaps I will be pardoned for giving my own definition.

Applied to meditation I would say that this exercise is not religious if one is meditating to improve one's general health or to relieve one's backache or to cure a migraine headache or to enhance one's business acumen. However noble and laudable these objectives, even the broadminded will scarcely call them religious. But if, over and above these things (without necessarily excluding them), one is searching for ultimate truth, for values, for wisdom; if one is preoccupied with what we now call "ultimate concern", then one's quest is religious. In a nutshell, what makes meditation religious or non-religious is one's sense of values and one's motivation. These are the all-important elements in the whole business.

In this sense I believe that many of the self-styled agnostic meditators are religiously motivated because they are searching for truth. And sooner or later, if they continue their practice, they will be confronted with ultimate questions of life and death and faith and the Absolute.

It will be perfectly clear by now that everything I have said presents a tremendously stimulating challenge to the traditional religions in their institutional forms. I myself believe that they have a great role to play in directing and promoting and inspiring this meditation movement. For the fact is that the development of human potential is a two-edged sword. It simply means that man will have increased powers either for good or for evil, for love or for hate, for war or for peace. More human potential will enable businessmen to exploit the poor or to build the *noosphere*. It may help politicians to enslave millions or to alleviate distress – to make better bombs or to purify the air we breathe. Everything depends on motivation. It is well known in all the great religions that mystical powers can be used for evil as well as for good; and when they are used for evil, the consequences are very, very evil. That is why the meditation movement is a challenge to the great religions, which are called to give values and motivation. They have to give guidance about what is important in life and about the goals towards which increased human potential should be directed. This, religionless meditation will not do. The role of religions will be to teach their gospel to the new, mystical man now emerging in the *noosphere*. They must save him from the quagmire of illusion and insecurity and mystical evil.

Christians have sometimes asked me about the relevance of TM and biofeedback and mind-control for their faith; and I have answered that whatever develops human potential should also develop Christian faith, provided this faith is alive and nourished by scripture and liturgy. I mean that if human potential is enhanced, then the totality of one's commitment to Christ can also be deepened. Having said this, however, I hasten to add my conviction that the Judaeo-Christian will soon have its own, vital part to play in the evolution of this meditation movement. Part of this role will be the sharing with others of the riches of the Western mystical tradition, just as others have generously shared with the West. In order to do this it will be necessary to revitalize and live this Western mysticism, making it relevant for the men of our day, whether they be students or scientists, businessmen or professors, housewives or labourers. If institutional religion has somehow failed those in search of meditation, this is partly because it has been unable to keep pace with the sudden evolutionary leap in consciousness that has characterized the last decade. We are now faced with a new man, a more mystical man, and it is on the mystical dimension of religion that we must fix our attention.

2

The new science

Perhaps the most intriguing aspect of the meditation movement is not the interest of students, professors and businessmen, but that of the scientists. For the scientists are the prophets of our day; when they praise a commodity the populace hastens to buy. But why this scientific interest?

For one thing it stems from a growing preoccupation with "altered states of consciousness". At the beginning of the century William James shrewdly observed in a famous sentence that our normal waking consciousness is but one special type of consciousness, while around it, parted from it by the flimsiest screens, there lie potential forms of consciousness entirely different. In other words, within the human mind are many, many worlds that are uncharted and unknown. Now psychologists become increasingly interested in these worlds; they become aware of the almost infinite possibilities for exploration in the field of human consciousness. It would seem that all the popular talk about exploratory trips in inner space is not just science fiction. Inner space is going to be quite as enthralling as outer space. LSD, mescalin and suchlike drugs (whatever may be said about their abuse) do reveal a new environment, a new world, another dimension of reality; and the psychophysiology of awareness promises to be one of the most exciting adventures of our exciting age. In short, we find ourselves at the threshold of a new science. This is the science of consciousness, of mind-expansion, of enhanced awareness.

This new science has received a boost from a series of conferences held at Council Grove in Kansas over the past few years and attended by psychiatrists, physicists, theologians, physicians, mathematicians, psychologists and engineers, from Denmark, Iceland, India, Japan, Germany, Canada, France, Chile and England. For the first session called the "Interdisciplinary

Conference on the Voluntary Control of Internal States of Consciousness", the invitation to the participants contained the following paragraph:

> The calling of a conference on states which have been variously termed altered states of consciousness, expanded consciousness, or states of internal awareness, is precipitated by the need for research in the domain of consciousness itself. We have reached a point in history at which the exploration of "internal states" has become not only a legitimate, but also a high-priority business of science. In addition, many people are conducting their own explorations in consciousness with unknown chemicals in psycho-actively-unknown dosages in an attempt to enhance life or escape from it. This can be a dangerous route to "freedom". The Conference Committee feels that at this moment it is especially important for stabilizing forces to be brought to bear that link what is useful from the past with the present and the future, uniting in some degree the existential wisdom and psychology of the East and the different psychological insights of the West.
>
> (Green(1))

The above reminds me of Teilhard's contention that we now stand at a unique point in human history, when the time is ripe for the development of a science of man; it also reveals the great contemporary interest in consciousness. Today even the man in the street (about whom we now hear so little) gets interested in recording his dreams and daydreams, while the scientist turns his attention not only to dreams but also to hypnotic trance, drug experience, and all that goes by the name of altered states of consciousness. A few serious psychologists begin to say that in the process of evolution man's brain and nervous system are developing a psychological and physiological need for these altered states – a need for a new kind of "high" that has not been found through drugs, alcohol and sex.

Now obviously anyone interested in states of consciousness

will enjoy something of a field-day when he comes to meditation, particularly to the meditation of the mystics who, centuries ago, experienced states that the psychologist is only now beginning to envisage. All meditation, once it gets deep, produces changes in the electrical activity of the brain, bringing the conscious and unconscious mind into closer proximity. The conscious mind impinges, so to speak, on the unconscious and is thus opened to receive messages and enlightenment from the dark and subliminal depths of one's being in a process that is analogous to, but different from, dreaming. "Zen is the prayer of the unconscious", remarked a bright student of mine. I would prefer to say that it is the prayer of the unconscious made conscious or becoming conscious. But be that as it may, the traditional metaphors for describing contemplative prayer – about spiritual sleep and so on – indicate the working of new levels of consciousness in the mystical depths of the mind, and cannot fail to attract the attention of the researcher in inner space.

Yet it is only in recent years that the scientist has begun to take notice of this profound human adventure that we call meditation. Asserting that scientific knowledge of this meditative realm of psychic life is totally inadequate, Dr Charles Tart of the University of California at Davis pleads for more research in this field:

> It seems likely that research in this area has been too long delayed through a combination of ignorance and prejudice. Scientists in general simply have not known anything about the rich tradition of meditation, and the intimate connection of meditation practices with religion has further removed it from the area of "acceptable" topics of study . . . Although prediction is premature, the potential contributions of the experimental study of meditation to such diverse areas as perceptual vigilance, psychotherapy, and creativity, in both a theoretical and practical sense, warrant a greatly expanded research effort. (Tart, p.176)

Since the above was written in 1964, considerable progress has been made. Yet it can still be said that, while altered states have been around for milennia, the science that investigates them is still in its infancy. Most researchers gladly admit to their appalling ignorance of the human mind. Even vocabulary-wise we are at a loss. In Sanskrit there are more than twenty words for what we blandly call "mind". But scientific jargon is being born. Now, not only ASC for *altered states of consciousness*, but also MSC for *meditation states of consciousness*, and HSC for *higher states of consciousness* and EIA for *enhanced internal awareness*. Personally I am glad and happy about the distinction between altered states of consciousness and meditation states of consciousness because I believe that the states arrived at through meditation are not "altered" in the sense of being bizarre or abnormal. Rather are they the most normal states – states that every man should pass through to fulfil his great vocation of hominization or becoming a man.

So we have a new science. And it is interesting to see that for a number of scientists the study of meditation states of consciousness is not just academic. It is also practical. I personally have met a number of scientists who themselves practise meditation and experience to some extent the states of consciousness that are the object of their research. They say they would feel unqualified to talk about these states without some degree of personal experience.

After the fourth meeting at Council Grove, one of the participants described the proceedings in a paper entitled "Towards a Science Concerned with Ultimates". The very title surprised me. Though it is true that Aristotle, wise old Greek, was an astronomer and a physicist and a historian who jumped the traces and entered the field of ultimates which he called metaphysics, I did not expect modern scientists to follow his example. For Aristotle metaphysics was the science of causes and the greatest science (the so-called "first philosophy") was the science of ultimate causes or of *the* ultimate cause. That was how he got involved with the Prime Mover and "the thought that thinks itself". And do modern scientists now follow his example? Are they, too, going to look for a Prime Mover? If so, they would follow the example of Teilhard, whose science led him to the conclusion that there must be an Omega, a Prime Mover ahead, the point of convergence of the evolutionary process. Or Jung, who at the end of his life declared that he had always seen something permanent beneath the eternal flux. Or Einstein, who said that God does not play dice with the Universe. These are big names. They risked their reputation and jeopardized their credibility by talking like this. But things have moved since they lived and thought; and now we find scientists following in their footsteps, "extrapolating" in the same way, asking about ultimates and even about religion. The fourth Council Grove meeting, called for the study of transcendental things, ended with a declaration which is both novel and profound:

Our group decided he [the scientist] should admit he doesn't know anything.
Our group thought he should study transcendental things in a questioning way.
A scientist is a human being, and should deal with personal matters in a human way.
He should read the "scientific journals" [i.e. great spiritual systems] of other cultures. The science of consciousness has already been written.
Most science of consciousness material is related to personal escape.
But Mohammed lived in society.
These inner forces are very powerful. Beware the great dangers that exist when work like this is done, especially by large numbers of people, without the high values and lifelong discipline of the great ancient systems.
The role of science is testing out old ideas.
What makes old ideas new is taking them seriously.

(Weide, p. 84)

As a statement from scientists this has a fresh and humble ring. I think it was Plato or Socrates who said that the first step towards wisdom is the acknowledgement of one's own ignorance; and these scientists have done just that. And then the feeling that they really must read the great spiritual systems with their "scientific journals". By this I suppose they mean that the researcher in consciousness must get to work and read the Upanishads, the

Sutras, the Bible, the fathers of the Church, St Teresa of Avila, *The Cloud of Unknowing,* the Koran, and all the rest. Pretty enthralling reading for the scientist indeed. Again, profound is their realization that powerful forces are unleashed with consequent dangers. Anyone with the slightest experience of meditation knows about the uprising of the unconscious and the possible resultant turmoil, to say nothing of the increased psychic power that meditation brings. All this could have the greatest social consequences if meditation becomes widespread. Yes, the high values, the lifelong disciplines and the wisdom of the great spiritual systems are not to be overlooked. When you build a tower you'd better sit down and count the cost.

The only statement in the above declaration that makes me hesitate is that which asserts that the science of consciousness has already been written. That it has partly been written I do not doubt. But is it finished? Has the curtain come down? I prefer to believe that it has a pretty bright future and that there is another act. More will be experienced; more will be written; more facts will come to light. Is it not possible that we will continue to have mystics of the calibre of Paul or the Buddha or Mohammed or Augustine or Ramakrishna? Why not? There is a Buddhist saying that the disciple who does not go beyond his master is not worthy of his master. And did not Jesus say, 'He who believes in me will also do the works that I do; *and greater works than these will he do*, because I go to the Father'' (John 14:12)? Going to the Father, he would send the Spirit to teach his disciples all things.

But let me not quibble over details. The significant thing about all this is that some leading scientists are at last stretching out a friendly hand of dialogue towards religion. And I do hope that this time the religionists will not let them down. Surely this dialogue is long overdue. In the past two centuries these two great forces have moved successively from friendship to enmity and on to peaceful co-existence. What progress for humanity if once again they could get really reconciled and go about the work of building the earth!

Some time ago, I and my colleagues invited a number of friends, Buddhist and Christian and scientist, to our place in Tokyo to discuss the inroads of science into meditation and religion. This topic is particularly relevant in Tokyo where a couple of universities (Komazawa and Tokyo University) are sponsoring rather extensive research on the psychophysiology of meditation, measuring the activity of the brain, plotting its course and tabulating the results. It seemed like a good idea to exchange views on this whole thing; and we did so over a *suki-vaki* dinner with beer and then coffee. I must confess that a few of the guests reacted negatively; they felt that the inner life was just too sacred for this kind of experimentation. Meditation in the laboratory, like sex in the laboratory, was the dehumanization of something sacred. Moreover they agreed with à Kempis that the grace of devotion should be concealed by humility and so they took a dim view of people who would get themselves wired up to machines, thus manifesting their *samadhi* to the world. But this was not the opinion of the majority. Most of the participants felt that the time had come for dialogue — that we should stop talking about the *limits* of science and talk instead about the *contribution* of science to meditation and religion. It was even suggested that religion had better have dialogue with science or run the risk of going out of business.

While I myself was all in favour of dialogue with science, I could sympathize with those who reacted negatively to experiments in the neurophysiology of meditation. After all, it would be pretty sad if churches and meditation halls were turned into laboratories for experimentation on the human mind. Shades indeed of the brave new world! But, on the other hand, this need not be so; and such an idea is far from the minds of the scientists I have met. What they want to do is to measure the physiological repercussions of the sacred practice of meditation, always respecting the area of mystery which science cannot enter and which is the special field of the religionist and the mystical theologian. Seeing the trepidation with which their scientific effort is greeted by some religious people, I am reminded of the storm over depth psychology and psychoanalysis. Seventy or eighty years ago psychology was "the new science". Religion generally feared and opposed it. This was a pity since religious influence might have served and helped direct a science that was to make a strong impact on society. Only after several decades did religious people awaken to the immense significance of psychology and the incalculable value of its findings for religion and for meditation. Now at last religious psychology is an indispensable part of theology and, as is well known, it exercised considerable influence on Vatican II. Will the same hold true for neurophysiology? Some of our guests seemed to think so.

Coming to practicalities, we finally felt that the psychologist, the psychiatrist, the neurologist and the rest have a lot to offer to the meditators and their directors. For one thing there is the fact that meditators sometimes get sick. "Zen attracts sick people!" exclaimed one psychologist who practises Zen. And I believe that the same can be said of most forms of silent meditation. Not infrequently consultation with a doctor is necessary before even starting on the meditational journey; and later to distinguish between enlightenment and sickness, between the joy of *satori* and the manic phase of a manic-depressive personality. But apart from this, science is investigating the ideal external conditions for meditation – the place, the lighting, the bodily posture, the diet, the sleep. All this is not without value and it is interesting to see how often scientific research confirms ancient religious traditions about diet and posture. Though it is also true that science sometimes will do away with ancient taboos.

More important than this, however, are the discoveries now being made in the field of consciousness itself. Not long ago people (both wise and not so wise) tended to lump together mysticism, hypnosis, schizophrenic experience, drug experience and other altered states, as though they were all variations of a single theme. And this was not so terribly foolish because to distinguish these states scientifically is not easy. Yet now, thanks to rigorous laboratory experiments, it becomes possible to distinguish between the consciousness of Zen and that of Yoga; it is possible to demonstrate from the brainwaves that hypnosis is not the same as *samadhi* or the prayer of quiet. Even within Zen, fine research is showing a difference between the *Rinzai* and *Soto* consciousness. All this will help masters and directors who, after all, should know as much as possible about the kind of consciousness they wish to produce and the kind they wish to reject.

Granted, then, that there should be dialogue between religion and science on the subject of meditation, let me say a word on the process of *dialogue*, about which a whole philosophy is already in the making.

Quite clearly the aim of dialogue is not to prove that I am right and you are wrong; nor is its aim to win you to my way of thinking. In dialogue one *explains* with courage and clarity and without pretence, while the other *listens* as sympathetically as possible. Neither party need *compromise* on basic issues, but both *share*. A good example is the dialogue between Zen and Christianity in which I have had the privilege of taking part. As a result of this dialogue no Christian has become a Buddhist nor has any Buddhist become a Christian; but we have shared and greatly profited from our meetings. And in the same way, as the religio-scientific dialogue comes into its own, each party must retain its own identity. Religion must remain religious and science must remain scientific. Only then will there by any real dialogue, any real sharing, any real growth.

Now to do this properly it seems to me that mysticism must be recognized as an autonomous and unique science with psychological, physiological and neurological dimensions – but with a deeply religious core that is not determined by other disciplines. This is frequently recognized by scientists, as for example by one distinguished professor of Tokyo University who explained to me that he was not studying consciousness itself but only the neurophysiological basis of consciousness. And this, he said, is a different thing. It is one thing to study the psychological and physiological repercussions of a human activity and it is quite another to study the activity itself. For the fact is (and this professor grasped it intuitively) that there is something in man that escapes all attempts at delineation and can never be measured by human methodology. For example, psychology and neurology cannot tell us who is a good man. In the eschatological age, people will stand before the Master and say, "Lord, we worked miracles in your name. We cast out devils. We produced alpha waves; we altered our consciousness; we expanded our minds like elastic." And the Master may well answer, "Amen, I say to you, I know you not." For all these exterior criteria and measurements,

however valuable, don't get to the heart of the matter; they don't
penetrate to the deepest caverns of motivation and love. That
these deep caverns are not known to others nor even to ourselves
is one of the great points stressed in the leading religious traditions
and more especially in the gospel. Here again we read that the just
will be surprised to hear themselves called just. They'll raise their
eyes in astonishment and say, "Lord, when did we see thee hungry
and feed thee . . . ?" (Matthew 25:37) And yes, by human
reckoning it was pretty reasonable that the men who slaved all
day in the vineyard should get more pay than the fellows who
turned up later. But that is not the way things worked. There is an
element of mystery here. And in the same way we can never equate
the attainment of wisdom or the actualization of one's Buddha
nature or union with God with any empirical experience that can
be measured by man or machine or the most delicate computer.

Most scientists will, I believe, accept this; but the problem with
science is that it does not remain pure science for long. It quickly
becomes technology and then there arises the danger of glorifying
technique at the expense of human values. We have seen this in
other areas. At one time there was a great cult of technique for
getting the maximum pleasure out of sex. A whole literature
appeared on the art of sexual intercourse, complete with up-to-
date translations of the *Kama Sutra* and the yoga of sex and all the
rest. And then some leading psychiatrists began to protest that all
the emphasis on technique destroyed something that was
primarily an expression of love. Next an attempt was made to
turn friendship into a technique of how to win friends and
influence people with all the tricks of the trade. But this, too, had a
hollow ring. And this is very relevant when we come to practise
meditation or mysticism. Here also is a way of love – it is the
deepest love for the Lady Wisdom who cries out in the streets. Let
us not overwhelm it with technique. One shudders to think of the
advertisements: "*Satori* in one week or money back."

Meditation in the Judaeo-Christian tradition is nothing less
than a love affair between two free agents. That is why it finally
cannot be tied down and analysed in terms of alpha and beta and
delta. A strange love affair this, a strange kind of intercourse,
where the beloved is "the mountains, the solitary wooded valleys,

strange islands . . . silent music". "O that his left hand were under my head, and that his right hand embraced me!" (Song of Solomon 2:6) This aspect of the loving relationship is eminently clear in the Bible where Yahweh is the bridegroom and the people are the bride – sometimes the faithful wife, often the wanton harlot. In the writings of the Church fathers frequently it is the human person who is the bride, while Christ is bridegroom.

This notion of the love affair is less evident in Buddhism, where wisdom is not personal. Yet even here I have sometimes found a hint of something similar. I was impressed when a Buddhist monk once remarked to me that *samadhi* is the bodhisattva's wife, and he said that this was reiterated in the early sutras. He was speaking in the context of celibacy, but his remark indicates that the notion of the loving relationship can be close to the heart of the Buddhist meditational ideal. Indeed, the Buddhist, the Jew and the Christian are lovers, foolishly in love with wisdom. That is why they can understand one another well. For the Buddhist, this wisdom is the exquisitely beautiful *prajna*. For the Jew, it is the Torah, and the Lady Wisdom who cries out in the street. For the Christian, wisdom is a person, Jesus Christ, since he is, in the words of Paul, "the power of God and the wisdom of God" (1 Corinthians 1:24).

Here is the real contribution that religion can make through dialogue to a scientific or secular meditation. It can save it from a mechanistic end by adding the distinctively human dimension. We all know that the great tragedy of the brave new world and other scientific paradises is precisely that they are inhuman. One role of religion is to humanize and to introduce love.

Let me conclude, then, with the suggestion that we take an interdisciplinary approach to the vast and complex field of religious meditation. Broadly, I would divide the study of meditation into two autonomous sciences, one secular and the other sacred. The secular science, containing many subdivisions, would study the psychological, physiological, neurological dimensions of consciousness, leaving the theologian to speak (or, perhaps we should say, stammer) about the area of mystery and faith and grace that lies beyond the cloud of unknowing. Then by dialogue between these two disciplines we may progress into the future.

Brainwave and biofeedback

The science of consciousness suffers somewhat from its popularizers. Having had the opportunity to speak with specialists both in
Tokyo and the US, I have been amazed at the difference between
their attitude and that of the popular magazines. These latter talk
blithely about alpha, biofeedback machines and the entrance into
blissful states. The researchers, on the other hand, keep saying that
they know almost nothing about the human brain and even less
about the human mind. Faced with new discoveries in the area of
consciousness, they are (as one researcher put it to me) like
Columbus when he set foot on a new continent. Or they are "like
stout Cortez, when with eagle eyes he stared at the Pacific',
confronted with uncharted territory, with unexplored continents,
with undreamt-of universes. Moreover they are not a little alarmed
by popularization that may bring their work into disrepute.

Having said all this, let me hasten to add that it is not my
intention to write here with scientific rigour, and in this sense I am
among the popularizers. Having become aware of the great
complexities of the matter, I simply intend to summarize aspects of
recent scientific research with a view to discussing their
implications for religious meditation. For what I say about this
scientific study I am greatly indebted to Dr Tomio Hirai of Tokyo
University with whom I have had the privilege of doing some work,
and also to other specialists in the US who were generous to me with
their time, with their learning and with their publications.

Research in the field of consciousness owes a great debt to the
German scientist, Hans Berger, who in the 1920s discovered
brainwaves and their relation to varying states of consciousness.
Thanks to his pioneering work we now know that the brain emits
faint electrical impulses which can be measured in microvolts by an
electroencephalograph or EEG. Concretely, in their work of

experimentation the researchers paste electrodes on the scalp of the subjects to be tested and hook them up to the EEG, which contains an amplifier. This amplifies the tiny electrical potentials as much as ten million times. Then the brainwaves or brain rhythms are traced with automatic ink pens on a revolving scroll. Since there are many types of brainwave, the EEG may be equipped to filter out the particular brainwave one wishes to record.

There are four principal brainwaves, measured according to frequency or speed of impulse and amplitude or voltage strength of the impulse. Researchers ask subjects being tested to describe their internal states while they are producing certain brainwaves; and in this way they are finding that certain internal psychological states of the mind are consistently associated with a corresponding activity of the brain.

The four principal brainwaves are as follows:

Beta is the most common in our waking hours. Beta consciousness, measuring 13 or more cycles per second, is associated with focused attention and the active thinking of a mind turned towards the outside world. In this rhythm the highest degree of cortical excitability is manifested. The reader of these pages is now presumably producing a good deal of beta.

Alpha is more restful. In it the frequency is lowered to 8–12 cycles per second and the internal state is described as one of "relaxed awareness" with a move towards interiority or what are called "internally focused states". Though about 10 per cent of the population of the US are non-alpha-producers, most people produce alpha when they close their eyes and relax. But to continue in alpha consciousness steadily with open eyes is not easy. Indeed it can rarely be done without ascetical training and is one of the characteristics of adepts in Zen. Alpha can be of high or low amplitude according to the production of microvolts by the brain. High-amplitude alpha indicates that the subject is in a rather deep state of concentration; this rhythm is associated with more advanced meditation and with mysticism.

Theta (4–7 cycles per second) is associated with drowsiness. It is the rhythm that appears when one slips towards unconsciousness or towards sleep, and it is often accompanied by dream-like hypnagogic imagery.

Delta (0–4 cycles per second) is the rhythm found in deep sleep.

Perhaps the brainwaves can be understood more easily by glancing at the following two diagrams:

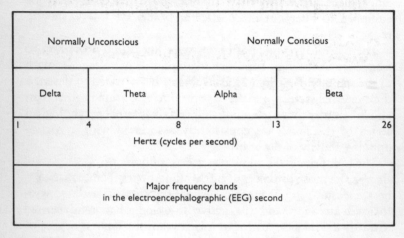

Normally Unconscious		Normally Conscious	
Delta	Theta	Alpha	Beta
1 4	8	13	26

Hertz (cycles per second)

Major frequency bands
in the electroencephalographic (EEG) second

(By kind permission of Dr Elmer Green)

After the discovery of brainwaves a further advance was made of the discovery of biofeedback. This is a technique for human self-monitoring in which a person is made conscious of his brainwaves while at the same time reflecting on his internal state of mind. In other words, it is a mechanical device for presenting information externally about what is happening internally. Our state of consciousness is, so to speak, projected outside so that we can look at it objectively. Concretely, this is done by equipping the EEG with instruments which by sound (the sound of a beep, for example) or by the flashing of a light tell the subject that he is now producing alpha or theta or whatever it may be. By listening for the beep and associating it with certain internal states, he can gradually train himself to enter internal states of consciousness previously only accessible to very gifted people or to drug-users or to mystics. But again one must be cautious. The mechanism of

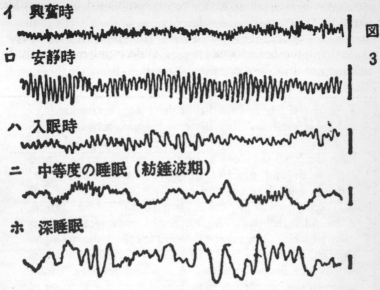

イ　興奮時

ロ　安静時

ハ　入眠時

ニ　中等度の睡眠（紡錘波期）

ホ　深睡眠

図
3

(By kind permission of Dr Tomio Hirai)

EEG graph paper showing the different brainwaves. The Japanese characters on the left describe the brainwaves. From top to bottom: excited state (beta); restful state (alpha); drowsy state (irregular theta); moderate sleep (spindle waves and delta); deep sleep (delta).

these machines is incredibly delicate. Good biofeedback machines, say the researchers, are not easily come by and they cost money. An inferior machine may cause absurdities. It may make twitching of the scalp sound like alpha, thus raising false hopes in the unfortunate practitioner.

Biofeedback is still in the early stages. But it may well point to a new form of mind-control and to new horizons in education. Its possibilities are enormous.

The rhythm that has evoked most interest in recent times is alpha; and it is already surrounded by myth, with talk of alphatology, alphagenesis, and so on. It seems moreover that a particular personality type tends to be an "alpha-producer" more or less naturally. Let me quote some descriptions of the alpha-producer from a leading researcher in the field. Dr Joseph Kamiya of the Langley Porter Institute in San Francisco asks subjects to describe their interior dispositions during the various brain rhythms, and this is what he says:

> Tentatively, I have found that there are certain kinds of individuals that do much better at learning how to control alpha, especially learning to increase alpha; and these individuals so far seem to be those who have had some interest in and practice of what I shall loosely call "meditation". It doesn't necessarily have to be of the Zen or Yoga school or any other formal school of meditation. If the individual has a long history of introspection on his own, he seems to be especially good at enhancing the alpha rhythm. Also he is likely to be an individual who uses words like *images, dreams, wants* and *feelings*. I have come to the conclusion that there are a large number of people who really don't know exactly what you are talking about when you talk about images and feelings. To such people the words describe something somebody else might have; but these people do not seem to have any degree of sensitivity to such things themselves. These people do not do well in my experiments, they do not gain a high degree of control over their alpha rhythms.   (Tart, p. 514)

So Dr Kamiya tentatively concludes that people who meditate enter easily into alpha. And probably the converse is also true; the alpha-producers veer towards meditation and the contemplative life. This thesis is confirmed by experiments on Zen in Tokyo University and on Transcendental Meditation in Harvard. In both cases it was found that the meditators moved quickly into alpha and the experienced meditators into high-amplitude alpha, thus showing that the frequency of the rhythms is lowered as one enters deeply into meditation. Another interesting point is the way of suppressing alpha, technically known as "alpha blocking". Here again is Dr Kamiya:

I would often hear that visual imagery was the answer [to the problem of how to suppress alpha], that all they would have to do was to conjure up an image of a person's face, hold it, and look at it very *carefully*, so much so that they could actually see the features of the person's face.

(Tart, p. 510)

From this it is clear that focused awareness blocks alpha. And blocking is also caused by any kind of agitation or excitement.

While in the US I had an opportunity to visit Langley Porter to see the equipment and to meet some interesting people. As the researchers kindly told me about their tests with *roshi* and *swami* and various *gurus* from the East, I asked in a flash of Irish chauvinism why they didn't test some Christian monks. They replied that they did. They tested some Catholic clergymen. But whereas the yogis and masters sat silently in majestic splendour registering exquisite and impeccable alpha, the clergymen read the Bible, sang hymns, wandered around the room and fouled up the machines. On hearing this, I blushed for the Holy Roman Church.

Undismayed, however, I reflected that they may have asked the wrong people, and I suggested that they experiment with Cistercian or Carthusian monks who have a long tradition of silent and imageless meditation.

Shortly after this I had occasion to visit a convent in north California where contemplative men and women had gathered for some days of silence and recollection. So I made use of the opportunity to invite a researcher to come along with a portable biofeedback machine and do some Christian contemplative experimentation. The contemplatives were very cooperative in getting wired up; and, as I had expected, all the persons tested produced high-amplitude alpha. This was more heartening; and although this experimentation could not be carried out with the scientific rigour of the laboratory, it would seem to confirm Dr Kamiya's insight that not only Zen and Yoga but any form of contemplation brings into play the lower-frequency brainwaves.

Seeing this, one can understand why the old spiritual masters discouraged conceptualization and discursive thinking in time of contemplation. What they were discouraging was the focused awareness or the superficial visualization which characterizes conceptual thought. This, as Dr Kamiya has shown, blocks alpha and brings one into beta, thus destroying the conditions most favourable to contemplative experience. Put in scientific terms, what the spiritual masters wanted was to bring their disciples into an alpha state and keep them there, intuitively realizing the value of this neurological conditioning.

Let me remark here, however, that while all contemplation is probably alpha, not all alpha is contemplation. This is important. Contemplation is much more than a certain kind of brainwave; and there is a whole area of motivation, of faith, of grace and the rest which transcends scientific experimentation to enter the cloud of unknowing. About this dimension of mystery more will be said; so let me pass on to some reflections about experiments performed in Tokyo.

Tokyo is a pretty good place for the psychophysiological study of meditation, since here one has sensitive equipment, able scientists and cooperative Zen masters. What more could be desired? Let me, then, say a word about the research on Zen consciousness made by Dr Tomio Hirai of the University of Tokyo.

The most basic experiment (and one that confirms the findings of Dr Kamiya) was done with practitioners of Zen – some with decades of experience, others with little experience, and some practising Zen for the first time. Electrodes were pasted to the frontal, parietal and occipital areas of the brain and hooked to the EEG. (I might add that, besides the brain rhythms, the pulse-rate, respiration, muscle relaxation and skin resistance were also tested – but this need not detain us here.) Results showed that whereas those with no experience of Zen registered beta with bursts of alpha when the eyes were closed, the Zen masters almost immediately entered alpha, even though their eyes were open. This alpha, beginning at the frontal and moving to the parietal and occipital areas of the brain, increased in amplitude and decreased in frequency as the meditation progressed. In some cases it developed into rhythmical theta trains.

After the meditation, alpha waves continued for some time.

Furthermore, it was observed that those disciples selected by the master as proficient in Zen conformed most closely to this pattern; and there was a clear correlation between the EEG graph and the number of years spent in *zazen*, which seems to confirm the correlation between brainwaves and internal psychological states. All agree that one of the most interesting aspects of this experiment is the long theta trains which frequently appear after thirty or forty minutes of meditation in the case of proficients. This seems to be a phenomenon the full significance of which is not yet fully understood. I shall return to it later.

A second experiment is called by Dr Hirai "the click experiment". The EEG shows that if a person in alpha hears a click or noise, the jolt will cause alpha blocking and bring him back to beta. But if the click is constantly repeated, the person may get accustomed to it and simply cease to react. Now one might expect that proficients in Zen would be so absorbed in their practice as not to hear the click at all or that they would habituate immediately. But the contrary is true. The proficient in Zen never habituates. The EEG shows that his reaction to the click is exactly the same each time he hears it. The extremely brief alpha blocking continues for a fraction of a second each time. This says something important about the Zen consciousness. It shows that the master always hears and sees with the same freshness as if he were hearing or seeing for the first time. To me this is beautiful and fascinating. Here we have a consciousness like that of the natural child, a consciousness filled with wonder and never losing its amazement at the beauty of the sunrise and the falling of the peach blossom. "Unless you . . . become like children . . ." (Matthew 18:2).[1]

Another interesting experience of Dr Hirai is what he calls "name-calling". When the subject, all wired-up, enters into Zen meditation, Dr Hirai or one of his colleagues calls out a name and watches for the repercussions on the EEG. In all he has 131 names

---

[1] "I believe the Adult's function in the religious experience is to block out the Parent in order that the Natural Child may reawaken to its own worth and beauty as a part of God's creation." Thomas Harris in *I'm OK – You're OK* (Harper & Row, New York, 1969), p. 234.

– the name of the Zen master himself, of his wife and children, the names of Nixon, Cleopatra, Stalin, Marilyn Monroe, famous Japanese movie stars, TV personalities, and whatnot. The person inexperienced in Zen will react very differently according to the name called. The name of his wife or loved ones may cause considerable EEG vibrations whereas the name of Stalin may arouse very little reaction. But in the case of experienced and enlightened Zen masters the reaction to every name called is *exactly the same*. Whether it be Nixon or his wife, the calling of the name causes an infinitesimally small blocking, followed by a return to deep alpha. From this Dr Hirai concludes that the Zen master does not react at all to the *content* of the word called but only to the sound impinging on his ears.

When I told this to some of my friends they expressed a certain amount of dismay. How cold and unfeeling! After all, they said, a man of flesh and blood should react differently to his wife than to Stalin or Cleopatra. Does this man love at all or is he indifferent to human affection? Yet I myself believe that the matter is not quite so simple. It is not, I believe, that the Zen master loves no one, but rather that he is not clinging to anyone or to anything. He is deep in a state of detachment or non-attachment to self-interest; he is in a state of pure beholding which is not only compatible with, but necessary for, the highest love. I came to this conclusion while reading a passage from *The Cloud of Unknowing* which is strikingly parallel. The medieval English author of this work was educated in an asceticism of detachment which valued non-clinging and freedom from self-interest as a path to love. And so he says that in the time of contemplation the contemplative has an equal love for everyone:

> But in the contemplative work itself, he does not distinguish between friend and enemy, brother and stranger. I do not mean, however, that he will cease to feel a spontaneous affection towards a few others who are especially close to him. Of course, he will and frequently, too. This is perfectly natural and legitimate for many reasons known only to love. You will remember that Christ himself had a special love for John and Mary and

Peter. The point I am making is that during the work of contemplation everyone is equally dear to him since it is God alone who stirs him to love. He loves all men plainly and nakedly for God; and he loves them as he loves himself.
(Johnston (1), ch. 25)

From the above one can see the similarity between the Zen consciousness and the Christian contemplative consciousness. In either case the names of Cleopatra, Stalin, Nixon and the meditator's wife will cause the same EEG reaction *during the work of contemplation*. Nor is this cold and unfeeling; because "the warmth of his love reaches out to them all, friends, enemy, stranger and kin alike. If there is any partiality at all, it is more likely to be towards his enemy than towards his friend" (Johnston (1), ch. 25). In this point, as in so many others, the English author of *The Cloud* displays characteristically admirable poise and balance.

But let me now just mention briefly some more conclusions arising from the work of Dr Hirai and others in this field.

First of all, no one can now say that Zen and mysticism are nothing but forms of self-hypnosis. The fact is that the person in hypnotic trance does not necessarily enter into protracted alpha at all. His brain rhythms are more or less like those of any waking, working person. Again, it cannot be said that Zen is just a form of light sleep. Needless to say, the Zen practitioner, like any mediator, might doze off from time to time. But if he does, there is a change in the EEG.

Another interesting conclusion (to which I have made reference in the previous chapter) is the scientific distinction that can now be made between Zen consciousness and the Yoga consciousness. To the superficial observer these two practices are exactly alike. Both are silent, supraconceptual, unified, imageless, wordless, beyond thought. Moreover in both the meditator produces high-amplitude alpha rhythms. But there the resemblance ends. EEG experiments have shown that if you make a noise, the Zen meditator hears it; if you flash a light, he sees it; if you stick a pin in him, he feels it. This is because his meditation is very much geared to the here and now, to a total presence to reality. In this sense, Zen is extremely incarnational. On the other hand, when the yogi enters into very deep meditation, he hears nothing, sees nothing and feels nothing. So much so that one researcher writes that "the control of attention achieved by the subject is so intense that neither flashing light, sounding gongs, vibration or the touch of hot glass test-tubes could disrupt the state of concentration and cause alpha-blocking" (Green (3), p.14).

It will now be clear that for the study of meditation probably the most significant rhythms are alpha and theta.

Fascinating research on alpha-theta trains has been done by Dr Elmer Green at the Menninger Foundation in Kansas. Dr Green associates the alpha-theta train with what he calls "reverie", a drowsy state found when the mind moves towards sleep or unconsciousness and characterized by the presence of hypnagogic, dream-like imagery (Green (2)). His subjects assert that this imagery is more vivid than that of dreams in that it is much more realistic. "What were these images like? They were different for each individual of course, yet they shared certain characteristics. They were dream-like rather than dream, hypnagogic imagery that emerged full-blown, so to speak, without consciously being willed; vivid visions of people, scenes, objects, known and unfamiliar to the subject. And they were changeful, as if a very private showing of lantern slides were being run through the theatre of the mind" (Segal, p.324).

From this it would seem that the mind is full of unconscious imagery of which we are ordinarily unaware. And now the aim of researchers is to make it conscious – to bring people to a state in which, so to speak, the unconscious will be luminous to the conscious. In laboratory experiments Dr Green uses certain stimuli to make people aware of the hypnagogic imagery latent in the mind. "Many gave reports that, were it not for the stimulus, they would not have become aware of these images. One subject reported that the stimulus caused him suddenly to become aware of little pictures in his mind that he did not know were there" (Segal, p. 323).

In terms of brainwaves, in order to become aware of hypnagogic imagery it may be necessary to produce many varieties of brainwave at the same time. This seems to be the opinion of Dr Green. Speaking of a Swami whom he tested, he goes on:

> When the Swami produced alpha, he did not cease to produce beta. And when he produced theta, both alpha and beta were retained, each about 50% of the time. Likewise when he produced delta, he was also producing theta, alpha and beta during a relatively high percentage of time. Perhaps this tells us something important. Since alpha is a conscious state, it may be necessary to retain it when theta is produced if one wishes to be aware of the hypnagogic imagery which is often associated with theta.
>
> (Green (5))

From this we get a fascinating picture of the human mind filled with a wealth of imagery that is largely unconscious but that can be brought to consciousness by entering the theta state and receiving some stimulus to enhance awareness and to ensure that in time of theta the alpha and beta rhythms will continue.

Now this may well confirm a very old technique for bringing people to enlightenment. In Zen the stimulus is the blow on the face or the shout or the hard word – or alternatively the gentle falling of the peach blossom or the sound of the temple bell. Whatever it may be, ordinarily some stimulus is necessary to ripen a person's enlightenment and make him aware of what is already in his mind. For he is already enlightened and the stimulus brings to the surface what was there all along. I believe that Jesus too sometimes used the hard word to shock his hearer into self-realization. "Why do you call me good? None is good but God alone" (Luke 18:19). It should be remembered that according to one Buddhist theory everyone is already enlightened by possession of the Buddha nature. And does not Genesis say that man is created in God's image? Which may be a kind of enlightenment with which man is born. As for the New Testament, it seems to highlight baptism as the great enlightenment. Spiritual training in these cases may be the art of leading a person to the realization of what he already possesses. This may have much to do with the realization and conscious grasp of the hypnagogic imagery that fills the mind with its richness and depth.

One thing that interests Dr Green is the relationship of this hypnagogic, theta imagery to creativity. It is well known that the creativity of poets, artists, writers and scientists is frequently linked to dreams and dream-like states. We have all heard stories about writers waking up in the night and furiously scribbling their great intuitions, or of mathematicians and scientists crying "Eureka" in the dead of night or at the moment of waking. Elmer Green quotes the chemist Kekulé, who urged his contemporaries: "Gentlemen, let us learn to dream" (Green (2)).

And again this is not without great relevance for meditation. It is not at all uncommon for religious people to receive deep enlightenment in the twilight zone between waking and sleeping, or at some time in the night. For this is precisely the time when the conscious mind is open to receiving communications from the teeming womb of the unconscious. "A vision appeared to Paul in the night: a man of Macedonia was standing beseeching him and saying, 'Come over to Macedonia and help us.' And when he had seen the vision, immediately we sought to go on into Macedonia, concluding that God had called us to preach the gospel to them" (Acts 16:9–10). Was this vision hypnagogic? The Scripture does not say that Paul was asleep; it does not say this was a dream but just that it was "in the night". Whatever it was, it was creative and Paul lost no time in following its message.

Dr Green, then, envisages the possibility of training people for creativity through theta. Talented people, by learning how to enter the alpha-theta state, may learn to develop themselves in that area in which they are creative. Artists and writers frequently look for methods to stimulate creativity and here may be one answer. Dr Green writes of "developing a training programme through which individuals could be helped to develop and sustain those internal states associated with low frequency alpha and theta rhythms in which hypnagogic-like imagery often appears, and of developing a method that would enable us to bring someone in such a state to focused awareness in which he could not only report the imagery but hopefully could learn to manipulate it in a creative way" (Green (2)).

All this brings us to the important and delicate question as to whether and to what extent religious meditation and religious creativity could be developed through biofeedback. Or could religious groups use these machines to teach their aspirants mind-control? to help them produce high-amplitude alpha-theta trains? I must confess that my natural feelings are somewhat jolted by the thought (I always fear the brave new world), but at the same time I cannot help reflecting again on the development of depth psychology – how religious people opposed it and then woke up to its great possibilities, so that now psychological tests are frequently used for screening candidates for monastic or contemplative living. If psychological tests are valid and helpful, why not neurophysiological tests too? If it is true that the alpha-producers are nature's contemplatives, would it not be a good idea to discover them as soon as possible? Quite clearly I am not saying that neurophysiology can tell the whole story (any more than psychology can tell the whole story) and I assume that the deeper things like motivation and faith and love and grace will never show up on the EEG. But granted this, could we make use of biofeedback as we make use of psychology?

In theory I see nothing against it. Only the very practical difficulty that at present biofeedback has not developed sufficiently to be a sure guide about a person's contemplative aptitude. This, I believe, is what most researchers would say. The science is still in its infancy and few would have the confidence to rely on it as a sure norm for the making of big decisions. But what the future holds no one knows. We had better not bury our heads in the sand. It would be sad if religious people were unduly fearful and defensive in the face of modern man's discoveries and explorations into his inner world. If they are open and positive towards scientific trends, they may learn a lot; and they may also help develop and direct scientific discoveries to greater good and greater human fulfilment.

4

The science of mysticism

I have called the study of consciousness a new science; but it is probably more correct to say that, like everything else, it evolved over many centuries. The author of Ecclesiastes was not completely off the mark when he observed that there is nothing new under the sun; and some rumblings of a real science (in the rigorously scientific sense) of mysticism have existed in the West for a couple of millennia. Psychoanalysis, the study of brainwaves, trips in inner space and experimentation with drugs are giving renewed vitality to a study that has its roots deep in tradition.

We are so conscious of the catastrophic rift between science and religion that we easily forget about the ancient harmony that existed between them. Monks were in fact the forebears of the modern scientist and their monasteries were, until the Renaissance, the main centres of Western learning – in which no distinction was made between philosophy and what was called natural science. It was a monk, the Venerable Bede, who in the seventh century proposed the notion that the earth was round. Albertus Magnus and his disciple Thomas in the thirteenth century dabbled in speculation about the nature of the universe; Galileo and Copernicus, however badly they fared at the hands of the authorities, were educated and nourished by monastic life. Roger Bacon, a Franciscan friar who is responsible for the so-called "scientific method", wrote that "the true scientist must subject all things in heaven and under it to experiment. He should blush to find out that he does not know more about the earth than the average person knows." Then there is Nicolas of Cusa, a mathematician, a mystic and a bishop. And a host of others who devoted their lives to science. I say all this to stress that the scientific approach was deeply rooted in the West. No doubt this was partly a consequence of Yahweh's command to subdue the earth and rule over it.

Now this scientific approach was not without influence on

prayer and the mystical states; so that there arose a body of teaching about the development of consciousness in the contemplative life – about various meditational states, about ecstasy, about visions and how to handle them, about the possibility of illusion and so on. Thus were evolved some of the great scientific treatises to which Council Grove referred.

Here I would like to say a word about one great scientist of mysticism, the French Jesuit, Auguste Poulain (1836–1919), whose monumental work *Des Grâces d'Oraison*, written at the beginning of the century, remains a classic. Poulain insisted that he was writing what he called "descriptive mysticism", that is, getting the facts, analysing them rigorously, sifting the evidence and drawing conclusions. So he read the works of the mystics meticulously (how much loving and patient toil he devoted to this task!), interviewed hundreds of mystics throughout France and reflected on his own mystical experience, which was not small. Great spiritual master that he was, he was convinced that the France of his day abounded in struggling, potential mystics who needed a helping hand. For them he wanted to write a practical book out of his own experience and that of the people he guided and loved. "For the past forty years", he writes, "I have made a study of these questions . . . I have read large numbers of treatises, ranging from duodecimos to folios. I have questioned at great length numbers of persons possessing the graces of interior prayer, and others who mistakenly thought that they possessed them when in fact they did not. An acquaintance with these last is also helpful" (Poulain, Preface, 3). This last sentence is typical of the shrewd insight that keeps popping up amidst the array of mystical scholarships that fills his pages.

For Poulain, descriptive mysticism depends upon two kinds of materials. First the descriptions found in the great classical writers and secondly the evidence supplied by living persons from their own experience. Both of these are indispensable and they throw light on one another. Indeed he claimed that there are many passages in the writings of the mystics that can only be understood by someone who has had a similar experience. In his research no aspect of mysticism is overlooked. The physical repercussions, the effects upon health, the influence on interpersonal relations, the possible aberrations – all are examined. And then his page upon page of "extracts" which he culled from his long and painstaking perusal of the Western mystics; these extracts are indeed a veritable gold-mine for the modern researcher in the field of consciousness. As for laboratory experimentation, he seems to have known something about that, according to the scientific milieu of his day. Speaking about ecstasy, for instance, he observes that "the heart-beat is weak and the breathing so slight that it is difficult even to detect it, *as can be seen from numerous experiments made with great care upon ecstatic persons*" (Poulain, Ch. 13, extracts). The italics are mine. What these experiments were he does not say and I have not been able to find out, but it would certainly be interesting to know. For all this situates Tomio Hirai, Elmer Green, Joe Kamiya and other researchers in a long pioneering tradition of meditational scholarship.

Furthermore, for Poulain mysticism, far from being a static science, was constantly in evolution. It had developed slowly through the ages and would continue to develop in the future:

> In the course of the centuries we see that descriptions become more and more accurate. Writers come gradually though very slowly to distinguish, one from the other, states of consciousness which had previously been confused; and they discover better comparisons with which to describe them. In this respect, mysticism partakes in the forward thrust that can be seen in all the descriptive sciences. There is no reason for thinking that there will be no more progress. Our successors will do better than ourselves. And it is in this direction that mysticism has a future. (Poulain, Preface, 2)

In all this is there not something of a prophetic ring?

For Poulain the writings of St Teresa of Avila in sixteenth-century Spain are a landmark in the development of the mystical consciousness and its scientific study. Teresa was the first, he claims, to analyse minutely the earlier states of consciousness which precede ecstasy; and he constantly appeals to her acute psychological analysis. Asserting that there are two great eras in the development of mysticism, the one before and up to the death of St Teresa of Avila and the other from her death to his own time, he goes on:

> During the first period, mystics devoted their attention only to those facts that stared them in the face: ecstasies, visions of Christ and the saints, and revelations such as those of St Gertrude and St Bridget. But the states of union on the way to ecstasy were more difficult to analyse, as is always the case with more rudimentary things. So their ideas on these states were very vague, their descriptions were brief and hazy and they failed to make distinctions between states of consciousness that were different. For example Blessed Angela of Foligno, whose writings contain such beautiful passages on the subject of raptures and visions, tells us almost nothing about the other states of consciousness. The same is true of Dionysius the Areopagite, Ruysbroeck, and so on. Speaking about the lower phases they were satisfied with such vague remarks as: "You find that you are taken possession of by a certain sweetness."
>
> It was St Teresa who was the first to take the trouble to study the states of consciousness below ecstasy under the microscope. Her personal contribution amounts to just this, and in this respect she brought about a true revolution. She has done us a great service, for these states of consciousness are the most common. And in addition to her power of description she had real ability for classification.　(Poulain, ch. 30, 2)

What a sense of history Poulain had! And together with a sense of the past, he had a sense of the future. Mysticism, he laments, has made almost no progress since the time of St Teresa. Scarcely any new facts have been discovered, and authors have been preoccupied with explaining and coordinating what has already been discovered.

Poulain wrote at the beginning of the century. Little did he know that the science of mysticism was on the verge of an earthquake that would shake it to its foundation and make his

Teresian revolution look like a tiny tremor. I mean the impact of psychoanalysis, the meeting between Christianity and the religions of the East, the discovery of brainwaves and the popularity of biofeedback and research in drugs. How many new facts now emerge for the West through our knowledge of Ramakrishna and Aurobindo and Dogen! What a contribution is made through the growing knowledge of Buddhist meditation with its divisions and subdivisions of states of consciousness that St Teresa did not know or, at any rate, did not depict. And then the new light thrown on consciousness by the astronauts and space travel. It is true, of course, that Poulain had some glimmering knowledge of psychological and neurological studies and that he was aware of the existence of mysticism in the East. But he was a man of his times, limited by the milieu in which he lived. Many of his observations on these subjects are now outdated and it is clear that he did not have the spirit of dialogue that we now take for granted.

At the same time, Poulain's research differs from that of contemporary scientists in that it includes a profoundly religious dimension. In the mystics whom he guided and interrogated, the dimensions of faith and charity and ultimate concern were all-important and these are less easily put under the microscope. Here is a whole dimension of mystery that scientific investigation cannot touch. For the traditional mystic the very centre of his practice is purity of motivation in such wise that he seeks the ultimate with what was called "pure and chaste love". Now there is no human way of judging another's motivation (hence, "Judge not, that you be not judged" (Matthew 7:1)) nor can we have certainty about our own. That is why we come up against mystery in a love affair where the beloved is "the mountains, the solitary wooded valleys, strange islands . . . silent music". There is no way of measuring and programming any love, much less divine love.

Again there is bound to be awful mystery in an exercise that is built on the belief that ultimate reality is dynamic, that it moves towards us as we move towards it, that it searches us out before we go in search of it. And the mystics directed by Poulain believed not only that ultimate reality is dynamic but that it has a face and a heart and a name. The whole mystical tradition in which Poulain stands is based on the Johannine sentence, "We love [God], because he first loved us" (1 John 4:19). That is to say, there is a prior action of ultimate reality inviting man to contemplative wisdom; and the mystical path is an answer to this call. This means that there is another factor in the drama and that we must, in consequence, reckon with the action of his love. This is technically called "grace".

Something like "grace" has to be taken into account in the lives of all the great mystics whether they be Jewish, Christian, Hindu or Buddhist. Assuredly Zen Buddhism rejects such an idea and glories in its self-reliance, called in Japanese *jiriki*. Yet even here masters sometimes get second thoughts. At one of our Zen-Christian dialogues, an old and highly esteemed master compared enlightenment to the chicken emerging from the shell. Push as it may, he said, the tiny chick cannot break out to freedom unless the mother pecks at the shell from outside. This, he went on, is equivalent to what Christians call grace. Something similar is found in the famous Oxherding pictures which describe the Zen journey to awakening. Here the searcher must see the footprints and feel the attraction of the ox before he can set out on his arduous journey.

The point I make here is that unless this mysterious religious dimension is taken into account in mystical experience and deep meditation, the picture will be falsified. Quite certainly this is the case in Jewish and Christian prayer. Here we are always confronted with an incalculable element of mystery because two free agents are somehow involved.

To preserve the balance between the strictly scientific dimension on the one hand and the religious and theological on the other is far from easy. Though Poulain's orthodoxy was never questioned, there was a rival school of speculative theologians who, looking askance at his methodology, approached mysticism almost exclusively from the standpoint of scripture and dogma. Though this approach has great validity (which Poulain explicitly admits), it can suffer from the disadvantage of talking about what the mystics *should* experience or what the theologian would like them to experience rather than what, in fact, they do experience. Moreover, theologians of this school spoke a language and used a terminology that other poor mortals, including the scientists, were unlikely to understand. Most disastrous of all, it was this school of theology that prevailed in the seminaries, wrote the text-books, got the *imprimatur* and influenced theological thinking. Consequently, when the modern flood of interest in oriental mysticism and states of consciousness swept into the West, the mystical theologians had already lost contact. What they said did not sound very meaningful; and many scientists working in the field of consciousness have dismissed the Western mystics as shallow or irrelevant. Now the theologian is faced with the unenviable task of picking up the broken pieces.

Poulain was clearly a man in advance of his times. If I were asked to define his role, I would call him not a scientist but a mystical theologian open to dialogue with science and with the world of his day. I call him a theologian because his prime interest was in the divine action on the lives of those whom he directed. In other words his first interest was the working of grace and of God's self-communication to man, about which he learned from scripture, from tradition, from the writings of the mystics, from the intimate disclosures of those he directed and from the action of the Spirit in his own heart. But he was also keenly aware of the vital importance of what we now call neurophysiology and psychophysiology. He was shrewd enough to see that just as the moral theologian cannot neglect psychology, economics, sociology and the other sciences that border on his specialization, so the mystical theologian cannot neglect the sciences that touch his field. In short he saw the necessity of the interdisciplinary approach; and in this sense he points to the path along which future research in mysticism must walk. This is the path of dialogue.

For the future of mysticism may well be in the balance. It could be bright or it could be pretty dark because of the enormous spiritual potential that will be unleashed as the human race becomes progressively more mystical. Let me here look on the bright side. Mysticism can be a unifying factor in a world searching for wholeness. Already it has done much towards bringing together the great religions. We now see that Hindus and Christians, Buddhists and Jews can dialogue and understand one another better at the level of mystical experience than at the level of philosophy. But mysticism can be a meeting ground not only for believers in the various religions but also for scientists and religionists. These latter approach the problem at the level of mystery, of ultimate concern, of transcendence; and they can dialogue with those who approach the same problem as psychologists, psychiatrists, neurologists, physicists, biologists and the rest. Who doubts that we have great need of some unifying science? And mysticism may well be the answer.

PART II

CONSCIOUSNESS

5

Initiation

In the meditation of the great religions one makes progress by going beyond thought, beyond concepts, beyond images, beyond reasoning, thus entering a deeper state of consciousness or enhanced awareness that is characterized by profound silence. This is the *silentium mysticum*. It is a state of consciousness in which there may be no words or images. Or if there are words, they spring from the depth of one's being and are not borrowed from books or outside sources; and if there are images, these again will be from within, more in the nature of hypnagogic imagery than that which we create by conscious visualization. Frequently this state of silent unification will be filled with peace; but it may at times be dry and even painfully filled with anguish. It is a silence that probably differs considerably according to the faith of the meditator, and it goes by different names in the different religious traditions. In Sanskrit the generic word *samadhi* is used, though this word has a wide variety of meanings; in Christianity it is called *contemplation* or, in its earlier stages, *the prayer of quiet*. In Zen it is called *san'mai*, which is a Japanese rendering of *samadhi*. Elsewhere it is called one-pointedness. Physiologically speaking, it seems to be characterized by high-amplitude alpha brainwaves. The breathing slows down (some Buddhists measure the depth of their *samadhi* by the rate of breathing), as also do the heart-rate and general metabolism, while the consciousness is greatly expanded.

There are so many divisions and subdivisions of mystical silence that researchers in consciousness have no vocabulary that will encompass the whole complex thing and they are anxiously looking for one. Perhaps that is the reason for their growing interest in mysticism and the mystics. The problem is by no means easy because it is impossible to speak accurately about altered or expanded states of consciousness in terms taken from ordinary, normal, waking consciousness. It is like denizens of two different worlds or universes trying to communicate with one another.

Hence mystics usually resort to silence or to symbolism. In the West the Church fathers speak of Moses climbing the mountain to meet Yahweh in the dark cloud of unknowing or of Mary Magdalen sitting silently at the feet of Christ; while St Teresa speaks of the successive interior mansions into which one enters to meet the king at the deepest centre. It takes the scientist some time to get accustomed to such language. And the matter becomes all the more complex when we reflect that among the many kinds of interior silence are some that are unhealthy. It is well said in Japan that any clown can tell the difference between wise talk and foolish talk; but it takes a good master to distinguish between wise silence and foolish silence.

The transition from the rational, wordy consciousness to a deeper, mystical and intuitive consciousness has been the object of considerable psychological study in recent times. What precisely happens in the process of passing from an excited state characterized by beta to a relaxed awareness in which alpha predominates? One of the more widely accepted explanations is the so-called filter theory (Naranjo, pp. 170 ff.). According to this, the brain and nervous system are fitted with restrictive filters or barriers of some kind which prevent total reality from entering consciousness, only permitting the entrance of such knowledge as man needs for biological survival. These filters are nothing less than a repressive mechanism calculated to impede the inrush of knowledge that would otherwise overwhelm and break us. In this sense they are a sort of protective screen: humankind, unable to bear too much reality, must find some way of blocking things out.

But these protective barriers, this theory continues, can be removed so that more knowledge enters, thus expanding the mind. Probably one way of removing them is by the intake of drugs. Or they are perhaps broken down in certain forms of mental illness. In these cases, the floodgates are opened and reality rushes in, often with horrendous and traumatic consequences. Or again, some people may be born with less restrictive filters; and these are the "psychics", who are open to telepathy, clairvoyance and other parapsychological sources of information. Meditation is also a human and natural way of opening the filters, welcoming the inflow of reality, and expanding the mind. It is a gradual process, a daily practice, in which the filters or barriers are slowly lifted to allow an almost imperceptible inflow of greater reality into the intuitive consciousness – though this unhurried process may, at times, give way to a sudden collapse of barriers that causes massive enlightenment or mystical experience. In all this, meditation is safer than drugs because the meditator, if properly instructed and guided, can integrate the new knowledge and preserve his equilibrium. This point I will take up again in a later chapter.

Let me now mention some ways, common to many religious traditions, by which one enters the unitive silence that lies beyond thought. These are techniques for restricting or rejecting the rational consciousness, thus allowing the deeper, intuitive consciousness to rise to the surface of the mind.

Zen Buddhism nurtures the intuitive consciousness by a radical rejection of the rational. Conceptualization of any kind is jettisoned. Here are the words of an ancient Zen master:

> Conceptualization is a deadly hindrance to the Zen yogis, more injurious than poisonous snakes or fierce beasts . . . Brilliant and intellectual persons always abide in the cave of conceptualization; they can never get away from it in all their activities. As months and years pass they become more deeply engulfed in it. Unknowingly the mind and conceptualization gradually become of a piece. Even if one wants to get away from it, he finds it impossible. Therefore, I say, poisonous snakes and beasts are avoidable, but there is no way to escape from mental conceptualization. (Chang, p. 86)

In Zen, then, one rejects reason, thought and imagery in order to enter the deeper area of *san'mai*. In *Soto* Zen this is ordinarily done by attention to, or concentration on, the breathing, which has the effect of brushing away all thoughts and images, and of restricting consciousness to the one single process of breathing. When conceptual thought is thus abandoned, intuitive consciousness begins to rise to the surface, giving one a sense of well-being and of interior integration.

In the Western mystical tradition as it evolved since the

sixteenth century, it was usual to begin meditation with a certain amount of reasoning and thinking about the scriptures, about the life of Christ and so on. This was called "discursive prayer" and in time it was simplified to the process of repeating aspirations (this was technically called "affective prayer") and finally to the repetition of one aspiration and the entrance into intuitive silence. This last stage was called "the prayer of simplicity" or "the prayer of the heart" or "the prayer of simple regard" or "acquired contemplation".

It will be noticed that in the West (unlike Zen Buddhism) rational thinking, far from being rejected, is the very road that leads to intuition. Perhaps there is here a valuable Western insight, based on an intensely incarnational view of life: the whole man should be involved in meditation – the whole man with his rational and intuitive capacities. Only by developing and appreciating and then *going beyond* the rational can he reach the intuitive in an integral way. I believe this approach to meditation produced men who were great in reason and great in intuition. I mean men like Augustine and Thomas Aquinas and Bergson and Teilhard.

But let me now continue to describe some techniques for entering into *samadhi*.

One of the most common is the repetition of a *mantra* or sacred word. This is the method employed in transcendental meditation, where one simply adopts a comfortable position (though it is advised that the back be kept straight), closes one's eyes and repeats interiorly the *mantra* in a passive way. What is important is not the meaning (most practitioners do not know what their *mantra* means) but the vibrations, which have the effect of leading one into deeper and more subtle layers of consciousness and of psychic life. And all this without the rigours of Zen. The most famous Indian *mantra* is OM. In Japan, while Zen was always for an élite, the repetition of the *mantra Namu Admida Butsu*[1] had enormous influence on the masses of believers in Pure Land Buddhism. In Christianity the word "Jesus" is a very traditional "*mantra*", but others, too, were used. Here is the advice of a fourteenth-century English mystic on the use of the *mantra*:

[1] "I take refuge in the Buddha, Amida."

If you want to gather all your desire into one simple word that the mind can easily retain, choose a short word rather than a long one. A one syllable word such as "God" or "love" is best. But choose one that is meaningful to you. Then fix it in your mind so that it will remain there come what may. This word will be your defense in conflict and in peace. Use it to beat upon the cloud of darkness above you and subdue all distractions, consigning them to the cloud of forgetting beneath you. Should some thought go on annoying you, demanding to know what you are doing, answer with this one word alone. If your mind begins to intellectualize over the meaning and connotations of this little word, remind yourself that its value lies in its simplicity. Do this and I assure you these thoughts will vanish. Why? Because you have refused to develop them with arguing.   (Johnston (1), ch. 7)

For this author, the *mantra* is a kind of weapon for warding off reasoning, thinking and conceptualization. By it, too, the horizon of rational consciousness is narrowed and prepared for the breakthrough. Interesting is his paradoxical advice to choose a meaningful word and yet not to bother about the meaning. Anyone who uses a *mantra* will tell you that his word is extremely meaningful but he doesn't bother about the meaning. Perhaps this is because a *mantra* is above all symbolic – it points to something other than itself.

It should be noted that in the use of the *mantra*, monotony, far from being an obstacle to enlightenment, is central to the practice. This is because monotony is another way of restricting the reflective consciousness. If things become too interesting at the rational discursive level, one may want to stay there; one may cling to one's interesting thoughts, losing the desire to break through to something deeper. If, on the other hand, monotony predominates at the discursive level, the intuitive is allowed to act. Hence the monotonous repetition of litanies in the West:

> Ora pro nobis
> Ora pro nobis
> Ora pro nobis

Or again, the constant recitation of the Ave Maria in the rosary. These are ways of introducing people to mind-expansion and enlightenment.

Somewhat similar to the use of the *mantra* is the recitation of the sutras in Buddhism and of the Gregorian chant in Christianity. Here also rhythm and monotony are important elements in introducing the chanter to the prayer of quiet. That is one reason why the psalms were recited in common by the monks for centuries. But again it is interesting to see that whereas Japanese Buddhists frequently recited Chinese sutras which they did not understand, Western monasticism never rejected meaning. It aimed at going beyond the rational meaning to a deeper, primordial and transcendent meaning. That is to say, it went beyond wordy meaning at the discursive level to find deeper meaning in wordless wisdom.

Yet another way of restricting rational consciousness and entering a deeper level of mind is the use of the *mandala*. This is a visual image, sometimes very complex and sometimes just a simple circle, on which one fixes one's gaze. Its use is common in the Tibetan tradition of esoteric Buddhism. Within Christianity I believe the principal *"mandala"* has been the crucifix, upon which people have fixed their gaze for hours and hours without words or images or thoughts of conceptualization and in this way have broken through to enlightenment and resurrection. Or again, the tabernacle has been a *mandala* upon which simple people, who, of course, never heard the word *mandala*, have fixed their eyes in silent expansion of consciousness or *samadhu* or one-pointedness or the prayer of quiet.

Another way of enhancing awareness, found in Zen, is the process of listening to every sound. There is a *koan kikunushi* usually translated, "Who is the master that is hearing?" Using this *koan,* one listens to every single sound, all the time asking who is the subject that hears. In this way, it is said, the bodhisattva, Kannon, found enlightenment. Like the other *koan*, it restricts rational consciousness and forces the mind to a breakthrough. Again, in Christianity I believe that the crucifix, besides being a *mandala*, is a *koan*. Paul makes this pretty clear when he says in Corinthians 1 that Christ crucified is a scandal and a stumbling block, but once understood, it is wisdom. Quite a good definition of the *koan* from Paul.

I have insisted that in all these methods the technique is that of limiting rational consciousness to one process. That is to say, the stream of consciousness being restricted, the mind is forced to work vertically downwards, and is in consequence expanded. The same effect, however, is sometimes achieved simply by fixing the mind on God without any of the above techniques. Here is the clear and direct advice of the author of *The Cloud*:

> This is what you are to do: lift up your heart to the Lord, with a gentle stirring of love desiring him for his own sake and not for his gifts. Centre all your attention and desire on him and let this be the sole concern of your mind and heart. Do all in your power to forget everything else, keeping your thoughts and desires free from involvement with any of God's creatures or their affairs whether general or particular. (Johnston (1), ch. 3)

This seemingly simple advice cannot be put into practice, however, without tremendous control of the mind. In fact one generally cannot do it without training in the other methods for entering *samadhi* already referred to.

Yet another way to the silent state of consciousness and one that deserves special mention, is the process of visualization. This can be of many kinds, as may be evident from what has already been said about laboratory experiments in hypnagogic imagery. One can close one's eyes and imagine a scene – or, on the other hand, one may suddenly and unexpectedly become aware of dream-like-imagery that is already present in the mind. This latter is clearly of another order, enacted at a different level of consciousness from the ordinary process of conjuring up a scene. In short, there is a type of visualization that destroys alpha (and on this point I quoted Dr Kamiya in an earlier chapter) and there is a visualization that springs from alpha and more often from the combination of alpha and theta.

A Buddhist monk told me that in his sect (he belonged to esoteric Buddhism) one of the best ways to enlightenment was to visualize the Buddha with which you wish to identify, be it Amida or Kannon or whatever – and in this way one loses self and becomes a Buddha. He told me that some monks were so good at visualization that they could actually bring themselves to see the Buddha of their choice. He confessed, however, that this kind of visualization did not appeal to him personally and that he was not expert in its practice.

Yet deeper than all this, and deeper than hypnagogic imagery, is an area of psychic life that is associated with what Western mystics have called "the interior senses". Here is seeing and feeling and hearing and touching of a different kind and in a new dimension. St Teresa, for example, writes: "One day, when I was at prayer . . . I saw Christ at my side – or to put it better, I was conscious of him, *for I saw nothing with the eyes of the body or of the soul*" (Teresa (1), ch. 27). This experience, frequent in the life of Teresa, differs from the Buddhist visualization I have spoken about in that it is not conjured up or deliberately fostered. It is something that just happens, a spontaneous activity arising from within. Moreover it differs from the hypnagogic imagery that appears in the alpha-theta experimentation of Dr Elmer Green. This latter was described by subjects as being vivid like lantern-slides, whereas Teresa's images are not seen at all.

What St Teresa and the mystics say about seeing is paralleled by what they say about hearing. Locutions can be heard at many levels, not only at the level of the bodily ears. I believe that the prophets of Israel heard locutions of this kind. They really heard something or someone speaking in the depths of their being; they really heard themselves called by name, "Abraham, Abraham . . . "; but the voice of Yahweh did not impinge upon their bodily ears like the vibrations of a human voice. Something much deeper was going on. "Now the word of the Lord came to me saying, 'Before I formed you in the womb I knew you . . . ' " (Jeremiah 1:4–5). Or with Paul: "And I know that this man was caught up into Paradise . . . and he heard things that cannot be told, which men may not utter" (2 Corinthians 12:3). I do not believe that Paul heard a human voice or that sonic vibrations struck in his ears. He was beyond all this, hearing beyond hearing.

Today, also, locutions are by no means unusual with people who meditate deeply. And the most common is still the sound of one's name being called in the core of the being without reference to the physical ears. "Do not be afraid, Mary . . . " (Luke 1:30). In the Hebrew tradition the name has marvellous significance and penetrates to the innermost self. And the experience of being thus called by Yahweh in a personal, loving encounter is central to the Bible. Needless to say, in all this the name is not one's ordinary given name. Rather does one have the sense of being called by that which is of one's personal essence. It is something that cannot be reiterated in human speech. One just knows it and, in a sense, remembers it in so far as it was a *creative word* and one knows the self it created.

It will be readily seen that we are here dealing with a whole area of psychic life ordinarily dormant but opened up through meditations. The mystics claim that they see and hear and smell and touch and embrace in a way that is totally different from the ordinary experience of man. How astonishing their talk of being inebriated with wine and of the kiss of love and all the rest!

Poulain tackles the problem of interior senses in his usual scientific and matter-of-fact way with the question: "Has the soul intellectual, spiritual senses which in some way resemble the bodily senses so that in an analogous manner and in different ways she can perceive the presence of pure spirits and of God in particular?" (Poulain, ch. 6) He answers in the affirmative and then sums up:

> The physiognomy of the mystic union can be described in the following way: during the union, when it is not too deep, we are like a man seated beside one of his friends in darkness and in silence. He does not *see* him therefore, he does not *hear* him; he only *feels* that he is there by the sense of touch since he is holding his hand. And so he goes on thinking about him and loving him.
>
> The material touch may, as it increases in strength, turn into a clasping and an embrace. It is the same with the spiritual touch. In the prayer of quiet, when it is not very strong, it is a simple drinking in which is tranquilly enjoyed. But sometimes the two spirits embrace one

another, which is to say that sudden and affectionate claspings between them take place.

This abundance of grace is not, I believe, common with beginners; and when they at length come to experience it, it is at first only for a few seconds at a time. Afterwards, if they were to try to reproduce this special impression they could not do so.

(Poulain, ch. 6)

It goes without saying that we are here confronted with a psychic dimension which is of the utmost importance for the full understanding of man. A century ago some people were content to look on mystics like St Teresa as oddballs; others preferred to think that they received special powers from God. Now I believe we can say that they were normal people, making use of faculties inherent in man though the majority of people are unaware of their existence. How little of our potentiality we use! It may well be that, as Bergson observed, the mystics are in the vanguard of evolution, men and women before their time – what they experienced may well be an ordinary thing in the years that lie ahead. Be that as it may, I do not believe that these interior faculties are purely spiritual – Platonic rejections of matter. I prefer to use the Teilhardian terminology of "spiritualized matter" and to think of them as highly developed human activities. Probably hominization will not be complete until these faculties are actuated and man is fully alive. But I also believe that the interior senses will never be brought into play until one is able to transcend the monopolizing power of the exterior sense. That there is a tremendous need for renunciation all the mystics agree. But more about this later.

I am aware of the paradoxical nature of everything that I here say. One the one hand I began with the assertion that mysticism is an entrance into silence and then I spoke about words; I said it was imageless and then I spoke about seeing. Yet this is precisely the language of the mystics. They talk about emptiness, darkness, the void, the nothingness, using a string of words that suggest total negativity; and then, in the next breath, they begin to describe it in terms that are rich, joyful, beautiful, erotic. It would seem that the void and the nothingness of the mystics is not a repelling spiritual poverty but an ocean of indescribable wealth, a treasure-house of unearthly beauty. Nothing is all; darkness is light; suffering is joy. How this can be is difficult to say unless one has had some experience. Then the whole thing seems obvious. All I can do here is repeat what was said earlier; namely, that this is an expanded or altered state of consciousness and to explain it in terms of the ordinary day-to-day consciousness that makes up our language is almost impossible. Language from one state of consciousness just does not fit the other. This also explains why mystics will say that everything is one and yet that everything is not one. At one level of consciousness we see the unity and at another we see the diversity. Both statements, I believe, are true; both express something about reality. And modern Western man simply must learn to accept the validity of paradox if he wants to understand.

I have described some ways and techniques for expanding the mind and entering into mystical silence. More could be mentioned. There is fasting, for instance, which has the effect of expanding consciousness. The precise repercussions of fasting – its influence on the flow of blood to the brain and the general metabolism – are now being studied, and the forthcoming conclusions will surely be of the utmost significance for the meditation movement. Or again, in some religious traditions dancing leads to one-pointedness, as in the case of the famous whirling dervishes.

These are all techniques. But let me now hasten to add that in deep meditation there is more than technique. In the heart of the man of good will, whatever his religious affiliation, I believe that the Spirit is at work. And this is the incalculable element which escapes definition and which cannot be circumscribed. I further believe that faith in the action of the Spirit deepens meditation immeasurably. If we believe in something beyond self, beyond consciousness, beyond our own spiritual faculties however refined, then meditation enters a new dimension.

Mention of the Spirit reminds me of yet another way to

enlightenment which many of my readers will undoubtedly have experienced. This is the way of love.

If two or more people love one another deeply, they may be brought to the profound level of awareness and mind-expansion that the great religions speak of. They may come to that *samadhi* in which no words are necessary because their intimacy is not built on words. And the stronger the love, the more profound will be the silence and the deeper will be the enlightenment. Furthermore, if this love goes to the core of their being, it brings a realization of something more than the people involved – it brings a consciousness of the all; it contains an element of universality. This, I believe, is a truly religious experience, very central to the Bible, which tells us that "he who loves ... knows God ... for God is love" (1 John 4:7–8). The Bible does not say that he who *loves God* knows God; it says that he who *loves* knows God. And if this is so, human love must be the supreme way to *samadhi*, to enlightenment, to God. Nor need this, in the case of a man-woman love, be sexual in the physical sense. Psychologists will surely agree with me that, ideally speaking, sexual intercourse is an expression of something deeper – and it is this deeper thing that I am talking about here. It may, of course, be expressed sexually or it may not. That depends on the persons, their relationship and their circumstances. In itself it is a deeply spiritual communication, going beyond the emotional and intellectual to the intuitive consciousness. It is one of the most human roads to contemplation.

That love leads to enlightenment is a recurrent theme in the Western mystics. Love they compare to a candle which gives light and enables us to see both our own misery and God's great goodness. No doubt it helps us to see the great goodness of other people too – if we love them, we are enlightened about their value and worth and goodness. St Teresa says quite simply of the prayer of quiet that it is not necessary to know much (in the rational sense) but to love much. That love should lead to enlightenment is easy to comprehend when we recall that the essence of the oriental awakening is the loss of self (called *muga* in Japanese and *anatta* in Pali) and that self is radically lost through love. Aquinas calls love "ecstatic" because it, so to speak, goes out and lives in what it loves. Perhaps his idea is best expressed in poetry like that of St John of the Cross who exclaims: "O life, how canst thou endure, since thou livest not where thou livest?" – as if to say that his life has gone out from himself to live in the beloved and he wonders that it can continue to dwell in his breast. And then there are the beautiful words of the poet-martyr Robert Southwell, "Not where I breathe, but where I love, I live!" Here is a dramatic loss of self through love.

Needless to say, the love that leads to enlightenment is of a very high order. It is the love Teilhard speaks of when he declares that at the level of the person union differentiates. Teilhard makes a good distinction between union and absorption. Two people can be fascinated with one another, lost in one another, absorbed in one another – in total oblivion of everything, even of themselves. Such love is adolescent. It may be a stage in growth towards maturity, but it is still self-centred. Love of union, on the other hand, differentiates in that the two people find their true selves, are transparent to one another, live in one another, and are in consequence opened up to the all. Early in his life, Teilhard was faced with the awful mystical dilemma of how to become the other while remaining one's self; and here he found the solution; union between persons differentiates. It is this person-to-person love that is a road to enlightenment.

Union differentiates! Insufferable paradox you will say. Yes, but we are learning to think in paradox. And we must think in paradox if we want to reach enlightenment. To the person with experience of love the paradox will present no difficulty. "Give me one who loves", says Augustine, "and he will understand what I say . . ."

To enter the mystical path through love may sound attractive and easy. Attractive indeed it is; but not easy. Anyone can gaze for hours at a flower or a flame or a *mandala* with the safe assurance that it won't hit back, it won't hurt him, it won't betray him. He can be united with a flower in great security. But with other persons much more is involved. The fear of being hurt, or betrayed, or unrequited – the fact that free persons are interacting on one another. All this makes for deeper purification, deeper anguish, deeper love and, in consequence, deeper enlightenment.

Moreover the enlightenment that comes from love is necessarily incarnational. It involves us in society and never cuts us off from reality. This point is worth noting. Talk of altered states of consciousness, of interior senses, of ecstasy and the rest might give us the impression that meditators and mystics are divorced from reality – whereas the contrary is true. Gandhi, Martin Luther King, Dag Hammarskjöld, Thomas Merton still speak to us of a mystical life integrated with service to men. And apart from these giants there are a host of unknown people who integrate mysticism with the humdrum waking consciousness and with daily living in community or family. This is important. For it is mainly through this ordinary life in society that we can distinguish sound mysticism from some forms of mental illness and from Gnostic meanderings in a phantasmal world of inner space.

My contention throughout this book is that this love is the essence of the deepest meditation. To try to understand Teresa or Poulain or Ramakrishna or Martin Buber while neglecting it would be to falsify the whole picture. This love can exist between people of the same sex ("Simon, son of John, do you love me . . .?" (John 21:15)), or between those of the opposite sex, or it can be love for a community. My point is that whether one recites the *mantra* or gazes at the *mandala* or wrestles with the *koan*, the whole process should be undergirded by love if the enlightenment is to go the whole way. In fact, the development of meditation can be compared to a love affair. When two people begin to love, they may chatter and use words a good deal; but as their intimacy grows, words become less necessary and are even superfluous. The two maintain a total and unitive silence, enjoying one another's presence in love. And the same holds true when the beloved is "the mountains, the solitary wooded valleys, strange islands . . . silent music".

6

The road to ecstasy

Writers in many of the religious traditions have depicted successive states of consciousness which the meditator passes through on the way to enlightenment or resurrection. In the West, one of the best known of these is St Teresa of Avila whose *Interior Castle* will always be a classic and a source-book for the researcher in states of consciousness. In this book Teresa divides the interior odyssey into seven mansions of which the last four are deeply mystical and of great relevance today. The soul is a castle in the interior of which dwells the king; and the meditator, at the invitation of this king, makes a journey into inner space to find him enthroned at the centre of the soul.

The experience of St Teresa tallies with that of many Western mystics; so let me describe this journey into inner space, once more following the lead of Auguste Poulain. Relying mainly, but by no means exclusively, on St Teresa, Poulain divides the mystic states of consciousness broadly into four.

The first is the prayer of quiet:

> This comes abruptly and unexpectedly. You are suddenly possessed by an unusual state of recollection which you cannot help but notice. You are overtaken by a divine wave that fills you through and through. You remain motionless beneath the influence of this sweet impression. And then it all disappears with the same suddenness. Beginners are surprised at this, for they find that they are overtaken by something that they cannot completely understand. But they surrender themselves to this inclination because they realize at once that it is something holy. They postpone to a later date the task of examining it more closely.
>
> (Poulain, ch. 16)

This, then, is the initial awakening. In the mystical life it is a

moment of the greatest significance, which Teresa describes in
great detail. If one were to take this experience lightly or forget it,
or misunderstand it, a priceless treasure might well be lost.
Buddhists say something similar. A Buddhist monk once asked me
bluntly if I could recall the moment when I first entered *samadhi*, I
was taken aback by the abruptness of the question which seemed
like an invasion of privacy. He then told me that this question was
frequently asked in the monastery where he did his training. It was
considered helpful for a monk to reflect on the first stage of his
spiritual journey.

If one values these moments of enlightenment and fosters them,
this state of consciousness will become habitual. In general it can
be said that the mystical life consists of peak experiences which
eventually become plateaux. This state, initially surprising and
abrupt, becomes the ordinary thing. So says Poulain:

> Finally a time comes when the prayer of quiet is not only
> very frequent but *habitual*. Now we have it as our state
> whenever we want it. It will occur outside the time of
> prayer and whenever the thought of God is presented, as
> for example in conversation. This is enough for us to be
> seized by the divine action. If this action is powerful, then
> we may find that it interferes with our occupation, but
> usually it all disappears quickly. At other times the divine
> action seems to have a mute influence which continues in
> the midst of a busy life.   (Poulain, ch. 16)

From this it can be seen that meditation is not just something
that one practises night and morning. It perdures. It comes to take
over one's life. If a person's *samadhi* only arises in time formally
devoted to meditation, this indicates that it is still superficial. Zen
meditators will frequently say that Zen is walking, Zen is eating,
Zen is sleeping, Zen is life . . . And all the traditions teach much the
same thing.

In this first state of consciousness, which we have called the
prayer of quiet, two levels of psychic life are at work
simultaneously. The upper, imaginative level may be roaming and
romping and roaring wildly (St Teresa calls it "the fool of the
house") while the deeper level is silently unified and at peace. In

the stage which follows, however, known as "the prayer of union", a unification of these two levels is effected so that one is "without distraction" – two worlds are, so to speak, united. In this way the personality is greatly integrated in a state of consciousness which Poulain describes as follows:

> It is a mystical union of such power that the soul is totally occupied with the divine object. In short, there are no distractions. Yet the senses keep on acting, at any rate partially acting. Furthermore, with a certain amount of effort it is possible to re-establish relations with the external world, to make movements and to come out of this state.   (Poulain, ch. 17)

Poulain then quotes St Teresa, who in her fifth mansion compares the prayer of quiet to drowsiness and the prayer of union to sleep. One is asleep as regards the world and oneself, and during the brief time that this state lasts, one is deprived of all feeling and unable to think discursively.

The third stage is ecstasy. To understand this it should be noted that from the outset of the prayer of quiet the meditator has had some difficulty in using his discursive faculties and he eventually finds himself in a situation technically known as the "ligature" because he is as it were "bound". "In the prayer of quiet", writes Poulain, "the ligature does not constitute a complete impossibility. Thus we can begin to formulate a vocal prayer such as the Paternoster. But after a few words some unknown and secret force hinders us. We hesitate and we stammer. By a renewed effort, however, we can start again; and so it goes on. If we attempted to continue the struggle we would soon be very tired. The right thing to do is to resign ourselves" (Poulain, ch. 14).

As the union deepens, however, the ligature grows and develops into ecstasy, which is "a state which not only at the beginning but during its whole course contains two essential elements. The first, which is interior and invisible, is a very keen attention to some religious object; the second, which is corporeal and visible, is the alienation of the sensible faculties" (Poulain, ch. 13). As for the description of ecstasy:

Ecstasy is found when the divine action is of great force,
and all communication with the external sense is broken or
almost entirely so. We are no longer able to move, at least
voluntarily, not are we able to come out of our pray at
will.[1]

(Poulain, ch. 3)

There are degrees or grades of ecstasy. "Simple ecstasy" comes
upon the meditator slowly. "Rapture" is sudden and violent.
Then there is "flight of the spirit" in which St Teresa affirms that
she does not know whether or not the spirit remains in her body.
Her words remind one of Paul – "whether in the body or out of
the body I do not know, God knows" (2 Corinthians 12:2). The
secrets and revelations that Paul refers to in this state are shared
by other ecstatics. About rapture St Teresa affirms that it is very

---

[1] Poulain devotes a good deal of space to describing ecstasy. See chapter 13:
(1) *The senses* cease to act, or they convey only a confused knowledge...
(2) As a general rule, *the limbs* become motionless, and it becomes impossible
to speak or to walk or to make any gesture...
(3) *The respiration* almost ceases; sometimes it seems to cease altogether.
The same is true for the heart-beats as well as for the pulse. In all these
things there are differences of degree, according to the depth of the
experience. Sometimes at certain moments there has been reason to fear
that death has supervened.
(4) *The vital heat* seems to disappear and a coldness sets in at the
extremities.
To sum up, everything seems as if the soul were losing in vital strength...

Later in the same chapter Poulain describes the effects of ecstasy in greater
detail. For example:

The effect upon the eyes. It is only possible to observe this properly if, while
the body is motionless, the eyes remain wide open and fixed. Several people
have told me that they then saw the things around them as though they were
veiled in a white mist. It is something like an evenly dispersed fog, or like the
smoke that rises from incense...

And again:

In the case of ecstasy we sometimes come across the following phenomena in
regard to the body:
(1) The body rises up into the air. This is called *levitation*;
(2) Or it is surrounded by a luminous *aureole*;
(3) Or it emits a sweet fragrance.

This chapter of Poulain should be interesting for the researcher in the
psychophysiology of meditation.

alarming at first, that often it is irresistible (though simple ecstasy can be resisted) and that one remains in the position in which one was before the ecstasy came. One comes out of the ecstasy at the command of a superior or some authorized person – this was called "the recall".

Poulain's fourth and final state of consciousness is the "transforming union", called by Teresa the "spiritual marriage". There is no ecstasy here because, once again, the peak has become a plateau. The meditator, now accustomed to the powerful inflow of spirit, is able to control it. Hence no more suspension of the sensible faculties, no more loss of control, no more ligature, and in place of these a great freedom to act and to work and to love. This in some ways resembles the Zen "return to the market-place", a stage in which the enlightened person comes back to ordinary life to redeem all sentient beings. In Zen, it may be remembered, there is the first stage, in which trees are trees, rivers are rivers and mountains are mountains; followed by a second stage, in which trees are rivers, and rivers are mountains, and mountains are trees; only to be followed by the final stage of enlightenment, when once again trees are trees, rivers are rivers and mountains are mountains. In some such way, the transforming union is a completely ordinary and normal state in which, however, one is moved and motivated by something deeper than oneself. Hence the Christian mystics' constant appeal to the Pauline, "It is no longer I who live, but Christ who lives in me" (Galatians 2:20). One is moved by the Christ within who speaks and acts and loves and blesses and cries out, "Abba! Father!" (Galatians 4:6) This is the peak-point of hominization when one has found one's true self and, in the case of Christians, has found one's true self in Christ. St John of the Cross puts it well when he says that at the beginning one sees the Creator through the creatures but at the end one sees the creatures through the Creator.

In the above four stages of mysticism I have followed Poulain. It is interesting to note, however, that the majority of his contemporaries had different views on the role of ecstasy. The French Jesuit, Joseph de Guibert (1877–1942), for example, maintained that ecstasy was by no means an integral part of the mystical ascent. It was, he claimed, simply a consequence arising from the weakness of the human organism unable to stand such a powerful inflow of spirit without losing the use of its physical and psychological faculties. Consequently, the person who was physically and psychologically strong would undergo no ligature, no physical ecstasy, no suspension of the faculties. Nor would this lack of the extraordinary indicate that his experience was less profound than that of the person who lost the use of his external senses. It would simply mean that he was strong in body and in psyche. Consequently de Guibert preferred to speak of three stages: prayer of quiet, union and transforming union; and he looked on ecstasy as no more than an occasional and unimportant by-product of the second stage (Guibert, pt. 7, ch. 2).

De Guibert's theory is probably closer to the truth. Much as I admire and respect Poulain, I think that in this point his scientific bent led him to a false emphasis. Besides, here he sings out of tune with the great chorus of Western mystical thought. It is significant, too, that in Zen, even in the deepest spiritual experiences, physical ecstasy is virtually unknown. If anything like this does rear its head, it is promptly crushed. Indeed, the whole Zen training is calculated to counteract anything like ecstasy. The open eyes keep the meditator in contact with his surroundings; then the scolding and the shouting and the beating with the stick and the general atmosphere of the meditation hall militate against anything like ligature or suspension of the faculties. Dr Suzuki often insisted that Zen was not "mystical". I suspect that he disliked this word mysticism precisely because of its association with phenomena like physical ecstasy: the great scholar felt intuitively (and how wisely!) that these bodily things were not what mattered.

Granted all this, however, I still would not reject ecstasy as a stage in mystical development. But I would modify the meaning of the word. I believe that underlying the unimportant physical phenomena is a spiritual experience of the greatest significance which merits our attention. It is an experience that is undoubtedly present also in the deepest stages of Zen; an extraordinarily powerful uprising of spirit in the human mind and heart and the transition to a new level of consciousness. It is this that I call ecstasy (prescinding entirely from ligature and levitation, which may, or may not, be there) and in doing so I believe that I am following a Christian tradition that antedates Poulain and goes back to the thirteenth and fourteenth centuries. For the medieval mystics, ecstasy (the Greek *ekstasis* or *standing out*) was a going out from, or a relinquishing of, the self. This is the root meaning of the term.

Taking it in this sense, I would like to examine more closely this mystical phenomenon and discuss its significance for human life and, more particularly, for human death.

Describing ecstasy, St Teresa speaks of "a feeling of great joy and sweetness". "You realize . . . and indeed see that you are being carried away and know not where. For although this is delightful the weakness of our nature makes us afraid at first . . . often I should like to resist . . . especially in a public place" (Teresa (1), ch. 20). From her accounts, as well as others, we can distinguish two aspects of ecstasy: joy and fear. There is joy because of the change in consciousness, the inflow or ascendency of spirit, the finding of the new self, the increase of being. There is fear because of human weakness and the possible loss of control. One is, so to speak, overwhelmed like a sinking ship. Yet this fear diminishes as the meditator becomes capable of controlling the new force that has entered his life. Then gradually the peak, as already noted, becomes a plateau.

In recent times some psychologists have proposed the hypothesis that a similar phenomenon takes place at the moment of death. Studies on sudden death (gathered from people who fell from mountain-tops or whose parachutes did not open – people who came to the brink of death yet still lived) have revealed that the dying person is frequently overwhelmed by what can only be called a mystical experience resembling ecstasy. This and other studies have led to the hypothesis that dying persons pass through three psychological stages – resistance, life-review and transcendence. In the first stage they fight back because, like the ecstatic, they fear the loss of control. But once they have submitted to the inevitable, memories of their whole past may arise, all in a flash and in the most minute detail. Finally comes the mystical consciousness, often described in terms remarkably like those of the great ecstatics.

No one, of course, claims that everybody dies in ecstasy. The most that can be said is that ideally speaking this is the way life should end. And indeed some ancient cultures have felt this way about death. The task confronting us now is to examine the dispositions and the attitudes we should cultivate if we are to die in this way. Such knowledge will be of the utmost value and significance. And here St John of the Cross (who in some ways confirms this psychological hypothesis) comes to the rescue, telling us of one type of person who dies "with the most sublime impulses and delightful encounters of love". This is the mystic. The great Spaniard makes his point quite clearly:

> The death of such persons is very gentle and very sweet, sweeter and more gentle than was their whole spiritual life on earth. For they die with the most sublime impulses and delightful encounters of love, resembling the swan whose song is much sweeter at the moment of death. Accordingly, David affirmed that the death of the saints is precious in the sight of the Lord (Psalm 115–15). The soul's riches gather together here, and its rivers of love move on to enter the sea, for these rivers, because they are blocked, become so vast that they themselves resemble seas. The just man's first treasures, and his last, are heaped together to accompany him when he departs and goes off to his kingdom, while praises are heard from the ends of the earth, which, as Isaiah says, are the glory of the just man (Isaiah 24:16).
>
> (John of the Cross p. 592)

Here is a beautiful description of ecstatic death.

Psychological discoveries about ecstasy at death dovetail with modern theological studies about the ageing process. These speak of a double curve in the graph of human life; the downward curve of physical disintegration as the vital forces diminish, and the upward curve of spiritual energies as the core of the personality is liberated.[1] Not, again, that this happens in every case; but ideally speaking it should happen if all goes well. From the earliest times, the Hindus have had the same intuition and they have divided human life into four stages in the course of which the personality is increasingly spiritualized. In the third stage (coming after that of the student and the householder) the now ageing man retires to the forest or to a quiet place to devote himself to the reading of the scriptures and to meditation; while in the final period he embraces the monastic life, rising above all the cares of the world in equanimity and the cultivation of God-consciousness. And then there is Jung, with his thesis that beginning with the middle period of life (thirty-five to forty-five in the West of his day) a person should become increasingly contemplative.

All these theories point to one central idea: that the life of man is (or, more correctly, ought to be) a process of spiritualization which reaches its climax with death. If this is so, what happens abruptly in ecstasy and sudden death may happen gradually in the ageing process. There is the same inflow of spirit, the same expansion of consciousness; but the very slowness of the process makes integration easier. In either case, death is the door to the ultimate ecstasy (call it resurrection or *nirvana* or what you will), and in the lives of the mystics we find foretastes or adumbrations of this final beatifying ecstasy.

I have constantly spoken about the uprising or transcendence of *spirit*. Now I think the word needs to be explained with more precision. I use it in two senses. First there are the spiritual energies that lie deepest in man, making him cosmic and universal, making him see deeply into reality, making him truly and distinctively human. It is, presumably, about this spirit that Jung and other psychologists speak. But in the Christian tradition, joined to this is another uprising of the Spirit – of the Holy Spirit, of the Spirit of Jesus who cries out, "Abba! Father! (Galatians 4:6)

---

[1] See Roger Troisfontaines, *I Do Not Die* (Desclée, New York, 1963); Ladislaus Boros, *The Mystery of Death* (Herder & Herder, New York, 1965), published in Great Britain under the title, *The Moment of Truth: Mysterium Mortis* (Burns & Oates, London, 1965).

This is the Spirit that animated Paul when he exclaimed, "It is no longer I who live, but Christ who lives in me" (Galatians 2:20). Paul quite surely had both of these meanings in mind when he wrote of the Christian life as a transition from flesh to spirit. We know that the Pauline flesh is not just sensuality, and the Pauline spirit is not the Platonic soul. Rather is the spiritual man the one whose human faculties are highly spiritualized and who acts under the influence of the Spirit. As such, the transition from flesh to spirit represents a movement towards hominization, towards becoming a man fully alive, towards submission to the Spirit of God.

But can we probe a little more into the cause of this ascendency of spirit that we call ecstasy.

Again, I would distinguish. About the uprising of man's spiritual energies we can say something, since this is a psychological phenomenon. But about the rising of the Holy Spirit we can say almost nothing except from theology. For the Spirit is like the wind that breathes where it will. This makes the whole phenomenon drastically charismatic. But about the uprising of the other spiritual energies, I repeat, it should be possible to say something; and, indeed, some psychologists have put forward hypotheses and explanations. Let me, then, refer to one such hypothesis (with which I beg to differ) about the pre-death ecstasy; and then let me tentatively propose my own explanation.

It has been suggested that the ecstasy that precedes sudden death is caused by hopelessness and despair. The future is a blank. Man is faced with inevitable extinction. And so, his vital energies concentrate on the beautiful experiences of the past, which then surge up in a transfigured way. Hence the joy and the ecstasy.

I myself cannot accept a theory which makes ecstasy an emotional reaction against extinction. It does not fit the facts. Even if it accounted for the transfigured life-review, it still would not explain the subsequent mystical experience. Besides, we know that something like ecstasy may take place when people are brought to what psychologists call "survival level" – even when there is no hopeless prospect of immediate death or extinction. When the body is kicked and beaten and broken and starved and treated as an object, the most profound psychic powers, ordinarily dormant, may be released and something like ecstasy may ensue. But this seems to happen not with the people who have no hope; but on the contrary, in the people who have strong faith and hope and love and motivation. Let me give one striking example.

The story of Viktor Frankl's suffering in concentration camp is well known. Deprived of food and clothing and human comfort of every kind, he had the most beautiful experiences of mystical communion with his deeply loved wife. I cannot believe that this was caused by fear of extinction. He does not indicate that he feared death at all. His account implies that there were two contributing elements: the first was his love, constituting the most powerful motivation, and the second was the total deprivation that he was forced to endure. These two factors opened up a new layer of psychic life that can well be called ecstatic. Frankl himself draws the conclusion that the most important thing for human survival in such circumstances is motivation or faith (hence his logotherapy) but he was also keenly aware of the role of deprivation and detachment in ecstatic experience.

Viktor Frankl's experience is not unique. In the case of the mystics is was precisely when they clung to faith in the most radical detachment that the ecstasy took place. A Buddhist monk once told me that he had his most beautiful interior experiences when he was cold and tired and hungry in time of *sesshin*. I believe that Jesus confirms this when he says that the poor and the persecuted and those that mourn are happy and have their reward. This reward is not just pie in the sky after death; it is a reward here and now. "Rejoice and be glad, for your reward is great" (Matthew 5:12). As if he were to say, "If you have faith in me and do not waver, then in suffering and persecution your latent spiritual powers will be brought into play and the truest human joy will well up from the core of your being. So rejoice and be glad with ecstatic joy." Such is the power of faith; and such is the power of suffering.

Returning to the ecstasy prior to sudden death, then, I would propose that it also is the result of these two elements. On the one hand there is the total deprivation of all that is familiar, the prospect – not of extinction, but of total loss, and the ensuing detachment. And just at this moment, faith wells up in the human heart. In the face of the greatest adversity human faith comes to the fore. Graham Greene speaks somewhere of "the kind of faith that issues from despair"; and I would hazard the guess that in the person with religious faith the ecstasy is more likely to occur. But in others also, a basic faith in man, a kind of primordial hope that lies deep in all of us – this surges up ecstatically in the human breast. As such I speak of a psychological phenomenon. But from theology we can also say that the action of the Spirit may penetrate this whole process and cry out, "Abba, Father!"

Asked about the deepest significance of ecstasy, I would say that it is a foretaste of resurrection. It is a step forward in the spiritualization of man; it is a movement to a deeper level of consciousness that is ever more cosmic; it is the death of the old man and the birth of the new. All this reaches its climax, I believe, in resurrection, when man, definitively spiritualized, becomes cosmic in union with Christ who is cosmic and coextensive with all that is. People who have experienced ecstasy have somehow savoured resurrection and that is why they often long for death, like Paul, who wanted to be dissolved and to be with Christ (Philippians 1:23). Having experienced the shadow, he wanted the reality. But only through death is this reality reached. "Unless a grain of wheat falls into the earth and dies, it remains alone; but if it dies, it bears much fruit" (John 12:24).

Ecstasy is indeed a foreshadowing. It is never the ultimate thing. The pre-death ecstasy is no more than a tiny glimpse, an inkling of what the post-death ecstasy might be. The pre-death ecstasy is still an act of faith: the post-death ecstasy is an act of possession. All the great religious traditions stress that the final consummation is not found in this life. Zen Buddhism says this by its insistence that the meditator never reaches the end. There is always a further step: there is always something beyond: the most sublime states of consciousness are no more than beginnings. How often the self-complacent monk who thinks he has reached the end receives a blow with the salutary reminder that there is no end.

In the Hebrew-Christian tradition, too, it is constantly reiterated that the highest ecstasies and the most profound spiritual raptures are no more than tokens of the final experience of God. They are never the last stage. Moses may meet Yahweh in the cloud of unknowing, but the great prophet never sees Yahweh's face. "You cannot see my face; for man shall not see me and live" (Exodus 33:20). This is a literary way of saying that consciousness of the absolute is never direct: knowledge of God will never be complete. We can see the rays of the sun: never the sun itself. John of the Cross, humble and patient mystic though he is, gets shrill and angry at the very thought of self-satisfied mystics naïvely believing that their elevated states are the final consummation. To think this is to demean God and to forget that he is beyond anything man's little mind can grasp. The ultimate vision of God is reserved for the resurrection that is attained through death.

So in the last analysis we are left in darkness about the ultimate vision. Ecstasy points to the end. But it is not an end itself. We know very little.

7

Return to the market-place

In my last chapter I described the mystical states of consciousness as outlined in Poulain. In Zen a similar attempt to trace the meditational journey is made in the famous Oxherding pictures which depict man in search of the ox – the sacred animal of the East, symbolizing the true self. Successive sketches show man lost in illusion until he gets a glimpse of the footprints of the ox; then of the ox itself. Next he tames the ox and rides it home. Then the ox disappears, leaving the man alone. But the drama reaches its climax with the eighth picture where not only the ox but also the man disappears and nothing remains. Not a thing is. And this is represented by the famous and powerful symbol of nothingness in the form of a circle.

八　　　　　人牛倶忘

(By kind permission of Kobori Nanrei, Daitokuji, Kyoto)

Thus ended the original set of Oxherding pictures, with the last stage depicting a state of consciousness beyond subject and object in which it is impossible to make a statement or a judgement about anything. This is the undifferentiated or non-discriminating consciousness about which Zen talks so much.

In twelfth-century China, however, other pictures were added, so that the series ended with the enlightened old man returning to the market-place to save all sentient beings:

(By kind permission of Kobori Nanrei, Daitokuji, Kyoto)

These two sketches help us to understand the meditation we are discussing in this book. Such meditation is, ideally speaking, a growth from rationalization to the undifferentiated consciousness represented by the circle, and then on to the loving and compassionate consciousness radiating from the wise old man as he returns to the market-place to save all sentient beings.

Let me say a word about each of the pictures.

The undifferentiated consciousness represented by the circle is a fact of experience. No use denying it. As the human mind penetrates more deeply into reality, it becomes increasingly aware of unity. It comes to perceive that everything is one. And, at the same time, it knows that everything is not one. This is the great paradox of mysticism East and West. Experientially, indeed, it is no problem: the person who has delved deeply into reality knows quite simply that everything is one and yet it is not one. But the Greeks (in this point, as in some others, the villains of the piece) were much less open to paradox than their cousins east of Suez; and they built up this problem into the central riddle of all philosophical thinking. They called it *the problem of the one and the many*, and gave it the honoured place in all those philosophical disputations that shook and shaped the Western world. From Parmenides and Hercalitus to Plato, and from Aristotle to Thomas Aquinas the words rang out in syllogistic disputations: "How can it be that there is only one thing and yet there are many things?"

As I have already said, in the simple experience of the mystic this is a non-problem: the two poles are naturally reconciled. But, like many simple things, it becomes desperately complicated when you begin to theorize about it. While Eastern philosophy scarcely considered the problem, its Hellenistic counterpart set up two opposing and irreconcilable systems, two opposing camps: monism and dualism, pantheism and monotheism.

I do not believe that these systems contradict one another. Rather are they complementary. And this becomes a bit clearer in the thought of less Hellenistic Westerners like Bergson and Whitehead and Teilhard de Chardin. Earlier in this book I have said that it is mainly a question of different states of consciousness: the undifferentiated or non-discriminating consciousness which sees unity, and the differentiated or discriminating consciousness which sees multiplicity. Both of these states are, I believe, valid; and human perfection reaches its climax in a new consciousness where unity and diversity are somehow simultaneously operative in the same person. Just as a person can produce alpha and beta brainwaves at the same time, so he can possess a consciousness that is at the same time discriminating and non-discriminating.

Let me, then, outline three stages of growth to illustrate what I mean.

The first stage is that of the discriminating consciousness where we perceive principally duality. This consciousness is at work in the world of business, science, scholarship. It is a consciousness filled with imagery and thinking, ordinarily producing beta brain-waves. I have already said that Zen, rejecting this consciousness as illusory, works towards the non-discriminating consciousness; whereas the Western mystical tradition values it as a stage in meditational growth, a *path* to the non-discriminating consciousness. Western mysticism has always tried to enter into the intuitive with respect for the rational.

The second stage, represented by the circle, is the undifferentiated consciousness. Here one sees the unity of being. Everything is one. To the person who experiences this oneness in a momentary intuition, it may become difficult to believe again in duality; just as the person without experience of unity can only believe in duality. Perhaps a simple metaphor might help. If I see water, I see one thing. Yet this same water can become two things: hydrogen and oxygen. A simple person might find it difficult to believe that this single liquid can become two gases. Or he might find it equally difficult to believe that the two gases could form a drop of water. Yet we know this is true.

The third stage is found when the above two states become luminous to one another, growing into yet a new consciousness in which there is a total unity and a total alterity, a realization that all is one and yet all is not one. It is to this that Teilhard refers when he claims that union differentiates at the level of the person and that in union with the other I find my true self. This is the experience of the mystic who realizes in a flash of ecstatic love that only God exists and that God is the all – and yet, at the same time, that he himself also exists as a unique person, called by name and loved definitively. "Abraham, Abraham!" (Genesis 22:11) I doubt if this consciousness can be experienced apart from ecstatic love encounter. Yet it perdures in what I have called the transforming union. Like the first consciousness it can be at work in business, science and scholarship. For the wheel has turned a full circle.

The wise old man has returned to the market-place.

Let me make a few more comments on these stages of consciousness in relation to the mysticism of the West.

First of all, it seems to me that the Western insight about developing both the discriminating and non-discriminating dimension in man is valuable. The balanced and integral human person needs both rational and intuitive power. This, it seems, can even be shown biologically from recent research on the human brain. It has become clear that each of the two giant hemispheres which, joined by the *corpus callosum,* go to make up the human brain, has a distinctive role. The left hemisphere deals with words and thinking and reasoning and what are called verbal skills, in such wise that a lesion in this hemisphere will cause one to forget the words of a song even when one remembers the melody. The right hemisphere, on the other hand, is concerned with music, art, contemplation, silent meditation, in such wise that a lesion here will cause one to forget the melody of a song even when one remembers the words. Some scientists working in the Langley Porter Institute in San Francisco begin to talk about a *left-hemisphere culture* and a *right-hemisphere culture* (Segal, p. 328). The former is rationalistic, philosophical, technological – the kind of culture that has predominated for the past few centuries in the West. The right-hemisphere culture, on the other hand, is artistic and contemplative – I would say that in spite of its tremendous technological advances Japan's culture is still predominantly right-hemisphere.

The point I wish to make here, however, is that for human perfection both hemispheres should be developed. Otherwise man remains one-sided and unbalanced.

I have always believed that respect for rationality is something that Zen can learn from dialogue with the West. The great Zen philosopher Nishida Kitaro seems to have seen this. Rooted in Zen, he was also steeped in Western philosophy. Perhaps he was looking for a rational system that would balance and strengthen the silent intuitiveness of Zen.

The Judaeo-Christian tradition has always made much of the

dualistic element since its notion of prayer centres around a relationship of love between two free agents. "You shall love the Lord your God with all your heart . . ." (Deuteronomy 6:4). But the first, purely discriminating consciousness is no more than a stage towards the third experience of unity and diversity.

This third stage stands out gloriously in the seventeenth chapter of the fourth gospel where Jesus prays that his disciples may be one, that they may be perfectly one, that they may be completely one – "even as thou, Father, art in me, and I in thee". And yet they are not one; because each retains his own personality.

Something similar is found in St Paul. His first encounter with Christ on the road to Damascus takes the form of a dialogue: "Who are you, Lord?" (Acts 9:5) But in the later epistles a new dialogue appears. For now Paul is "in Christ" and the Spirit of Jesus within is calling out, "Abba! Father!" (Galatians 4:6) So we find enacted within Paul a dialogue between the Father and the Son, who are perfectly one yet remain distinct. As for Paul himself, he can claim that his very life is the life of the Son of God who loved him and gave himself up for him (Galatians 2:20); and Christ is "the fullness of him who fills all" (Ephesians 1:23). Paul has died and his life lies hidden with Christ in God (Colossians 3:3). What *koan* Paul used! And they can be understood only in the light of a consciousness in which everything is one, and yet it is not one.

Before going on to discuss the second picture let me quote two more examples of these stages of consciousness. The first is from Zen. I was greatly impressed when I heard a master say that after attending to the breathing for some time, one realizes that there are two distinct stages in Zen. One is:

I am breathing.

The next is:

The universe is breathing.

This is a fine example of the undifferentiated consciousness and the loss of self.

My second example is from St John of the Cross, and it also deals with breathing and awakening. It is at the end of his exquisite little poem *The Living Flame,* where he comes to write about the great enlightenment:

> How gently and lovingly thou awakest in my bosom,
> where thou dwellest secretly and alone!
> And in thy sweet breathing, full of blessing and glory, how
> delicately thou inspirest my love!

Note that he does not say *I* am enlightened, or *I* awaken – because this *I* is gone. Rather does he say (and he explains himself more at length in his commentary) that *the Word awakens in me.* This has something in common with the universe awakening and breathing; except that the Word inspires his love, and this is the love of the Son for the Father. Here again we have a wonderful example of that consciousness in which all is one and yet all is not one.

The second sketch depicts the return to the market-place. The charming, enlightened old sage, having entered the supreme consciousness of unity and duality, returns to save all sentient beings. That there is indeed an element of duality here can scarcely be denied. If the kind old man returns to save all sentient beings, then must there not be sentient beings to save?

Though the final picture is a twelfth-century appendage, it nevertheless forms a fitting and beautiful climax to the Zen journey, in which presence to reality and incarnationalism have always been stressed and are now doubly stressed with the additional dimension of exquisite Buddhist compassion, the highest form of activity.

Here is a typical passage from a Zen master who asserts that the deepest enlightenment is found by hurling oneself into the maelstrom of activity:

> The superior work you have done so industriously in
> quietness should be applied when you are submerged in
> the tumult of your daily life. If you find it difficult to do so,
> it is most likely that you have not gained much from the
> work of quietude. If you are convinced that meditating in
> quietude is better than meditating in activity, you are then

["falling into the trap of] searching for reality through destroying manifestations, or of departing from causation to pursue Nirvana. *The very moment when you are craving quiet and abhorring turbulence is the best time to put all your strength into the work. Suddenly the realization which you have searched so hard for in your quiet meditation will break upon you right in the midst of turbulence.* Oh, this power, gained from breaking-through, is thousands and millions of times greater than that generated by quiet meditation on your straw seat and bamboo chair.
(Chang, p. 88)

As far as practical advice is concerned, the above might well have been written by the soldier-saint, Ignatius of Loyola. He also wanted to hurl people into the turbulence of action, there to experience the divine and to find enlightenment. Nor in this was he a revolutionary innovator. Through the centuries Western mysticism waged a constant and relentless battle against Gnosticism, Neoplatonism and flight from matter. Though the states of consciousness outlined by Poulain may at first look escapist, the opposite is in fact true. No one insists on incarnationalism more than St Teresa. For her the mystic must have both feet planted firmly on the ground, must never let himself be divorced from reality

Here are some typical sentences from *The Interior Castle:*

Oh, my sisters, how little we should think about resting . . . For if the soul is much with him . . . it will seldom think of itself. Its whole thought will be concentrated on finding ways to please him and upon showing him how it loves him. *This . . . is the aim of prayer; this is the purpose of the Spiritual Marriage of which are born good works and good works alone.*
(Teresa (2), Seventh Mansion, ch. 4)

And in the same chapter she continues:

You may think that I am speaking about beginners and that later on you may rest; but as I have told you, the only repose that these souls enjoy is of an interior kind; *of outward repose they get less and less and have no wish to get more.*

And again:

> We should desire and engage in prayer not for our
> enjoyment but for the sake of acquiring this strength which
> fits us for service.

It should be noted that this stress on active service appears in
Teresa's seventh mansion, which is the very pinnacle of the
mystical life. In this respect it parallels the return to the market-
place which comes at the end of the Zen journey.

But how keep in touch with reality? How keep one's feet on the
ground in such a lofty business as meditation? In Zen this is done
by a series of techniques such as a deliberate policy of keeping the
eyes open, of never closing the doors of the senses, of always
remaining close to the environment, and so on. For Teresa,
however, incarnationalism is ensured by never abandoning the
humanity of Christ, even in the loftiest flights of contemplation. If
any one point is stressed and stressed again in the saint of Avila it
is the centrality of the humanity of Christ. To this she constantly
returns as the main norm for judging the authenticity of Christian
meditation. And she claims that meditation rooted in the
humanity of Christ will avoid the danger of airy-fairy floating in
inner space.

However, it is very important to discover what Teresa means by
the humanity of Christ. One thing is clear; she by no means insists
that the meditator entertain thoughts and concepts of the
historical Jesus as he lived in Nazareth or in Galilee. Rather is she
concerned with the universal Christ – who is, of course, the same
Jesus since there is only one Christ. But now he is seen in his risen
existence. In her *Life* she writes:

> Withdrawal from bodily objects must no doubt be good
> since it is recommended by spiritual persons . . . But what I
> should like to make clear is that *Christ's humanity must
> not be reckoned among these bodily objects. This must be
> clearly understood and I wish I knew how to explain it.*

> (Teresa (1), ch. 22)

And again in *The Interior Castle*:

> This secret union [the spiritual marriage] takes place in the deepest centre of the soul which must be where God himself dwells and I do not think there is need of a door by which to enter it . . . all that has been described seems to have come through the medium of the senses and faculties and this appearance of the humanity of the Lord must do so too. *But what passes in the union of the spiritual marriage is very different. The Lord appears in the centre of the soul . . . just as he appeared to the Apostles, without entering through the door, when he said to them "Pax Vobis" . . . he [St Paul] . . . says, "For me to live is Christ and to die is gain." This, I think, the soul may say here . . . because Christ is now its life.*
>
> (*Teresa* (2), Seventh Mansion, ch. 11)

Remember that the above words are written about the very summit of contemplation. There is no question here of the discursive, imageful prayer of beginners but of the highest stages of mysticism. And Christ is there. He is not, she says explicitly, the "bodily" Christ, even though he is quite surely the same person as the historical Jesus. In short, Teresa is quite certain that Christ is present, that it is not the "bodily" Christ, and that she simply does not have concepts to express Christ as he is ("I wish I knew how to explain it"). That it is the risen Christ (and therefore the cosmic Christ) is amply clear from the whole context which speaks of the Lord who appeared to the disciples and passed through doors – the Lord with whom Paul identifies his very life.

I myself believe that she means what Teilhard calls the cosmic Christ, a reality beyond images and concepts, fully compatible with the highest stages of imageless, nonconceptual prayer. I am not saying that Teresa talks explicitly about the cosmic Christ; but that she was striving for words to express something that centuries later was formulated by Teilhard in this way.

Let me speak briefly about the background to Teilhard's doctrine of the cosmic Christ.

Reading the New Testament quite simply, the chief point that stands out in the whole text is that Jesus who died is now alive. He is among us and will be with us all days even to the consummation of the world. In what shape or form he exists among us is not clearly said; and St Paul, when asked about the nature of the risen body, simply answers, "Don't ask foolish questions!" (But some one will ask, 'How are the dead raised? With what kind of body do they come?' You foolish man!..." (1 Corinthians 15:35).) So about the nature of the resurrected body, either of Christ or of anyone else, we can say little. Only two things are clear from the New Testament. On the one hand, it is the same Jesus as before, still retaining his wounds. On the other hand, it is a transformed Jesus – so much so that his intimate friends do not recognize him for some time.

Of the many interpretations of this phenomenon of the risen Christ I myself incline to the Teilhardian which I regard as a valid development of St Paul's and which, I believe, is somehow present in St Teresa. In death, says Teilhard, Christ becomes cosmic and is present among us as the Christ of the universe, who now possesses a new relationship to matter. He is physically present (and in this sense he is "bodily") but with a new kind of matter. Teilhard uses words like "hyperphysics", but he is trying to express the inexpressible.

All this may sound a bit complicated and abstruse, but it is of the utmost importance for the Christian who wishes to make his meditation Christocentric while retaining the imageless silence of contemplation. Without in any way downgrading the meditation that reflects on the words and life of the historical Jesus of Nazareth, it can safely be said that this is not the kind of meditation Teresa of Avila teaches in the deeper mansions. When she insists on the centrality of Christ, she is talking about the cosmic Christ who is coextensive with the universe and of whom no adequate picture can be formed. This is indeed the Christ who appears all through the fourth gospel saying, "I am the true vine, I am the true shepherd; I am the true bread; I am the way", and so on. "I, when I am lifted up from the earth, will draw all men to myself" (John 12:32). By his resurrection he is the reality in which every other reality exists.

Once we grasp this, we see that the Christian must perforce remain with the risen Jesus just as the Buddhist cannot escape the Buddha nature. But this does not mean that he *thinks constantly about* Christ any more than the Buddhist thinks constantly about the Buddha nature. Rather will he turn to the Father whom Christ has revealed and to whom Christ points. That is why when one has put on the mind of Christ there comes a time when, in a true sense, only the Father remains. But both feet will be firmly on the ground. Because the Christian believes that the risen Christ is the deepest reality (just as the Buddhist believes something similar about the Buddha nature) and that by remaining with Christ he remains close to the heart of the universe.

Finally let me say that we should not take this return to the market-place in a too literal or too simplistic way. In a sense, the dichotomy between contemplation and action is a false statement of the problem. Since contemplation is activity – the highest form of activity – it is in itself a return to the market-place and a building of the earth. This is clear in Teilhard, who, among the many ways of forwarding the thrust of an ongoing evolution, regards mysticism as the most effective and the most powerful. This is because in mysticism the very highest form of human energy is brought into play, a human energy that is nothing other than love at the core of one's being. It is precisely this that builds the earth. Zen hints at this when it claims that the Zen master "sits" for the whole universe. And *The Cloud of Unknowing* speaks of it, too, when it declares that this little love is helping all mankind and giving joy to the hearts of the dead. Here a whole cosmic energy is unleashed and the world shakes. More things are wrought by prayer than this world dreams of.

Writers like John of the Cross tell us that one act of pure love achieves more than all the exterior works in the whole world. And, of course, we have tended to dismiss all this as pious hyperbole. But now some scientists are beginning to say things like that. Some scientists are open to the hypothesis that in meditation a life-force is released which is more significant than nuclear energy. The energy that science looks to is not, of course, the whole story. Bioplasmic energy and passive energy (about which I shall speak in a later chapter) may be a basis for the even higher energy of faith and love that no instrument can measure.

So contemplation and action may not be opposed. One will

often return to the market-place while remaining on one's
meditation cushion or at the prie-dieu. The return to the market-
place need not be a further step. It is part of the very activity of
meditation.

8

A perilous journey

If travel in outer space is fraught with danger, in such wise that we need intrepid astronauts, even more perilous is the inner journey into the caverns of the mind. The astronaut might lose his life; the inner explorer might lose even more precious things. This point was made by a group of scientists whose words, quoted in an earlier chapter, might bear repetition here. "These inner forces are very powerful", they wrote. "Beware the dangers that exist when work like this is done, especially by large numbers of people, without the high values and lifelong discipline of the great ancient systems" (Weide, p. 84). Clearly these scientists are aware that religious people, rooted in the great spiritual systems, are less likely to have a bad trip than the psychologist or the layman.

The reason for this, I would suggest, is not only the high values and lifelong discipline of the great ancient systems. Other forces are at work. There is the action of ultimate reality moving towards man (action which we call grace), and together with this there is the extremely powerful and unifying motivation that underlies the journey of the mystic searching for that which he loves. "Seeking my beloved, I will go over the mountains", writes St John of the Cross. "I will pluck no flowers, I will fear no wild beasts." As if to say that even if all kinds of seductive images and frightening beasts rise up from the womb of the unconscious, he will pay no attention to them because he has heard the even more seductive call of his beloved – who is "the mountains, the solitary wooded valleys, strange islands . . . silent music". This depth of faith and singleness of purpose make his trip infinitely safer than that of the person who begins to roam around in the caverns of his own mind. Such a person might easily get lost.

But before going on, let me digress for a moment to make clear my distinction between the mystic and the explorer in consciousness. This is important because I believe that some modern people think they are practising religion when in fact they are exploring their inner world. The world of the mystic and the world of the psychic explorer, it is true, have much in common and they overlap. Both are inner mansions of hynagogic imagery, unconscious locution, exquisite symbolism and violent upheaval. But whereas the interest of the psychic researcher lies in this world itself, the mystic is passionately in love with a reality that lies beyond consciousness. His main interest is in something or someone he loves but can never fully grasp. For him expansion of mind and states of consciousness are unimportant consequences of his great love.

Yet the dividing line is fine. Jung and Huxley, primarily psychic explorers were also deeply religious men. And Poulain, primarily a theologian, was also an acute psychological researcher. So their terrains overlap.

Here, first of all, I would like to select two psychological dangers of snares that confront both the psychic explorer and the mystic. The first is flight from reality, withdrawal into one's own world: the escape syndrome. The second is a too rapid or premature entry into higher states of consciousness. When either of these things happens, a person may find himself unable to control and integrate the images and the knowledge that suddenly flood his psyche. Let me illustrate this with an example that may be of interest.

In a study of mysticism and schizophrenia, Kenneth Wapnick compares St Teresa of Avila with an anonymous schizophrenic who left a diary containing detailed descriptions of her inner life. In the experience of these two persons Wapnick discovers certain parallels such as the working of a similar psychological mechanism. But he finds more differences. Chief among these is the fact that the schizophrenic, totally unadjusted to ordinary life, retreated into her own world whereas St Teresa kept integrating her inner experiences with daily living. She led a happy life in community with other people and succeeded in doing an enormous amount of work. Wapnick considers this (which, in fact, is Teresa's return to the market-place) to be of the greatest significance. He indicates that in both cases many of the psychic experiences have a similar ring, but their adaptation to life is radically different; and he concludes that "the mystic provides the example of the method whereby the inner and the outer world may be joined, the schizophrenic the tragic result when they are separated" (Wapnick, p. 66).

In the same article, Wapnick goes on to elaborate the distinction between the mystic and the schizophrenic. In the latter, he says, a protective shell is suddenly and prematurely broken whereas the mystic goes to the depth of his being in gradual stages and in a controlled way. Consequently there is an organic growth in the psychic life of the mystic, who becomes more and more a person. Wapnick quotes Jung, who, at a time when he was exploring the deepest levels of the psyche, felt the need of family life and professional work to keep him in touch with reality, to reassure him that he was after all an ordinary person, and to preserve him from a too sudden exposure to his own inner world. Like Teresa he had to keep integrating the emerging data of consiousness into daily living, and without this he might well have become psychotic. We know that drug addicts often break down because they cannot cope with the images released by the ingestion of drugs. Therapy, then, consists in helping them integrate these images.

All this perhaps confirms the age-old Western teaching that the best norm for distinguishing the mystic from the neurotic is daily life. The great masters put less store on what was happening in the mind during prayer than upon the person's life outside prayer. No doubt St Teresa would have asked few questions about a mystic's scores on the EEG even if she had known all about the psychophysiology of contemplation. Rather would she have asked about his adaptability to community living, his humble service to others, his habits of hard work, his ability to do drudgery. It was by these common-or-garden norms that she, and others like her, judged the quality of mysticism. Above all, she put great store on the person's ability to submit to truth; and she kept saying, "Humility, humility, humility!", as if to say that the ego vanishes when the experience is real.

Because of the great perils involved, most religious traditions have sought to initiate their devotees into mystical silence rather than allowed them to wander freely into the deeper caverns of the mind. This is done in various ways. In Zen, for example, the master will tell the disciple when the time has come to give up breath-counting and enter into deep and imageless silence. Or he will give him the *koan* which he thinks will help him. In Western Christianity direction was considered important (though less important than in most Eastern systems), but it was supplemented by certain signs for discerning the right time for entrance into the subliminal depths of contemplation. These signs, however, were more than psychological norms for judging the aptitude of an aspirant to mysticism. They were ways for judging the action of the Spirit. For the whole Christian tradition asserts that Christian contemplative prayer is a response to a divine call ("Let us love God 'because he first loved us'" (1 John 4:1)) and that one should not enter hastily into the interior mansions lest one anticipate the invitation of the Spirit. "Stir not up nor awaken love until it please" (Song of Solomon 2:7) was a scriptural text constantly used to warn the would-be mystic that only the Spirit can awaken his contemplative love. Here let me summarize these traditional signs.[1]

---

[1] My sources for these signs are principally *The Cloud of Unknowing, The Book of Privy Counselling,* and St John of the Cross. All do not have the same number of signs or exactly the same descriptions, but they are remarkably similar in what they point to.

The Ascent of Mount Carmel, 11, 13 gives signs for discontinuing discursive meditation: (1) Inability to receive satisfaction as before. (2) Disinclination to fix one's attention on things extraneous to prayer. (3) Attraction to solitude in order to remain in loving awareness of God (4) That all three are present together.

The Dark Night 1, 9 gives signs indicating that one's aridity in meditation is the beginning of the night of sense: (1) Absence of sense of satisfaction from things of sense or spirit (2) Memory turns towards God in painful anxiety lest it may not be pleasing him. (3) Inability to meditate as before.

The Minor Works: Maxims and Counsels, 40. There are three signs of inner recollection: first, a lack of satisfaction in passing things; second, a liking for solitude and silence and an attentiveness to all that is more perfect; third, the considerations, meditations and acts which formerly helped the soul now hinder it and it brings to prayer no other support than faith, hope and love.

The Cloud of Unknowing, ch. 75: (1) Purified conscience. (2) Strong attraction to contemplation. (3) Desire for it when it seems to be absent.

The Book of Privy Counselling: (1) Meditation becomes impossible because of the intrusion of contemplation. (2) Increasing joyful attraction for contemplation. (3) The presence of both together.

The first sign was that the person aspiring to contemplation should have undergone a conversion and be totally dedicated to good. It is obvious why this stipulation was made. All the religious traditions know of a mysticism of evil. I remember being shocked when I first heard of a "*samadhi* of pure evil". I thought of Shakespeare's Iago and the cold-blooded mystical hatred with which he calmly plotted the overthrow of his noble friend Othello. No doubt he would have produced high-amplitude alpha on the EEG; but it would have been an alpha of evil. It was to obviate such enormities that tradition asked for a conversion prior to entry into the contemplative path. The person with mystical gifts must not use them for destructive ends. If he does, God help us all.

The second traditional sign was the desire for solitude and the longing to be alone. "How dearly you will love to sit apart by yourself," writes *The Book of Privy Counselling*, "knowing that others who did not share your desire and attraction, could only hinder you. Gone will be all your desire to read or to hear books, for your only desire will be to hear of it" (Johnson (1), ch.19). The "it" is the contemplative urge, the action of the Spirit which the same author calls "the blind stirring of love." This is all important. The desire of solitude itself could be neurotic (indication of "bad humours", says St John of the Cross) unless it is accompanied by a longing for the infinite.

The third sign was the inability to think discursively in time of meditation – or, at least, a disinclination to do so. At the beginning of the spiritual odyssey one has, perhaps, reflected on the Bible and prayed with psalms and colloquies. But now one is, as it were, held in the grip of something deeper which impedes thought; and one takes no satisfaction in pious reflections as before. Perhaps this is because the first stage in the development of human consciousness (the rational stage) has been gone through and one is ready for the intuitive: the left hemisphere of the brain has done its work and the time has come for further development of the right hemisphere. Unable to think discursively, one rests in silence. It is a situation like that of two people in love, who prefer to sit silently side by side because thinking and talking would only dissipate their loving union. They are not idling: they are united by a bond that needs neither word nor thought. And it is the same with the person who is beginning to commune with the inner flame of love.

The fourth sign is the constant presence of the contemplative urge. This interior movement at a subliminal depth begins to guide and to dominate in one's life. It has been variously called "the living flame of love", "the dark night", "the blind stirring of love", "the naked intent of the will". *The Book of Privy Counselling* says well that all that is said is "about it" but not "it". This author insists that such an interior motion of love must always be with the contemplative. If it is only present sometimes, then one cannot be sure that the contemplative call is real. "So abounding will it be, that it will follow you to bed at night and rise with you in the morning. It will pursue you through the day in everything you do, intruding into your usual daily devotions like a barrier between you and them . . . " (Johnston (1), ch. 19).

St John of the Cross and the author of *The Cloud* insist that all these signs be present at the same time. The presence of only one is no proof of the contemplative call. But all together indicate the action of the Spirit and not just a psychological state symptomatic of neurosis.

I have spoken about the psychological dangers lurking in the path of one who would enter deeply into the interior castle. But there are perils of another kind, more spiritual and peculiarly mystical. Chief among these is the danger of being seduced by the sirens of bewitching beauty that one encounters on the way. For there may be delectable experiences – voices and visions and profusions of joy. Or there may be a serene and restful silence that inundates one's whole being and fills it with peace. Or it may be the siren of discursive thought and reasoning that beguiles – beautiful thoughts about God and his angels and saints. Thinking, as I have repeatedly pointed out, has its part to play in the mystical life; but there is a stage in which it can be a snare. In fact all these experiences, good and holy in themselves, are snares in the mystical life when one makes them an end or seeks them for themselves. They are snares if one clings to them as if they were absolutes: because then one sticks there, stagnates, makes no progress. One must go on and on, clinging to nothing, absolutely nothing, in order to be free and attentive to the living flame of love that burns quietly and wounds the soul in its deepest centre. Yet there is another temptation even more subtle than this.

It is well known that with growth in mysticism comes growth in human potential – greater insight, refined perception, intuitive power and even extrasensory perception. In all the great religious traditions, these powers, known in Sanskrit as *siddhis* are a by-product of the true mystical experience and must never be sought for themselves. They can be a snare, a dangerous fascination distracting the mystic from his true goal which is wisdom in emptiness, the all which is nothing. In early Buddhism, misuse of psychic powers for self-glorification was one of the sins which merited expulsion from the monastery. That is why researchers and experimenters who want subjects to demonstrate such powers in the laboratory may have a hard task of finding cooperative monks. It is not, I repeat, that these powers are evil in themselves. On the contrary, they are good and can be used to help and to heal, as we see done in the New Testament; but like money, which is also good but difficult to use well, they can be a temptation. Clinging to them blinds insight and hinders progress.

That they can be a tremendous temptation must be clear to anyone. If all power fascinates and corrupts, how much more fascinating and corrupting is the lure of psychic power over the minds of other men! This is a terrible temptation: Dr Faustus, selling his soul to the Devil for psychic power, is a truly archetypal figure. Who would not be tempted to a deal with Mephistopheles with the promise of controlling the minds and the actions of other men? Undoubtedly this is one of the great temptations of those who go the whole way in mysticism. Can one not even find a hint of it in the temptations of Jesus? "The devil took him up, and showed him all the kingdom of the world in a moment of time, and said to him, 'To you I will give all this authority and their glory; for it has been delivered to me, and I give it to whom I will. If you, then, will worship me, it shall all be yours'" (Luke 4:5–7). What a mystical experience this was, seeing "in a moment of time" the totality of things! And then the temptation to power!

Of course our outlook on all this will depend to some extent on our interpretation of the Faust motif – whether we interpret Mephistopheles as a really transcendently existing evil or as a projection of the mind of Faust. Are the witches in Macbeth or the ghost in Hamlet or the evil spirits and Satan and the rest – are these real entities or are they no more than projections of the interior ambition and fear and anger and hatred that lurk in the heart of man?

On this point I would like once again to quote Dr Elmer Green of the Menninger Foundation in Kansas. He is treating of precisely the subject that occupies us here; namely, the dangers of a hasty descent into the deeper realms of the mind. After speaking about illusion and hallucination, he goes on:

> According to various warnings, the persistent explorer in these . . . realms . . . *brings himelf to the attention of indigenous beings who, under normal circumstances, pay little attention to humans* . . . Systems for inner exploration describe these indigenous beings as entities whose bodies are composed entirely of emotional, mental, and etheric substance, and say that at this level of development they are psychologically no better than average man himself. They are of many natures and some are malicious, cruel and cunning, and use the emergence of the explorer out of his previously protective cocoon with its built-in barriers of mental and emotional substance as an opportunity to move, in reverse so to speak, into the personal subjective realm of the investigator. If he is not relatively free from personality dross, it is said, they can obsess him with various compulsions for their own amusement and in extreme cases can even disrupt the normally automatic functioning of the nervous system, by controlling the brain through the *chakras*. Many mental patients have made the claim of being controlled by subjective entities, *but the doctors in general regard these statements as part of the behavioral aberration, pure subconscious projections, and do not investigate further.*

(Green(4))

The above surprised me a little. Not because of its contents (which are fairly orthodox in any religious tradition) but because it comes from the pen or the typewriter of one of the leading neuropsychiatrists in the US, who also worked for fifteen years as a physicist on rocket and guided missile research. It is one more example of the interdisciplinary approach. A scientist extrapolates into the field of religion. I reflected that a decade ago religious people were affirming the existence of devils, while the scientist smiled with amused incredulity. But now, just as we find religious people doubting about devils, we find scientists affirming their existence. And so the wheel turns.

For Dr Green, then, a great peril in this inner journey is the confrontation with these indigenous beings. Interesting too is his suggestion that they may influence the brain through the *chakras*. These latter are centres of psychic energy that play an important role in Yoga; and the notion that indigenous entities act on them parallels the traditional Christian teaching that the evil spirit takes his stand at the gateway between sense and spirit, making his impact not at the deepest point of the spirit but upon the imagination. If only one could get beyond sense to the core of one's being, said the old doctrine, one had nothing to fear from the evil spirit. "Have no fear of the evil one for he will not dare come near you. Be he ever so cunning he is powerless to violate the inner sanctum of your will, although he will sometimes attempt it by indirect means. Even an angel cannot touch your will directly. God alone may enter here" (Johnston (1), ch. 34). The suggestion of Dr Green that this impact is made on the *chakras* is an interesting physiological addition to the traditional doctrine.

About these indigenous beings not much can be said. Perhaps it is enough here to recall that orthodox Christianity has never accepted the notion of a Manichaean principle of evil. If beings are evil this is because, originally good, they chose to be evil. They were not created so; and their destructive power is limited and restricted.

All this brings us to the problem of false mysticism. The great religions are at one in affirming the existence of a mysticism that is true and a mysticism that is false. For modern people, it must be admitted, the terminology is none too attractive. How can an experience be "false"? Psychologists speak of states of consciousness that are *adaptive* or beneficial and *maladaptive* or harmful. But false mysticism says more than this. In general it means that certain states of consciousness are undesirable because they are irrelevant or morbid or regressive, or because they lead away from reality and wisdom, or because they lead to evil or to self-glorification or to destruction or to hatred. All of which are real possibilities. The term "false mysticism" is taken from the Western mystical tradition. Buddhism speaks of *miccha samadhi* (Pali) or *mithya samadhi* (Sanskrit), literally "left-handed contemplation", meaning that one gets one-pointed about the wrong things. Certainly, call it what you will, the phenomenon of mystical aberration is well known in the history of any evolving religion. Nor is discernment easy, because one seldom, if ever, finds mysticism that is one-hundred-per-cent "true". Even in the greatest mystics one finds elements of self-deception or illusion as well as emotional disturbances and the ordinary mental sickness to which mortal man is heir.

In the West, ability to distinguish between true and false mysticism, as between true and false prophets, was called discernment. This was a charismatic gift of the Spirit, given to certain people for building up the community (1 Corinthians 12:7). The person with discernment could judge intuitively. Having the Spirit himself, he could recognize the action of the Spirit in others while being sensitive to the action of less desirable spirits too. Stories are told of how great masters like St John of the Cross, hearing of the ecstatic prayer of certain mystics, would sniff the air of the convent and state confidently, "No, no! This is not it!" Something a little similar (though not quite the same) is found in Zen where the master often judges in a flash that the disciple is enlightened. Sometimes, it is said, he can judge from the very face of the disciple before a word is spoken. Or even from the sound of the disciple's footsteps on the corridor outside.

Unlike Zen, however, Christian mysticism has always insisted that any intuitive judgement should be backed up by a rational check. This is in keeping with a whole frame of mind (to which I have referred several times) which always respects the rational while going beyond it. And the norms for discernment were summed up in certain formulae which came to be known as "rules for the discernment of spirits".

These rules have their roots in the New Testament. "Beloved, do not believe every spirit, but test the spirits to see whether they are of God; for many false prophets have gone out into the world" (1 John 4:1). So we are to test the spirits; and for Christian prayer the New Testament gives a clearcut norm: "By this you know the Spirit of God; every spirit which confesses that Jesus Christ has come in the flesh is of God, and every spirit which does not confess Jesus is not of God (1 John 4:2). In other words, the norm is Christ: if a person's meditation leads him to deeper faith and commitment to Jesus Christ who came in the flesh, then it is true; if not, it is false. Meditation should somehow culminate in the act of faith: "Jesus is Lord!" (1 Corinthians 12:3)

Obviously this norm is only for Christians, but it may not be without value for others also. Because underlying it is a stress on incarnationalism that is of interest for any kind of meditation – the keeping in touch with reality, the keeping one's feet on the ground that I have spoken about in reference to St Teresa. John's words seem to have been written at a time when dualistic Gnosticism and flight from matter were rife in the Mediterranean world. Hence his emphasis on the flesh and blood of Jesus. "That which was from the beginning, which we have heard, which we have seen with our eyes, which we have looked upon and touched with our hands . . ." (1 John 1:1).

Following on this, the acid test of meditation in the New Testament is its fruits. "But the fruit of the Spirit is love, joy, peace, patience, kindness, goodness, faithfulness, gentleness, self-control; against such there is no law" (Galations 5:22). To judge the validity of interior motions and inspirations is not easy; but the effects or the fruits are more apparent. Among these, it is interesting to see how the whole Christian tradition stressed the great significance of peace. *Non in commotione dominus* ran the old Latin tag – "The Lord is not in commotion". And spiritual masters like Ignatius of Loyola give detailed norms for distinguishing between true and false peace. And again they always asked about the fruits of this peace.

It is scarcely possible here to enter into detail about these rules.

Only let me refer in conclusion to an important one: people who meditate were always counselled to open their hearts to a director, particularly in time of stress and temptation. Here is the quaint advice of St Ignatius:

> The enemy also acts like a false lover who wishes to be hidden and does not want to be known. For when this deceitful man pays court, with evil intention, to the daughter of some good man or the wife of a good husband, he wants his words and suggestions to be kept secret. He is greatly upset if the girl tells her father, or the wife her husband, his deceitful words and depraved intentions, for he sees clearly that then his plans will fail. In the same way, when the enemy of our human nature tempts a just soul with his tricks and deceits, he wants and desires that they be received and kept secret. When they are revealed to a confessor or some other spiritual person who understands his deceits and evil designs, the enemy is greatly displeased for he knows that he cannot win in his evil plan once his obvious deceits have been laid bare.   (Ignatius, p. 132)

The above has something in common with our modern counselling. Except that its aim is to discern the Spirit. Once again it is part of a whole incarnational thrust in Christian meditation. Any inspiration or enlightenment or action of the Spirit is not complete until it is manifested to another and thus "incarnated". How clear this was in the case of Paul! His great enlightenment on the road to Damascus was not complete until manifested to Ananias. With the imposition of those hands, the scales fell from Paul's eyes and he sat down to eat and drink. His enlightenment was now complete (Acts 9:18).

I have written a lot about the perilous journey. My intention is not to make people scared. "Pay no heed to anyone who tries to frighten you or depicts to you the perils of the way", writes Teresa. "What a strange idea that one could ever expect to travel a road infested by thieves for the purpose of gaining some great treasure without running into danger!" (Teresa (3), ch.21) The treasure is the thing. And it is worth any effort and risk. But the thieves are there too, and it would be unrealistic to overlook them in one's journey towards wisdom.

PART III

HEALING

9

Meditation, therapy and passive energy

Recent times have seen a good deal of interest in meditation as therapy. Western medicine, it is now recognized, has been desperately one-sided, largely ignoring the role of the mind in the healing of the human body. Assuredly it is acknowledged that up to eighty per cent of modern sickness is either psychosomatic in origin or has a psychosomatic dimension (in particular diseases which are peculiarly human and do not afflict animals are now regarded as psychosomatic); but while admitting psychosomatic sickness, the West has been slow in developing a process of psychosomatic health – that is to say, health of body that will stem from health of mind or from mental control of bodily functions. Only now with the growing influence of the East and talk about acupuncture, about the life-force, about *kundalini* and the rest – only now do we begin to grasp again the spiritual and metaphysical dimensions of healing. But interest is growing fast. And it is not unlikely that meditation will be one of the principal means of therapy in the future.

That meditation has strange and profound repercussions on bodily functions was recognized long ago by the British in India. While Rudyard Kipling sang blithely about the glories of the Empire, more penetrating and common-sensical British medical minds were examining stories about holy men, yogis, who reportedly walked on live coals, had themselves buried alive, stopped their hearts, listened during sleep, pierced their flesh with bloodless swords and defied the laws of gravity. What was the medical profession to think of all that? Was it fact or fiction or myth?

One of the first scientific studies on these phenomena was made by a French cardiologist, Thérèse Brosse, who went to

India in 1935 with a portable electrocardiograph and claimed to
have discovered a yogi who could stop his heart. But not everyone
took her seriously; and only in the last couple of decades have
more widely recognized studies been performed. Among these
one of the most striking was that of Dr and Mrs Elmer Green in
1970, with Swami Rama, a yogi from Rishikesh in the Himalayas.
A man in his middle forties, Swami Rama had been practising
Yoga since the age of four.

In a report issued from the Menninger Foundation, Dr Green
describes in considerable detail the swami's remarkable ability to
regulate bodily functions ordinarily outside human control
(Green (6)). For example, in a preliminary interview the swami
showed such control of blood-flow that he caused two areas on
the palm of his right hand to change temperature in opposite
directions – one part became ashen grey and the other bright red.
Later in the laboratory he stopped his heart from pumping blood
for a least seventeen seconds in what Dr Green describes as an
"atrial flutter" which ordinarily causes death. He also produced
at will alpha and theta waves, subsequently telling the researchers
about his interior state during these exercises. He was able to
diagnose physical ailments in others. And finally he lay down with
his eyes closed and, while gently snoring, produced the delta
rhythm characteristic of deep sleep. Yet after twenty-five minutes
he opened his eyes and repeated almost verbatim everything that
had been said while he was "asleep". He called this a "yogic
sleep" during which he had told his mind to record everything
that was happening while his brain slept. All the above has been
documented with scientific rigour by Dr and Mrs Elmer Green.

Swami Rama is obviously an exceptional man. At Harvard,
however, experiments of a more modest kind were performed
upon practitioners of transcendental meditation with no pre-
tensions to extra-ordinary powers. The subjects tested were
mainly young people between the ages of twenty and thirty who
had been practising TM from anything between six months and
three years (Segal, p. 377).

Results showed that from the physiological and metabolic
standpoint meditation is deeply restful, more so than the ordinary

relaxation found through lounging in a chair. In this latter situation there remains considerable muscle tension which is relaxed in time of meditation. Meditation, the researcher claimed, is a form of relaxation quite as natural to man as sleep or rest. Concretely they showed that after a few minutes of meditation the breathing slowed down, oxygen consumption was reduced, carbon-dioxide elimination declined. Blood-pressure also dropped and the heart beat more slowly. Skin resistance to electricity was measured by means of electrodes taped to the hands. It is well known that in a state of anxiety skin resistance to electricity drops (and on this principle the lie detector works) but in meditation skin resistance was shown to increase fivefold. Moreover lactate concentration in the blood declined, again showing a lowering of anxiety. Brainwaves registered high-amplitude alpha as in Zen; and all in all the claim of the researchers that meditation is deeply restful seemed to have ample foundation. One more extremely significant point was the number of meditators who claimed to have abandoned drug-abuse after starting meditation.

Studies performed on Zen in Tokyo showed very similar results. It was found that Zen is a deeply restful state in which blood-pressure falls, the heart beats more slowly than usual, anxiety is reduced and high-amplitude alpha is recorded on the EEG.

All this points to a fascinating conclusion; namely, that the person who meditates becomes physiologically different from the person who does not. Brain rhythms, heart-beat, blood-pressure, skin resistance – all are changed by meditation. And researchers have told me that people who go off to make a week's *sesshin* often return physiologically different. The great religious traditions, of course, have seen this intuitively and that is why people who meditate have instinctively taken on a different diet, different clothes, different sleeping habits and a different life-style. They have discovered that certain occupations are incompatible with the meditational thrust that fills their life; and sometimes they have made a strange option for celibacy. This confirms a point I have constantly made throughout this book; namely, that meditation is not just an occupation taken on night and morning for several hours each day. It is a whole way of life or, more correctly, a way of being. Once one gets into it, it tends to take over, to change and to transform. Anybody starting it had better sit down and count the cost like the sensible man who wants to build a tower.

In regard to the physiological benefits gained from meditation it is interesting to try to pinpoint the precise health-giving dimension. Some researchers in Tokyo have claimed that the beneficial effects stem from the lotus posture. They refer to the straight back, the balanced position, the slightly touching fingers and the slow breathing as conducive to the deepest human relaxation. Furthermore they claim that next to the lying-down position, the lotus is the posture in which the least energy is expended. All this contains much truth; and I believe that scientific studies on the flow of blood to the brain and the relaxation of muscle tension will reveal more and more the physiological benefits of the lotus. At the same time, I think it would be an exaggeration to put all the emphasis here and here only because similar benefits are reaped in transcendental meditation and other systems that do not insist on the lotus. Moreover, even in Zen the lotus posture, though highly desirable, is not essential. Zen can be practised on a sick-bed. Consequently we must look elsewhere for an explanation of the therapeutic dimension of meditation.

I myself believe that the secret lies in what scientists now call *passive concentration* and *passive energy*. This is a newly discovered energy which promises to be of immense significance for the future of science and for the future of man. It was introduced to the scientific world by the German scientist Joannes Schultz whose autogenic training (influenced by Western medicine, by hypnosis and by Yoga) first gained popularity in Europe around the year 1910. But before examining passive energy in detail I would like to glance at its role in meditational therapy.

The significance of experiments like that with Swami Rama does not precisely lie in the possibility of stopping one's heart or performing extraordinary feats. What is significant is the possibility of creating a new form of therapy through body-control. If people can learn to regulate body-temperature, blood-flow, heart-rate, and so on, enormous possibilities are opened in psychosomatic medicine. And if it is demonstrated that the automatic or involuntary nervous system is not involuntary after all, new vistas may well be opened.

At the Menninger Foundation in Kansas, volunteers are now being taught to control internal states by means of biofeedback, using audio and visual displays (Segal, p. 302). The method is rather similar to that which I described when speaking of control of brain rhythms. In regard to the regulation of hyper-tension, for example, the subject is wired to the machine in such a way that a light flashes any time his blood-pressure rises above a certain point. His job, then, is to prevent that light from flashing and so keep down his blood-pressure. It has been discovered that will-power or *active volition* (willing, willing that my blood-pressure go down) achieves nothing or may even have the contrary effect. But if I wish that my blood-pressure go down in a passive way and then simply allow the thing to happen – in this way, and by the use of biofeedback, I may attain to a great deal of control. The secret lies in the control of passive energy and the exercise of *passive volition*. And the whole process is a species of meditation.

A wide variety of experiments with this kind of therapy are being performed. There is, for example, training in muscle relaxation. It is known that in the process of relaxation the muscles in the forehead are of primary significance – if they are relaxed, a total relaxation becomes possible. So an electrode is pasted to the forehead, and when the muscle relaxes a light flashes or the meter goes down. And in this way muscle relaxation is learned. But the result is achieved not by striving and straining actively, but by passive volition.

Or again there is the possibility of curing migraine headaches. It was discovered that relief could be achieved through increasing the flow of blood to the hands in what is called "hand warming". Once again, active volition, with strong and determined resolutions that "I *will* warm my hands", achieves nothing; but if one relaxes, wishes the thing to happen and then allows it to happen, extraordinary results can be achieved. As before, electrodes are pasted to the hands and hooked up to a meter which immediately registers the slightest change in temperature. In this way the patient is immediately informed when his hands begin to get warm and can learn to regulate the temperature for himself: he is learning the art of passive volition.

It is still too early to predict the future of this new branch of medicine based on passive concentration and meditation. The suggestion has been made that a cure for cancer could conceivably be found – that voluntary starvation and absorption of cancerous growths through blood-flow control is within the realm of possibility. However that may be, one of the most significant aspects of it all is that we are coming to a form of medicine in which the patient will heal himself and in which the role of doctors and nurses will be radically changed. It seems to me that there is something right about this. It makes healing creative and positive rather than a process to be undergone.

From what has been said it will be clear that passive energy is not necessarily religious. It can be generated in a meditational therapy that has nothing to do with religious faith. Or it can be found to predominate in certain cultures. In Japan, for example, it is unmistakably present in the tea-ceremony, the flower arrangement, calligraphy, and even in traditional sports like judo and archery.

But it is found pre-eminently in religious meditation from ancient times. The *Bhagavad Gita* tells us to work without coveting the fruits of our labour. In other words, we want the fruit but we don't strain and strive to obtain it. In a sense we don't want it at all, and we are wholly detached. This is an example of passive volition. Or again, in Zen one's aim is *satori*. Yet one does not strive and strain for this experience; and if one does so, one will not get it. The striving must be done in a passive way – and this again is passive volition. In Christian contemplation, too, the love of God brings about a cessation of thought and a consequent generation of passive energy. Clearly in all these cases the passive energy is associated with (and is perhaps the cause of) the high-amplitude alpha that registers on the EEG of contemplative meditators. It is important to note, however, that religious meditation differs from meditational therapy in that it has a totally different motivation and (in most religions) a belief in the action of a divine power and in his grace. This changes the exercise radically: passive energy is no more than a psychological consequence of a deeper spiritual aspiration and communion that can never be measured.

But in either case the psychological process is similar. One goes beyond discursive reasoning and yet remains alert and aware. Here is the core of passive energy. It is found in a state of consciousness where the mind does not go out to an object in order to analyse it in a discursive way. Rather does it take in the whole to "contemplate" (literally "gaze upon") and identify with it. Passive energy belongs to the intuitive way of thinking just as active energy belongs to the discursive. Both are necessary for full human development.

This passive energy, then, may go in many directions. It is principally in Yoga that it is directed to body-control. The lotus posture (and this I believe is very significant) is a magnificent way to the fostering of passive energy. By sitting in the lotus position and entering deeply into Yoga one can become aware of one's body in a new way. One can become conscious of physiological functions that normally pass unobserved. Not only is one conscious of the breathing, but one may also listen to the heart-beat and, it is claimed, one may come to an awareness of digestion, metabolism and one's whole interior physiology. Having become aware of them by *passive concentration*, the next step is to control them by *passive volition*. But in the highest spiritual traditions of Yoga, such control of bodily functions is considered of little importance compared with the great ideal of union with the divine.

In truly religious exercises passive energy is something like a vehicle for the activity of the Spirit – an activity that transcends all measurable energy. Sometimes it is found in group prayer – the vibrations that unite the participants are almost palpable. Or it can exist between two persons. In the East the interesting word *darshan* speaks of the communion that can exist in a deeply spiritual contact between two people, usually master and disciple. Or the same exchange of energy can be found between two people who are in love; their communion is intuitive, beyond all words and discourse in a kind of fusion of consciousness. I would hazard the guess that passive energy plays a key role in clairvoyance, mind-reading, telepathy and other forms of extra-sensory perception. But, I repeat, it is not necessarily religious. Probably it is generated in large quantities in mass hysteria, and it could be used for evil as well as for good. What makes it religious is the further "super-energy" of grace and profound motivation.

The scientific discovery of passive energy may well turn out to be a major breakthrough in our day. For one thing it demonstrates to the scientist that the Carmelite monastery, the Carthusian hermitage, the Hindu ashram and the Zen temple are not a refuge for people who want to waste time. They are generating large quantities of a very high and precious energy. What happens to that energy and how it is used is another matter. I myself believe that it is the material basis for a higher, unmeasurable, spiritual energy that builds the earth.

10

The healing of the mind

In the last chapter I distinguished between meditational therapy on the one hand and religious meditation on the other. It was not my intention to make a value judgement, as though one were better than the other. Rather did I mean that they are different in much the same way as psychology and theology are different, if overlapping, sciences. To aim at producing a state of consciousness that will heal body or mind is a legitimate and laudable aim of meditational therapy. But religious meditation does not do this. It strives for ultimates. That it may also have therapeutic consequences (St John of the Cross speaks of the cure of bad humours) and that it may also embrace psychological goals is a point I wish to make later; but even in this case the healing cannot be ascribed solely to the psychological process. Other factors enter in.

Before speaking of its healing power, let me recall that meditation is not necessarily therapeutic. In *The Psychophysiology of Zen* Dr Tomio Hirai observes that many neurotics visit Zen temples in Japan in search of psychological health. But quite often they get sicker. He then states that Zen should not be recommended for the emotionally unbalanced or for those with latent psychoses. Such people may find it impossible to integrate the images and problems released from the unconscious. Besides, Dr Hirai feels that the great severity of Zen in its present form renders it unsuitable for the masses.

Yet some kinds of meditation, including a modified form of Zen, do seem to be beneficial and therapeutic for certain people. For example, as mentioned in the last chapter, transcendental meditation sometimes helps cure drug-abuse. Or again, in *The Still Point* I spoke about a Japanese psychiatrist who combines *zazen* with counselling (Johnston (2), pp. 59–60). Or again, it has been claimed that simply by entering into prolonged alpha consciousness through biofeedback a cure for neurosis has been effected. Wherein lies the therapeutic dimension of the meditational practice? This is the question I would first like to ask. And perhaps a clue is provided by considering the role of the memory in man's psychic life.

It is now axiomatic in psychology that most neuroses and emotional disturbances are connected with the memory. While we are still desperately ignorant about the millions of cells within the brain, one clear thing is that our past is recorded and stored and can be played back in the present. In other words, the brain is like a tape-recorder that retains every experience we have had since birth – and, perhaps, since before birth.

All this is colourfully expressed in transactional analysis, which tells us that within us, stored in our memory, are a Parent and a Child.[1] The latter is an obstreperous, neurotic child who causes trouble and anguish and fear, telling us we are not OK and building our inferiority complex. And side by side with him is a finger-wagging, legalistic parent who torments us with warnings, admonitions and unreasonable prejudices. If we want to make balanced decisions, the Adult within must be in control and we must not be dominated by the Parent and the Child. We cannot entirely get rid of these voices from the past. They are engrained in the tape-recorder of memory. But we can learn to be detached from them, to be uninfluenced by them. We can smile compassionately at our neurotic Child and say, "There he goes again!" Or we can ignore and by-pass the crushing admonitions of the Parent.

Whatever way we want to express it, the fact is that ghosts inhabit our memory, influencing our present conduct. And in order to be healed we must find some way of confronting them, or handling them, or being detached from them.

Now certain forms of meditation make a great impact on the memory and can effect a detachment from interior states of consciousness. Probably any meditation which brings us into high-amplitude alpha stimulates and brings to the surface half-buried memories. This, at all events, seems to follow from the results of certain memory tests made by Dr Green in which the alpha-

[1] *I'm OK – You're OK* by Thomas Harris.

producers had better scores (Segal, p. 304; Green (1)). One can understand how this could be so. In the kind of meditation that goes beyond discursive thinking into a new level of awareness, thoughts and feelings from the past may rise to the surface of the mind. The not-OK Child may shriek and shout. The Parent may complain and admonish. Half-buried fears may float up from the subconscious. But I pay no attention to these troublesome voices from the past because I have entered a deeper level of mind where I can be detached and silent and free from their domination.

And now a cure may be effected in any of several ways.

One is by the help of an analyst or counsellor with whom I confront the ghosts and goblins, driving them away or weakening their power over me. In this case, it will immediately be seen, the meditational process is a rather secondary thing. It is little more than a preparation or a way to discover the hidden problems. It has played a role somewhat similar to that of the couch. The psychoanalyst is the central actor in the drama.

But there is another possibility. It may be that I find such joy and satisfaction at my new level of awareness that the howling Child and the grumbling Parent no longer bother me. They shout themselves to death, or die of exposure, or they starve. And I am liberated and healed. Perhaps the awareness of my problems (while at the same time letting them be) leads to a kind of enlightenment in their regard and they lose their power. As Rollo May says, the demon is named; and having been named, he loses his power.

Yet another possibility is that the joy emanating from my new level of awareness is so great that lesser fixations become unimportant. Entrance into deeper states of consciousness through meditation produces psychophysiological effects of joy and calmness and integration which are the positive side of what is happening negatively in the memory. This calmness is a great treasure. It is found in transcendental meditation and may explain why TM sometimes cures drug-abuse: the new joy makes the drug experience look trivial.

At the same time I myself believe that the technique of entering into deeper levels of consciousness alone will not heal the mind in a human way. This healing will never be complete without the presence of two factors that are extraneous to the meditational process.

The first of these is love. It is a truism to say that people need to be loved and are not infrequently sick from lack of love. This is particularly true of the child, which may well die if not loved. Love is the great healer; and meditational therapy will not be complete without love from counsellor or friend or family or community.

The second is meaning. Jung, Viktor Frankl and the rest stress that no cure will be complete unless a man finds motivation and a reason for living. Meditation itself does not provide motivation. This must come from elsewhere.

In other words, even on the psychological plane, a mere technique of meditation (whether it be the recitation of a *mantra*, or the counting of the breathing, or the adoption of a given posture) will never effect a total cure. It may give temporary relief; but the deepest self of man calls for more.

Mention of love and meaning brings me to religion. As I have already said, religious meditation does not aim at therapy. But it can have therapeutic consequences; and its psychological pattern is similar to that of the meditational therapy already outlined. Let me illustrate this from Christian contemplation.

Christian contemplation is the answer to a call and the response to a vision. One cannot embark on the journey until one has heard the voice or glimpsed the footprints of the ox. In other words there is an initial awakening. One stops in one's tracks, amazed by the realization that one is loved. Christian contemplation begins with the belief, the conviction, the experience of God's love for me. It never starts with vigorous efforts on my part; it does not manifest itself through active energy; it does not begin with my violently drumming up some powerful love for God and man. This is stated explicitly by John: "In this is love, not that we loved God but that he loved us" (1 John 4:10). This love powerfully experienced has been compared to the call of the good shepherd inviting us to enter the sheepfold.

Now this call is creative. It creates a response, an interior movement, a motion of love that necessarily expressed itself in an altered state of consciousness. So deep is the call and so interior is my response that a new level of awareness is opened up and I enter into a changed environment. Christian contemplation is the experience of being loved and of loving at the most profound level of psychic life and of spirit.

This love is not directed to some imaginary world of escape beyond the senses. Rather does it go out to the great reality of the cosmic, risen Christ who loves me and whom I love. This is the Christ who is before our very eyes and ears and hearts and whose glory is all around us because he is "the mountains, the solitary wooded valleys, strange islands . . . silent music", and the people I meet every day.

The love affair thus initiated lasts until death and beyond death. It goes on and on. Sometimes it is violent and anguishing like the struggle of Jacob and the angel: at other times it is a peaceful reclining in the arms of the beloved: "His left arm . . . under my head" and "his right arm embrac[ing] me" (Song of Solomon 2:6). One enters new mansions: new areas of psychic life are opened up.

Examining the development of this love affair, one immediately sees its psychological similarity to the meditational therapy already described.

First of all there is the entrance into a deeper level of awareness under the gentle guidance of the Spirit. When this happens, the mind is expanded, the unconscious is opened up and (just as in meditational therapy) ghosts and goblins, as well as saints and angels, may rise up from the unconscious. The memory is stimulated. The past becomes luminous. The obstreperous Child and the admonishing Parent begin to raise their voices with excitement and clamour. Joy and sadness, love and hate may surge up. The meditator is aware of all this. But he lets it be. He pays no attention to it. He refuses to engage in any analysis of this turmoil. He will not have dialogue with it because the deepest centre of his being, beating on the cloud of unknowing with the shaft of love, is imbibing exquisite wisdom of a supraconceptual kind. It is this love that is all-important to him. As for the ghosts from the unconscious, they may shout themselves to death or they may die of exposure and neglect. Or the wounds from the past, now exposed to the healing power of the Spirit, may be beautifully transfigured – "because God's love has been poured into our hearts through the Holy Spirit which has been given to us" (Romans 5:5).

The angry rising of the ghosts and goblins is well expressed in *The Book of Privy Counselling:*

> Do not be overcome with anxious dread if the evil one comes (as he will) with sudden fierceness, knocking and hammering on the walls of your house; or if he should stir some of his mighty agents to rise suddenly and attack you without warning. Let us be clear about this: the fiend must be taken into account. Anyone beginning this work (I do not care who he is) is liable to feel, smell, taste or hear some surprising effects concocted by the enemy in one or other of his senses. So do not be astonished if it happens. There is nothing he will not try to drag you down from the heights of such valuable work.   (Johnston (1), ch. 7)

Without denying the existence of the fiend, all the author says can equally be applied to the tantrums of the neurotic Child and the admonitions of the dominating Parent, whose voices from the past may be working to destroy our house and wreck our true love. It is precisely by allowing them to ramp and rage, by compassionately acknowledging them but paying no attention to them, that their power is diminished and a cure is effected.

And how stable and rooted is the meditator! The schizophrenic and the drug addict, it is true, may enter similar levels of awareness; but in the ensuing turmoil their Adult is frequently tossed out of the saddle while the neurotic Child takes over. But the mystic is less easily dislodged. He is guided by love. "Nought but my love to be my guide", writes St John of the Cross.

So his great stability continues to stem from the knowledge that he is loved. It is to this faith that the Adult silently clings when the not-OK Child and the Parent are screaming their heads off; and it is this that makes the meditation therapeutic. Moreover (and this is important) the faith that forms the very core of Christian meditation is not faith that I am loved *because* I am good and holy and sinless; it is belief that I am deeply loved *in spite of* my sinfulness. So says Paul: "God shows his love for us in that while we were yet sinners Christ died for us" (Romans 5:8). Yahweh does not love his people because they are holy (how often they are unfaithful and stiff-necked!) but in order to make them holy. And this is the faith the meditator clings to in his journey into the profound caverns of the unconscious. If he loses this, he loses everything. His faith is not primarily a belief that God exists but that God loves; and it is this love that sustains him: "Because you are precious in my eyes . . . and I love you . . ." (Isaiah 43:4)

Now my point in this chapter is that this religious conviction of being loved is therapeutic in its consequences, a point made also by Thomas Harris in his best-selling work on transactional analysis. In an excellent chapter (which, the introduction tells us, was written by his wife) he comes to the crucial point of his work: how am I to come to the conviction that *I'm OK*? And he answers that this security comes from the realization that I am loved – and this, he says, is ultimately a religious experience. It is an experience of grace which, for Paul Tillich, means that I am unconditionally loved. Concretely, I come to the realization that *I'm OK* through a conversion experience like that of Paul: "The Son of God . . . loved me and gave himself for me!" (Galatians 2:20)

But it is not only the experience of being loved that is therapeutic. The very response to love is therapeutic too. This answering love, as has been pointed out, is not directed towards some abstraction but towards the living, risen, cosmic Christ who is in our friends and our enemies, who is in the poor and the sick and the afflicted. And the experience of loving him in himself and in others, no less than the experience of being loved, is therapeutic in its consequences because it purifies the whole person – mind and memory and unconscious. When one begins to love profoundly at a new level of awareness (as often happens in deep intimacy between a man and a woman) it may happen that latent or repressed forces rise to the surface of the mind: hatred, jealousy, fear, insecurity, anger, suspicion, anxiety, unbridled eroticism and the rest surge up from the murky depths of the unconscious.

And all this, it is well known, can coexist with true love. This violence, unleashed in human relations, can be unleashed also in the divine – the two are not so distinct, and divine love is incarnate. And one is liberated only by continuing to love. By fixing one's heart on the cloud of unknowing with deep peace, one becomes detached from these turbulent uprisings; and then they wither and die, leaving only love. It is by loving at the ultimate point, by going beyond all categories to the deepest centre, that one is liberated from jealousy and hatred and the rest. But this is an agonizing purification.

All this is particularly evident in that form of love which we call forgiveness. Most psychologists will agree that one of the most damaging traumas that can exist in the memory is suppressed anger and refusal to forgive. Because of early wounds, people refuse to accept others (you're not OK) and to accept themselves (I'm not OK) and end up in emotional upheaval. Often the root problem is an unconscious refusal to love and forgive their parents. And this makes it difficult to love and forgive anyone: because we are for ever projecting parental images on to the people we meet. One may succeed in forgiving in the conscious mind (and this is enough for salvation) but the unconscious lags behind, leaving our love so much less human.

But through meditation a deeper level of awareness is opened up. Love and faith, if only they are present, can now seep down into the more profound caverns of consciousness and into the subtler layers of the mind, enabling one to love and to forgive with a totality that was hitherto unthinkable. At the deep centre now reached, one can pass beyond parental projections, childhood fears, and other obstructions, to meet the person of the other. When this is done and one forgives from the core of one's being, an enlightenment takes place in a moment of total reconciliation with the universe. Barriers fall down; no one and no thing is rejected; all is one. In the act of forgiveness one realizes that one is forgiven; one loses self-hatred (which is the source of every other hatred); one is healed in an act of love.

From all this it is clear that the principal element in healing is not the psychological process and the entrance into internal states of consciousness. If that were so, drugs alone might heal. But what is really therapeutic is the faith and love which penetrate these deeper internal states. What is therapeutic is the experience of loving and being loved.

Finally, it is important to recall what is meant by healing. It is not the restoration of some stereotyped normality or social adaptability. It is not that the past is obliterated. It is not that wounds are patched up and the torn flesh restored to its pristine health. Neither will healing necessarily make the homosexual heterosexual; it will not give the alcoholic a taste for Coca-Cola. Healing is much more creative than that.

No, healing is progress and resurrection. It can best be understood by looking at the wounds of the risen Christ. These are still present. The resurrection did not take them away. But they are glorified, transformed, transfigured. Now they are beautiful: "Put your finger here, and see my hands; and put out your hand, and place it in my side . . ." (John 20:27). And in the same way meditation can remove the crippling effects of painful wounds and it can make beautiful what once was ugly. And it can give to the personality such depth of love and profundity of insight that the ghosts no longer frighten and the sirens no longer seduce.

And then comes the liberation of the true self. When the Parent and the neurotic Child have perished from exhaustion or neglect, the natural Child, nurtured by this great love, rises up from the depth of one's being. This Child, unlike the other neurotic, is innocent, wondering, religious, artistic – the source of creativity. This is the contemplative Child who is the subject of *samadhi* and ecstasy and the prayer of quiet. He now begins to love and to sing and to dance and to beget beauty. But above all, he cries out, "Abba! Father!" And in that moment of awakening we are healed.

Yet just as enlightenment is never complete in this world, neither is healing complete. More about this in the next chapter.

11

The deeper healing

From what has been said it will be clear that the healing power of meditation drives its roots deep down into the unconscious caverns of the mind, effecting a cure that can be physical or psychological. At the same time, it is an obvious fact that not everyone who meditates is a model of physical and psychological health. We know that many monks, both Christian and Buddhist, suffer from ulcers, malnutrition, consumption, and even from neurosis. The crippling effects of this neurosis, I have tried to say, may be removed. The whole thing may be transfigured – but the neurosis itself may somehow remain for life. St Paul was constantly sick, in addition to having some affliction which scripture scholars do not understand. "And to keep me from being too elated by the abundance of revelations, a thorn was given me in the flesh, a messenger of Satan, to harass me, to keep me from being too elated. Three times I besought the Lord about this, that it should leave me; but he said to me, 'My grace is sufficient for you, for my power is made perfect in weakness.' I will all the more gladly boast of my weaknesses, that the power of Christ may rest upon me" (2 Corinthians 12:7–9). This is a good example of a true healing which might not satisfy the local doctor. Healing there is, because Paul is cured of his pride and his tendency to be elated, while within him a new power, the power of Christ, arises. Yet, on the other hand, this healing does not come the way Paul wants.

The fact is that while all the great religions claim to heal, this healing process is often paradoxical, to such an extent that death cures and sickness strengthens.

But before going into that, let us ask ourselves about the basic sickness of man. What precisely is wrong with the human race?

If we were to ask psychology about modern man's basic sickness, we might hear that it is the sense of meaninglessness, of emptiness, of ultimate frustration. How agonizingly this was expressed by philosophers between the two wars with their talk of existential anguish and all the suffering summed up by Heidegger's terrible definition of man as "being-to-death"! Confronted with death, man is aware of his contingency, his incompleteness, his imperfection – and it is this that fills him with existential dread. So he has to find meaning. Not just meaning for his economic, or emotional or cultural life, but meaning for his existence. Hence Viktor Frankl's logotherapy. Hence Teilhard's affirmation of "Omega", the point of convergence and the term of evolution. Without this, claims Teilhard, there is no meaning to the whole business of life.

Or some philosophers might tell us that man's basic problem is his tendency to hate his fellow-men, his tendency to recoil from them in the Sartrian conviction that hell is the other. There is something destructive in man, a strange mixture of love and hate.

Now the great religions have never failed to recognize man's basic sickness and have attempted to give meaning to this puzzling predicament called human existence. They uniformly claim that man's existential problems run deeper than his chemistry and his psyche, existing as they do at the very root of his being. Let me say a word about both Buddhism and Christianity in this regard.

The Buddhist attitude to man's basic sickness is formulated in *The Four Noble Truths,* which may be summarized as follows:

(1) Existence is unhappiness
(2) Unhappiness is caused by self-centred desire
(3) Self-centred desire can be destroyed
(4) It can be destroyed by following the eightfold path which is that of
    Right views
    Right intentions
    Right speech
    Right conduct
    Right livelihood
    Right effort
    Right mindfulness
    Right concentration

"Existence is unhappiness"! This sounds like the existential anguish of the philosophers; and it is an emphasis that echoes all through Buddhism. Man is in illusion; man is suffering. Here are a few words from the famous *Fire Sermon,* reputedly preached by the Buddha at Benares after his great enlightenment:

> All things, O priests, are on fire. And what, O priests, are all these things that are on fire?
>
> The eye, O priests, is on fire; forms are on fire; eye-consciousness is on fire; impressions received by the eye are on fire; and whatever sensation, pleasant, unpleasant, or indifferent, originates in dependence on impressions received by the eye, that also is on fire. And with what are these on fire? With the fire of passion, say I, with the fire of hatred, with the fire of infatuation; with birth, old age, death, sorrow, lamentation, misery, grief, and despair are they on fire.   (Burt, p. 97)

And so it goes on, depicting eye and ear and nose and tongue and body and mind and ideas and impressions, all on fire.

I said that this resembles the anguish of the philosophers. But there is one important difference: Buddhism holds out hope of salvation. It indicates that there is a way out of the mess. Man can be saved from his existential suffering by the eightfold path of right views, right intentions, right speech, and all the rest. Here Buddhism asks for faith – faith that the situation is not hopeless, faith that there is a way out, faith that there is some meaning to it all, faith that man can be healed. And then faith that this eightfold path really does lead to the highest wisdom, *prajna,* through which man is liberated, saved, brought to *nirvana.* It is to this *prajna* or awakening or enlightenment that all forms of Buddhism point; and it is to the everlasting credit of the Buddha to have reminded the world that man is liberated through wisdom – beyond images and concepts, in the total cessation of desire. "The truth will make you free" (John 8:32).

It is worth noting here that in Buddhism the way to healing wisdom is not precisely meditation but the eightfold path. This is because, in the best Buddhist (as in the best Judaeo-Christian) tradition, meditation is not just a period of silent wall-gazing. Rather is it life. Zen is not just "sitting" or *zazen*; it is also eating, sleeping, walking, working and life. At the same time, "right concentration" does hold a privileged place in this life; and for this reason Buddhism is rightly symbolized by the majestic statues of the Buddha, deep in meditation and rising into the serenity of wisdom, as the lotus rises to the sunlight out of the dark, muddy pond.

A striking parallel to this Buddhist philosophy is found in Romans. In Tokyo I once had occasion to read this epistle with some Japanese students. I was amazed at their interest and their insights. Only later did it dawn on me that this might be because of its striking similarity to the Buddhist philosophy that is the backbone of their culture. With what vigour does Paul paint man in the mire! "They were filled with all manner of wickedness, evil, covetousness, malice. Full of envy, murder, strife, deceit, malignity, they are gossips, slanderers, hates of God, insolent, haughty, boastful, inventors of evil, disobedient to parents, foolish, faithless, heartless, ruthless" (Romans 1:29–31). With a masterly command of words and a rich vocabulary Paul depicts in lurid terms the Roman Empire of his day. And it was not only the Empire that needed salvation. Jew, Greek, Gentile, everyone was in the mess. For Paul is here describing the situation that subsequently came to be called *original sin*.

And again he asks the Buddhist question: Is there a way out? Is there salvation? How is man to escape from this anguished situation? How can he be healed? And once again he gives an answer which recalls that of the Buddha. Man is liberated or "justified" by faith. Romans plays on the theme that "he who through faith is righteous shall live" (Romans 1:17).

When he comes to explaining in more detail what this faith is, of course, Paul parts company with Buddhism. For him it is faith in God's love, based upon a historical fact: "While we were still weak, at the right time Christ died for the ungodly. Why, one will hardly die for a righteous man – though perhaps for a good man one will dare even to die. But God shows his love for us in that while we were yet sinners Christ died for us" (Romans 5:6–8).

Faith in God's love and the saving death of his Son is the way to salvation.

But the parallel with Buddhism continues in that Paul does not situate this faith in long periods of wall-gazing meditation. For him, also, faith is life. Rather than define it philosophically he simply tells the story of Abraham, pointing to the great patriarch's life as an example of living faith (Romans 4:1-4). Yes, faith is life, like the life of Abraham. And meditation (which is no more than an exercise of faith) is also life. As in Buddhism it is a life that leads to wisdom; but for Paul the wisdom that liberates and heals is Jesus Christ himself, who is "the power of God and the wisdom of God" (1 Corinthians 1:24). This is the risen Jesus who can only be grasped by love in an act that is beyond concepts and images in a new dimension transcending thought.

Both Buddhism and Christianity, then, situate man's sickness at a deeper level than migraine headaches, high blood-pressure and getting stuck in the Oedipus conflict. It is man's very existence that is somehow vitiated, and his existential anguish flows from a metaphysical sickness at the level of being. When we come to ask more in detail about man's ugly plight, we find *The Four Noble Truths* attributing the evil to self-centred desire. In Buddhism the great enemy is the self, which cuts man off from the all, separates him from the totality, hurls him into the illusion of multiplicity. And so this self must be annihiliated if one is to enter *nirvana*.

In Christianity the root problem is original sin. What precisely this means, however, is far from clear today. Recent advances in anthropology and in biblical studies have made theologians rethink the old doctrine of "the fall". It is hardly possible here to enter into their theories and niceties. Enough to say that when the smoke clears, the new thinking does not negate but reaffirms the basic traditional truth; namely, that man is in a sorry plight and needs salvation.

I myself believe that we find the most graphic account of original sin and its healing in the very heart of Paul. The Epistle to the Romans tells us of an existential struggle that runs deeper than the sharp physical pain that came as Satan's messenger. For this struggle is at the root of Paul's being – at the level of the self. Paul never sets himself above us; he never poses as the enlightened man; he never says that he has arrived. He is in the hurly-burly with the rest of us. And so in vivid words he describes the anguished struggle between the two selves at the depth of his being. "I do not understand my own actions. For I do not do what I want, but I do the very thing I hate . . . I do not do the good I want, but the evil I do not want is what I do" (Romans 7:15, 19). And he cries out for existential healing: "Wretched man that I am! Who will deliver me from this body of death?" (Romans 7:24)

Who will deliver Paul? The answer is Christ. He is the great healer, just as in his historical existence he cured the blind and the sick and the lame and the deaf to symbolize a deeper healing at the existential level of the self. Paul fixes his eyes on Jesus whom he loves and runs after him like the athletes in the Hellenistic games, they for the corruptible crown, Paul for the incorruptible. "I press on toward the goal for the prize of the upward call of God in Christ Jesus" (Philippians 3:14). Every Pauline line vibrates with Christ's love for Paul and Paul's love for Christ. For him life is a love affair with the risen, universal, cosmic Christ. "I betrothed you to Christ to present you as a pure bride to her one husband", he writes to the Corinthians (2 Corinthians 11:2), and just as the faithful are the bride of the risen Christ, so is Paul. And in this is he not the forerunner of one whose beloved is "the mountains, the solitary wooded valleys, strange islands . . . silent music"? It is this love which drives Paul; it is this love which heals him. "Who shall separate us from the love of Christ?" (Romans 8:35) As if to say that Christ's love is an irresistible force or a blinding light from which there is no escape. And Paul must share in this love and make it his own: "If I speak in the tongues of men and of angels, but have not love, I am a noisy gong or a clanging cymbal" (1 Corinthians 13:1).

The Christ who heals is the risen Jesus, now alive and intimately present to Paul and to all who believe. It is towards the risen Christ that he runs; and before his eyes stands out the second coming, the *parousia*. Now Christ is Lord, *Kyrios*; his is a name that is above all names; he is the cosmic centre towards which the human race is moving. Just as Christ rose, so will Paul rise. Just as Christ was transfigured, Paul will be transfigured. And this is the ultimate healing. Man is cured from his existential anguish and separation by union with the risen Christ and by resurrection with him. In the last analysis it is only the resurrection that heals.

But prior to resurrection is inevitable anguish and pain – principally the pain of separation. Paul longs and longs for the termination of this separation. He wants to leap over the gap that separates him from his beloved. "My desire is to depart and be with Christ, for that is far better . . . For to me to live is Christ, and to die is gain" (Philippians 1:23, 21). And so he longs for death. Not that he is in love with death itself (that would be morbid) but he sees it as the gateway to resurrection. "Far be it from me to glory except in the cross of our Lord Jesus Christ, by which the world has been crucified to me, and I to the world" (Galatians 6:14). Christ's death and resurrection are one single, inseparable, dramatic event. It might be nice to separate them; it might be nice to choose Christ's resurrection and forget about his death. But Paul knows that this cannot be. He must go through the whole process with Christ: ". . . that I . . . may share his sufferings, becoming like him in his death, that if possible I may attain the resurrection from the dead" (Philippians 3:10–11).

Death, being the one gateway to the resurrection, is glorious. What most people see as the great enemy is now transfigured in the golden light of the resurrection. Now it is a conquered enemy:

> Death is swallowed up in victory
> O death, where is thy victory?
> O death, where is they sting? (1 Corinthians 15:54–55)

Not only death but all that precedes it is transfigured. Hence Paul can glory in the cross and in his crucifixion to the world. Moreover, if we are moving towards him whom we love, then the other things in life are much less important. And the consequence is an almost absurd detachment. "Let those who have wives live as though they had none, and those who mourn as though they were not mourning, and those who rejoice as though they were not rejoicing, and those who buy as though they had no goods, and those who deal with the world as though they had no dealings with it" (1 Corinthians 7:29–31). What ridiculous detachment! It can only be explained in the light of an overwhelming desire for, and expectation of, the coming of one whom Paul loves more than life itself.

So Paul sings a paean of salvation, of love, of healing – which ends with the resurrection and the coming of him who is the soul of Paul's soul. He never loses sight of the goal; he never forgets the resurrection. If he were to do so, the whole fabric would collapse. "If for this life only we have hoped in Christ, we are of all men most to be pitied" (1 Corinthians 15:19). He is a song of triumph; but he never glories in the cross unless in the background there shines the resurrection.

Paul is the prototype of the Christian mystic. Those who follow sing the same song of love. They, too, love Christ unto foolishness; they, too, desire death and they glory in the cross that they may attain to the resurrection. They, too, fascinated by the divine eyes, throw off everything and run naked towards the goal where they are clothed in Christ. They, too, see their healing in the resurrection. This, I say, is the doctrine of the great Christian mystics. But the lesser people, the writers of little books and the composers of pious treatises often saw Paul glorying in the cross and they forgot about his greater glory – in the resurrection. And so a somewhat morbid doctrine of suffering and "love of the cross" crept into the Christian message. Morbid, because to glory in the cross while forgetting the resurrection is the stupidity of stupidities. "If for this life only we have hoped in Christ, we are of all men most to be pitied" (1 Corinthians 15:19).

Extremes bring reaction. Because of a morbid understanding of suffering and detachment and the like, some modern Christians tend to reject the whole thing. Detachment has become an ugly word and suffering is no longer a thing in which to glory. This is unfortunate. Because the cold fact is that there is no resurrection without death. "Unless a grain of wheat falls into the earth and dies, it remains alone; but if it dies, it bears much fruit" (John 12:24).

I have said that healing in Christianity is a process of death and resurrection in which man, anguished in his existential separation from Christ and from other men and from the cosmos, is once more united with the one he loves and for whom he longs. In

Buddhism there is a similar pattern. It is precisely because the self cuts man off from the whole that it must die; and it is by death and the loss of self that man enters into *nirvana* or union with the cosmos. A friend of mine, a Catholic priest, who practised some Zen told me that the Zen master once said to him with some severity, "God sent his only Son into the world to die. And you must die too. So die!" This is one more example of Buddhist ability to see the relevance of Christian dogma for daily living. How well he saw that as Christ died, his followers must die too if they are to enter into resurrection.

Buddhism, then, sees the necessity of death and of radical detachment as the gateway to *nirvana*. While I would not equate *nirvana* and resurrection (that would be an unpardonable oversimplification), I do believe that both concepts are striving to answer man's most terrible and most basic question – how to be healed from the anguish of separation and loneliness and isolation and death. In both religions death is conquered because it is the gateway to something else. Perhaps *resurrection* is a clearer affirmation of something hinted at by *nirvana*.

And in both religions prior to death there is the inevitable detachment. In Buddhism, as we have seen, selfish desire builds up the illusory ego and magnifies the gap that separates man from the all. That is why one must reject all desire and all clinging, not only to the comforts and luxuries and pleasures of life but also to knowledge and the process of thinking. The most rigorous detachment is demanded in the very practice of Zen; because one is constantly renouncing one's natural desire for conceptual knowledge. And the process in Christian meditation is rather similar. "Whoever of you does not renounce all that he has cannot be my disciple" (Luke 14:33). And here "all" means all. St John of the Cross demands detachment, never from God, it is true, but from thoughts and ideas and feelings of God. The justification for this is scriptural. God is above everything – ideas, idols, images and words of all kinds. Man's perennial temptation (as was Israel's) has always been to put God in a box or in a category and thus to be in control. Conceptual knowledge is a way of mastery that must be abandoned in favour of a non-conceptual knowledge, a whole new mode of knowing and loving which goes into the silence of the cloud or the dark night.

So we end with an awful paradox. From the viewpoint of science and common sense, sickness and death are the great evils to be conquered. And here we find religions claiming that they are conditions for true healing and that they lead to life. The practical conclusion is that sickness and death *are* great evils and that with the scientist we alleviate suffering; we fight death; we try to prolong life. We use medicine and biofeedback and even meditation in a relentless war against the great enemies, which are suffering and death. But when we have made the maximum human effort to ward off pain and postpone the end – only at this point are we justified in saying that death is swallowed up in victory. "O death, where is thy sting?" (1 Corinthians 15:55) Through death comes resurrection and the deeper healing.

12

Cosmic healing

We live in an age of planetization. That is to say, we live in an age when man longs to be liberated from the confining narrowness of nationalism in order to build the earth. Seeing the place of our little planet in the complex totality of the infinite universe, modern man thinks more and more in cosmic terms and aspires to act in a cosmic way. I was impressed to read how the astronauts, looking back on the earth from outer space, came to a new awareness of things. It is even said that several of them, detached from the earth and its little problems, underwent a change of consciousness resembling a mystical experience. This is highly significant. May it not be part of our movement towards a new cosmology and a new consciousness?

If the meditation discussed in this book holds an appeal for contemporary people, this is to some extent because of its cosmic implications. In an earlier chapter I said that the Zen master "sits" for the universe. This is not, I believe, just pious talk. It has a basis in psychology and even, perhaps, in physics. Because meditation entails an expansion of mind, a loss of self, an entrance into altered states of consciousness, a thrust into a dimension beyond time and space, in such wise that not only man's spirit but his very psyche and body become somehow cosmic. I have already spoken at length about the impact of meditation on the body, and I will not repeat it here. Only let me add that every religious tradition has stories of out-of-the-body experiences, of saints knowing intuitively what is happening in other parts of the world, of the impact of prayer on distant people, and so on. And while a good deal of this may well be legend, I doubt if we can dismiss the whole thing out of hand. There is in the human body a cosmic mystery that we will never fathom.

How modern physics would attempt to explain the cosmic dimension of the body I do not know. Everyone will admit that the whole question is exceedingly complex since we do not know what matter is, what the body is, what energy is. But one thing becomes increasingly clear: that the universe is so unified that every movement or action, however slight, has its repercussions throughout the whole. And man is part of this network. At one time he thought he could extricate himself from the totality to view the universe objectively as a serene and detached outsider. Now we know this cannot be. Receiving influence from every corner of the mysterious universe, he likewise influences it; and his actions are like the proverbial pebble thrown into the pond and causing endless ripples. I myself believe that next to God the most influential person in the cosmos is the mystic.

In Eastern meditation the body is prepared for its cosmic role by the emphasis on posture. One comes to a new sense of one's body and of its links with the universe. This is done more especially through attention to the breath. For in the oriental tradition, this breath is not just the air that fills my lungs, giving energy to my little body. Rather is it the breath of the universe. Through breathing I arrive at a harmony with the vibrating cosmos. Similar to this in the Western tradition is the breath or the wind or the *spiratio*, which speaks of the Holy Scripture breathing in me, uniting me to all men and to all creation and to the Father. This, in the New Testament, is "the Spirit of Jesus".

St Paul is well aware of the cosmic dimensions of the body, particularly of the resurrected body. For him the great prototype of man becomes cosmic in Christ in his glory. The body of Christ comes first, for he is "the first-born" (Colossians 1:18), and after it, and in him, all the saved become cosmic too. Christ is Son by nature: we are sons by grace. But when asked what the resurrected and cosmic body looks like, Paul answers almost abruptly: "Don't ask foolish questions!" He has been talking about the certainty of resurrection in Christ, and then he goes on: "But some one will ask, 'how are the dead raised? With what kind of body do they come?' You foolish man! What you sow does not come to life unless it dies . . ." (1 Corinthians 15:35–36). And then Paul goes on to say that there are many kinds of bodies, many kinds of flesh (how modern indeed!), and that there is a whole dimension of matter that we simply cannot understand. "For not all flesh is alike, but there is one kind for men, another for animals, another for birds, and another for fish. There are celestial bodies and there are terrestrial bodies . . . star differs from star in glory"(1 Corinthians 15:39–41). "Not all flesh is alike"! The bodies of the dead are with us in their resurrected form but they are in a new cosmic dimension which baffles our powers of imagination and intelligence. Yet for Paul this movement towards cosmification (if I may coin a word) begins at baptism, continues all through life in a movement from flesh to spirit, and reaches its culminating point through death. Now, no longer possessing a fleshly body, man has become a "spiritual body".

Nor is all this empty theory. In Japan, thanks to the Christian dialogue with Zen, some Christians are exploring forms of meditation that will bring the meditator to an experience of the cosmic body of Christ through a sense of his own body. To the Catholic Christian the notion of the universal body of Christ is already familiar because of his belief in the eucharistic presence of Christ transfiguring the world. And he believes that this presence is the risen body of Christ within his body, transforming it and making it cosmic. What is exciting about the whole thing is that this body of Christ which lives within him is united with the poor and the sick and the suffering and with the whole human race. It is also united with the Father, of whom Jesus could say, "I and the Father are one" (John 10:30). Such is the cosmic destiny of man – union with Christ, union with the Father, union with man and the universe.

In the above I may have digressed too much from the main point of this chapter, which was not to speak about the cosmic dimension of meditation but about certain people who, realizing their cosmic role, play a great part in the healing of the universe.

For the universe itself is sick. I have spoken about healing of body, healing of mind, and the deeper healing enacted at the level of being. But all the sickness here involved is linked to an even more fundamental sickness which is that of the universe itself. We have already seen the clear-cut Buddhist stand on this point. Paul, too, in Romans paints a fine picture of a universe sick and groaning as it waits for the promised deliverance:

For the creation was subjected to futility, not of its own
will but by the will of him who subjected it in hope;
because the creation itself will be set free from its bondage
to decay and obtain the glorious liberty of the children of
God. We know that the whole creation has been groaning
in travail together until now; and not only the creation, but
we ourselves who have the first fruits of the Spirit, groan
inwardly as we wait for adoption as sons, the redemption
of our bodies.   (Romans 8:20–23)

Here is a universe labouring in the pains of childbirth, unfinished,
incomplete, contingent. Just as the great suffering of the mystic is
his sense of separation from his end, which is the resurrection; so
the great suffering of the universe is its separation from the end
towards which it is straining and striving.

The sickness of the cosmos is due to a variety of causes. There is
the fact of contingency, the fact of incompleteness and unfinished
evolution, together with the anguished groaning that necessarily
accompanies parturition. There is the inevitable failure and waste
that goes along with growth. Then there is the evil arising from
man's refusal to build the earth, from the glorification of his ego,
from his refusal to love – and, even more terrible, from his
perversion of love. And there is the activity of one who put the
earth in bondage. All this makes the very universe itself shout out
with Paul: "Who will deliver me from this body of death?"
(Romans 7:24)

Yet the healing of the cosmos is not automatic or inevitable. It
will only be healed through man.

And here lies the vocation of the cosmic person who takes on
himself the totality of things and even the totality of suffering.
Here lies the vocation of the mystic. The Zen master "sitting" for
the universe is in a logical position, since in Buddhism the small
individual self is illusory and does not really exist. The only ego
that can be purified is the ego of the universe and this is purified in
him. In a somewhat different way, the notion of one person
healing the nation and the universe is dramatically portrayed in
Isaiah:

> Surely he has borne our griefs
>   and carried our sorrows:
> yet we esteemed him stricken,
>   smitten by God, and afflicted.
> But he was wounded for our transgressions,
>   he was bruised for our iniquities;
> upon him was the chastisement that made us whole,
>   and with his stripes we are healed.
> All we like sheep have gone astray;
>   we have turned every one to his own way;
> and the Lord has laid on him
>   the iniquity of us all.   (Isaiah 53:4-6)

Here one man suffers for the people. The cosmos is purified in him. This way of thinking is central to the New Testament, whose authors create a whole Christology from this servant of Yahweh in Isaiah. For them Jesus in Gethsemane and on the cross is this cosmic man who takes the woes of the world on his shoulders, who suffers not for himself (for he is sinless) but for man and the universe.

And the mystics follow after Jesus in that they become ever more universal. Paul is aware that his suffering is cosmic and can heal the broken totality of things: "Now I rejoice in my sufferings for your sake, and in my flesh I complete what is lacking in Christ's afflictions for the sake of his body, that is, the church" (Colossians 1:24). Nor is it only Paul. Any Christian who sincerely meditates is becoming one with the universal Christ in a process that reaches its climax in resurrection, the ultimate universalization of man. Yet this is full of paradox in that the further one enters the thicket of the joyful and ecstatic mystical life the greater becomes one's capacity for suffering – a suffering that is redemptive.

If it be asked, however, why suffering heals the universe, I would answer that in itself it heals nothing. What heals is love, which is most dramatically expressed in suffering. Love is the highest form of human energy; and in an earlier chapter I have already spoken of its incredible power to heal. This holds true in the cosmic dimension also. The universe is healed by men and women of universal love. It is not, I believe, the achievements of science themselves that build the cosmos, but the love for humanity that underlies them. And the same holds true for suffering – it is not the suffering itself that matters but the love that underlies it. The love that builds the cosmos is universal love, the highest love that can fill the human heart.

Though the working of mystical love and its power to heal are mysteries that no man understands, I would like to hazard a few remarks that may throw light on this cosmic adventure of the mystics.

First of all let me say that all knowledge and love open us up to new areas of experience by which we live in others and are necessarily affected by their joys and sufferings. Was it not Socrates who spoke of the inexpressible bliss of deep and dreamless sleep? Total ignorance, he realized, is a form of bliss, whereas to know and to love is to expose oneself to the beautiful possibility of joy and the awful possibility of sorrow.

Now this is particularly true of mystical knowledge and love. For this goes beyond images and concepts to a deeper level of awareness wherein we are one with the person we love. Here is a knowledge of identity, of empathy, of indwelling. And when it gets really deep we become part of others to such an extent that what happens to them happens to us – their joy becomes our joy, their sorrow becomes our sorrow. So the mystic, who loves all men with a universal love and who lives in all men, rejoices with those who rejoice and weeps with those who weep. This was the case with great-souled mystics like Paul himself or Pope John or Dag Hammarskjöld or Gandhi. These were people who by reason of their greatness loved more, rejoiced more and suffered more. Their very universality gave them greater capacity for joy and greater capacity for suffering. One is reminded of the great Bodhisattva who feels so deeply the suffering of the tiniest living thing that he refuses to enter *nirvana* until every sentient being is saved. And so he remains outside until the end of time.

And the Christian mystic who knows and loves the cosmic Christ takes on himself the joy and the suffering of the cosmos. His love, like Paul's, makes him live in Christ and Christ in him. But the Christ with whom he is now so deeply involved is the total

Christ who suffers in the wars and pestilence and social injustices that afflict mankind. Opening his heart to the cosmic Christ, the mystic opens his heart to the joys and sufferings of everybody as well as to the vast universe; for his beloved is "the mountains, the solitary wooded valleys, strange islands . . . silent music". All this dwells within him in its ecstasy and its agony. That is why the suffering servant in Isaiah is wounded for our sins and bruised for our iniquities.

And his love heals precisely because it makes him mystically present to all, precisely because through indwelling he can take upon himself everyone's burdens. His love heals just as a mother heals her child or as the lover heals the beloved. In the same way the universal love of the mystic helps heal the cosmos and man, in whom the cosmos comes to full flowering.

As for the goal of the cosmic healing process, I believe it is best understood in an evolutionary context. Surveying the vast stream of evolution, now led forward by the human spearhead, Teilhard asks where it is going. As a scientist and a man of faith, he cannot envisage such a process without an end or goal or point of convergence. If no such end exists, he declares, the human effort is valueless. If it does exist, it is personal, since the evolution of the universe is more and more in the direction of personalization. And so he comes to affirm the existence of Omega, the point of convergence, the Prime Mover ahead. But while Aristotle's Prime Mover was a thinking being ("the thought that thinks itself"), the Teilhardian Prime Mover ahead is a loving personal centre of attraction. Omega is at once transcendent, like a huge magnet that pulls the universe to itself, and at the same time immanently present to the universe which it propels towards its end. Omega stands at the apex of things like a lover luring to himself his beloved who is the totality of creation.

Besides being a scientist, Teilhard was a Christian. That is why he sees Omega as the risen Christ, while the point of convergence is the *pleroma* or fullness of time, the completion of God's plan "to unite all things in him, things in heaven and things on earth" (Ephesians 1:10). Such is the Christology around which Teilhard's thought revolves. He sees ahead the Christ who said,

"I, when I am lifted up from the earth, will draw all men to myself" (John 12:32). Drawing all men to himself, he is the point on which a world in evolution finally converges. This is the Son of Man who will come in the clouds of glory; this is the Christ of whom Paul writes, "Who shall separate us from the love of Christ?" (Romans 8:35) If Christ is the Prime Mover ahead, drawing all things to himself, then it becomes literally true that nothing can separate us from the magnetic power of his love, which penetrates the whole. Omega, then, is personalized love, the *agape* of the scriptures. Omega is the divine milieu.

How cosmic is the experience of one who loves "the mountains, the solitary wooded valleys, strange islands . . . silent music"! His is a love affair with the universe. And like every true love affair it is healing and strengthening and beautiful. It is through such love that the universe will be transfigured.

PART IV

INTIMACY

13

Meditation and intimacy

The modern world shows great interest in anything that concerns community and interpersonal relations. Perhaps we are beginning to see that if we are to live in harmony on this crowded planet we had better find some formula for community living – and pretty quickly. Teilhard put it well when he said that it used to be "Love one another if you want to be perfect", but now it is "Love one another if you want to survive". If we are to get on with the business of planetization and building the earth, we must learn how to live together. Hence our interest in communal living, interpersonal relations, group encounters, sensitivity training, and all the rest. It seems that community is one of the great preoccupations of our day.

And related to this is the modern interest in intimacy. New views on marriage stress the dimension of intimacy between husband and wife. New thinking on religious celibacy stresses personal love and intimacy in the single state. It seems that man has reached a stage in evolution where intimacy is not only one of his top priorities but also a psychological necessity of life.

In spite of all the talk about intimacy, however, there is little agreement about what the word means. Sometimes it is equated with sincerity in human relations, or with frankness and openness. Or it is put as the opposite of playing games. But what interests me here is that not infrequently deep interpersonal relations and intimacy are associated with profundity in meditation. Centres for sensitivity training and the development of human potential often hold courses both in encounter and in meditation, as though they instinctively felt that these two things are somehow related. And here I want to ask how, and to what extent, they are in fact related.

Faced with this question, I can immediately see two reasons why meditation might lead people to know and love one another at a deeper level of awareness. One is the non-attachment that necessarily accompanies the meditational process. The other is the empathetic knowledge already discussed in the last chapter. Let me say a word about these two points. And first about non-attachment.

Modern psychology reminds us that to be truly intimate we must not cling to people. We must let them be, leaving them the liberty to be themselves, to lead their own lives, to make their own decisions, to choose their own beliefs, to follow the spirit within them. The fact is, of course, that most of us cannot do this. We cling to those we love, trying to make them what we want them to be and to mould them according to our plans. This destroys union and intimacy.

It would be relatively easy to abandon our clinging fixations if they were in the conscious mind. But more often they are not. They are lurking in those nebulous, subliminal depths which are outside our control and even beyond the fringe of awareness. Sometimes we can only guess at their existence from the inexplicable anguish that crosses the mind in certain relationships. Often such relationships are partly projections: we are super-imposing our father or mother images upon others, clinging to others as a child clings to its parents. Or a mother will project into her child her own unconscious frustrations, forcing him to lead the life she wanted to live but could not. Needless to say, she is not aware of this; in her own eyes she is the loving mother. But she cannot be intimate with this child because she loves herself in him.

Depth can only be achieved when we get beyond projections to the core of the other's personality – that is to say, when person meets person. And this, in turn, can only be done when I am detached from my own subliminal imagery, self-centred desires, unconscious frustrations, childish projections, and all the rest. In other words, a first condition for intimacy is the purification of the conscious and unconscious mind.

Put in terms of the transactional analysis mentioned earlier in this book, intimacy, I believe, can only be achieved when a relationship is purified of excessive influence from Parent and Child. As long as the Child in me constantly relates to the Parent in someone else, the chances for intimacy are slim because the relationship is distorted by the interference of half-buried memories and voices from the past. If I am to meet the core of the other at the core of my own being I must "let go" of the neurotic Child and the finger-wagging Parent. And again this would be easily done if these phantoms were only in the conscious mind. But often they are not. They are lodged in subliminal areas, so that we cannot analyse the transaction even when we want to do so. Once more, purification of the unconscious is demanded. Only when this is done can person meet person without playing games. Only then does it become possible for adult to meet adult or, even more wonderful, for natural Child to meet natural Child. Only then is the stage set for a meeting that can be a real mystical experience. Detachment from one's internal states and purification from all clinging are the inexorable conditions for such mystical encounter.

Now vertical meditation that goes beyond thoughts and images to the inner core of silence is the arch-enemy of conscious and unconscious clinging. This is particularly true in Buddhist *samadhi*, with its emphasis on silence, nothingness, emptiness, the void and the cessation of desire. Buddhism declares (and how truly!) that clinging causes illusion, blinding us to the true nature of reality and making us live in a phantasmal world of ghosts. And so, in the silence of meditation that penetrates through layer after layer of consciousness, it liberates man from the tyranny of his internal fixations. It penetrates those murky subliminal depths and cleans them up. And then, liberated from clinging and possessiveness, I can see and relate to the other as other. No longer my idea of the other but the other as he is in himself. No longer my idea of myself by my true, deep and authentic self. Now I am free to love and receive love. Furthermore (and this is a characteristic of all contemplative experience) I become habitually present and open to the here-and-now. Conceptual ideas *about* persons and things withdraw us from the reality that lies before our eyes, bringing us into the past. The intuitive, non-attached person, on the other hand, is a now-person. He sees the other as he is today, not as he was yesterday. The discipline of detachment has led him to a continual freshness of perception (remember how this even appeared in the "click experiments" of Dr Hirai!) which makes possible a deeper authenticity and gift of oneself.

This non-attachment, so characteristic of Buddhism, is found in all those forms of vertical meditation that use the *mantra*, the *koan* the *mandala*, or just imageless silence. It is found pre-eminently in Christian contemplation. The meditational process clears the upper layers of the mind, opening up the unconscious, going beyond fixations to deeper layers of psychic life, thus bringing the meditator to an inner liberty in which he is freed from the tyranny of his own interior states, whether these be his Parent, his Child, or his inordinate desires. And all this is preparation for the phenomenon that we call intimacy.

Yet non-attachment, however valuable, does not constitute the essence of intimacy. It is no more than a condition, a preparation, a liberation. Indeed, as we have seen earlier, non-attachment in itself could be a condition for hatred and destruction: it could free the meditator to do evil with equanimity. Much more important is the second point I mentioned; namely, the knowledge of empathy, which forms the very core of religious meditation whether Buddhist or Christian. This is the knowledge that goes beyond thoughts and images and concepts. It springs from love and compassion, and it leads to indwelling. It is the knowledge and love of a Paul who discovers that he lives in Christ and that Christ lives in him. Paul keeps saying that he is "in Christ" and he also experiences that Christ is in him. the faithful, too, are "in Christ", and he prays that Christ may be in them – "that Christ may dwell in your hearts through faith" (Ephesians 3:17). Here is the very centre of intimacy and indwelling. And something like the Pauline intimacy with Jesus can be found in relationship between close friends who know and love one another at a deep level of awareness. In the *Introduction to the Devout Life,* Francis de Sales quotes the words of St Gregory of Nazianzen about his remarkable friendship with St Basil:

> It seemed as though there were but one soul between us, having two bodies. And if we must not believe those who say that all things are in all things, yet you must believe this, that we were both in each one of us, and the one in the other . . .
>
> (Francis de Sales, ch. 18)

These two men were mystics. They had experienced non-attachment and meditational states of consciousness so that their friendship culminated in an indwelling that reminds one of Paul's friendship with Christ. And the essence of such intimacy is a personal love, liberated through non-attachment, whereby two people meet at the core of their being in an ecstatic encounter.

I like to stress the role of empathy and love because it has been suggested in encounter groups that the psychological process alone can effect intimacy. As though the very fact of meditating, entering into deeper states of awareness and expanding one's consciousness, would effect intimacy without the religious dimension of faith and love. I do not believe that this is so. I do not believe that any psychological process, divorced from faith and love and commitment, can produce intimacy and indwelling. This was brought home to me on' reading of some laboratory experiments performed in the field of secular or non-religious meditation. These experiments resulted not in indwelling but in *merging*. Let me describe them briefly.

In one experiment, subjects are asked to meditate by gazing for long periods at an object such as a blue vase. As they stare and as their meditation deepens, some of them experience the sensation of merging with the vase and of becoming one with it. Or they feel that the vase is inside them. Here is a report from one researcher:

Merging was reported by subject A, who from the very beginning reported striking alterations in her perception of the vase and her relation to it. She reported, "One of the points that I remember most vividly is when I really began to feel, you know, almost as though the blue and I were perhaps merging, or that vase and I were. I almost got scared to the point where I found myself bringing myself back in some way from it . . . It was as though everything was sort of merging and I was somehow losing my sense of consciousness almost." This merging experience was characteristic of all of this subject's meditation sessions, but she soon became familiar with it and ceased to describe it as anything remarkable. Following the sixth session she reported, "At one point it felt . . . as though the vase were in my head rather than out there; I knew it was out there but it seemed as though it were almost a part of me." "I think that I almost felt at that moment as though, you know, the image is really in me, it's not out there."   (Tart, p. 206)

In addition to merging with the vase, subjects reported that they became personally attached to it; they felt disappointed when it was taken away or if it was missing when they entered the room. In other words, prolonged meditation had developed within them some kind of love for, and union with, the vase.

Merging with a vase or a flower is one thing; merging with a person is quite another. Here, too, laboratory experiments give us food for thought. After a series of sessions in mutual hypnosis, where two subjects, Bill and Anne, hypnotized one another, Dr Tart of the University of California at Davis made the following observation:

> The alteration that most impressed (and later frightened) the subjects, however, was the feeling of *merging* with each other at times, especially in the final mutual hypnosis session. This seemed like a partial fusion of identities, a partial loss of the distinction between I and Thou. This was felt to be good at the time, but later the subjects perceived this as a threat to their individual autonomy.   (Tart, p. 306)

Dr Tart himself is not convinced that this merging is always emotionally helpful, and he goes on:

> A . . . possible danger to be mentioned is that the "forced" intimacy produced by this technique may be unsettling . . . Our culture does not prepare people for sudden, intense intimacy. I know of a roughly comparable case of two married couples who took LSD-25 together; each experienced an intense merging of identities with the three others. Because of the sudden and unexpected intensity of these feelings the couples had a great deal of difficulty in their emotional relationships to each other for several months afterwards, all centred around feelings that they had seen too much of each other's real selves, more than

their previous relationship had prepared them to handle comfortably.   (Tart, p. 307)

In the mutal hypnosis sessions, Dr Tart tells us, Anne was willing to continue; but one sympathizes with Bill who was strongly opposed to any further exploration and subsequently lost interest in the whole business.

Finally, let me quote yet another researcher in meditation and consciousness, who suggests the following path to intimacy:

> Place yourself face to face with another person. Look at him and be aware when your mind wanders. Be aware when you treat his face like an object, a design, or play perceptual games with it. Distortions may appear which tell you what you project into the relationship: angels, devils, animals and all the human possibilities may appear in his face. Eventually you may move past these visual fantasies into the genuine presence of another human being.   (Tart, p. 186)

I have quoted the above experiments because I believe they shed some light on the reality which we call intimacy; and in them the strength and weakness of the scientific approach is evident.

In the deepest intimacy, it seems to me, there is no merging; but there is indwelling, to such an extent that people can live in one another and be part of one another even when separated by thousands of miles. What makes the difference between merging and indwelling is, I believe, personal love and commitment and trust. Two people can enter into deeply altered states of consciousness either through drugs or hypnosis, or even by the practice of non-attachment, and they can float into one another's psyche with a terrifying loss of identity. But where there is no love and trust, what human value can this possibly have? And where love and trust are lacking, how terrible can be this "forced" intimacy! Furthermore, love and trust must grow; and ordinarily this takes time. I cannot believe that we can blandly walk into the core of another's being by altering our consciousness with drugs or hypnosis or other techniques. Nor can we do so by staring for hours at another's face, unless our love and trust correspond to the length of our gaze. It must be awful to be stared at for hours by someone who does not love you; and it must be awful to stare for hours at someone we do not love. All this is so different from the ecstatic love affair in which the beloved is "the mountains, the solitary wooded valleys, strange islands . . . silent music". Without the mystical dimension of love and trust, meditation runs the risk of inhumanity and mechanical manipulation.

Obviously this is not meant to be a blanket criticism of scientific research in the area of meditation. All I want to say is that science needs the complementarity of religion if it is to be really human in this field.

To understand indwelling, as opposed to merging, it is helpful once again to recall the Teilhardian principle that union in the personal differentiates. When people meet at the level of personal love achieved through radical non-attachment, they do not merge; nor are they absorbed in one another; nor do they lose their identity. On the contrary, it is precisely in their union with the other that they find their true selves. There is at once a total unity and a total alterity.

Such intimacy and such indwelling is a central theme of the fourth gospel. "Abide in me, and I in you", says Jesus (John 15:4). And he prays that his disciples may be one, that they may be totally one, that they may be completely one (John 17:21–23). And yet they are not one, because each retains his autonomous personality. "In that day you will know that I am in my Father, and you in me, and I in you" (John 14:20). The model of intimacy is the union of the Father and the Son who are totally one God while remaining distinct, personal and autonomous. Paradox here reaches its climax. Yet I believe that hidden in these chapters of the fourth gospel are some of the greatest insights the world has ever heard. For here we have the notion of person – so central to any doctrine of intimacy – of the inviolability and uniqueness of the divine person and the human person, linked to the notion of total union. Never, never can the man or woman who has been called by name be lost in an amorphous mass of unified nothingness. On the contrary, the greater the union the more autonomous and free becomes the person. The impulse towards unity that characterizes all love results not in merging, not in absorption, but in a luminous presence of person to person.

This intimacy, however is bought at a high price. Non-attachment is a painful process in which the deep caverns of the psyche are purified from jealousy, hatred, possessiveness, anger and selfishness. Without this purification, husband and wife, parent and child, friend and friend can never be intimate. But (and this is the beautiful doctrine of the Christian mystics) it is love which purifies and detaches. The process is like that of the man who joyfully sold everything for love of the treasure hidden in the field (Matthew 13:44). In our case the treasure is the deep core of the other, the mystery of his or her personality. It is this that we love; and our search for this treasure demands the renunciation of lesser goods.

Realizing that love detaches, we can see how the quest for intimacy can be filled with joy and filled with pain. With joy because love is a joyful business, and who is more ecstatic than the lover? With pain because (in the words of D. H. Lawrence) "Love is the great Asker". It is always asking us to leave the lesser for the greater; it is always asking us to leave the rind to reach the core; it is always asking us to go on and on in perpetual exploration. And in the last analysis intimacy is less a *thing* than an *event* or a happening. That is why it defies analysis and escapes definition. It can never be circumscribed. "The mountains, the solitary wooded valleys, strange islands . . . silent music."

14

Mystical friendship

Earlier in this book I said that meditation opens up levels of psychic life that are ordinarily dormant. St Teresa calls these deeper levels of awareness "interior senses" and she speaks of a seeing, hearing, touching and embracing that are different from the seeing, hearing, touching and embracing that we associate with external sensation. A sixteenth-century Spaniard, Teresa used vivid and dramatic language to speak of a phenomenon which other mystics describe in simpler terms. They talk of relishing and savouring the deeper realities, while Bergson speaks of "deep, creative emotion". All are striving to describe a dimension of psychic life which most of us rarely actuate because we live at a superficial level of awareness.

In the case of Teresa these mystical faculties are operative chiefly in her relationship with Christ. It is Christ that she sees and hears and loves with the most profound faculties of her psyche. But (and this is the point I wish to make here) these same faculties can also be brought into play in human relationships. This was the case with the mystics. Their most intimate interpersonal relations were the outcome and extension of their profound contemplative experience. That is why in dealing with their fellow-men they could see and hear and touch at a new level. That is why they could sometimes read hearts and know intuitively what others were thinking. I am not speaking here about extrasensory perception but about a certain mystical awareness, an intuitive knowledge, a deep feeling. No superficial emotion this, but an extraordinary empathy. When two mystics were friends (and often they were) there arose between them a remarkable indwelling which enabled them to say one to the other: "As the Father has loved me, so have I loved you; abide in my love" (John 15:9).

One of the most attractive writers on the subject of mystical friendship is the twelfth-century Cistercian, Aelred of Rievaulx. Living in a religious culture which set great store on the beauty of friendship, he composed a little *Treatise on Spiritual Friendship* in which, like many of his contemporaries, he makes extensive and mystical use of the Song of Solomon. "O that you would kiss me with the kisses of your mouth!" (Song of Solomon 1:2) Aelred comments that a kiss can be exchanged at levels of consciousness transcending the physical. Just as Teresa speaks of a seeing that goes beyond the physical seeing with the eyes of the body, so Aelred speaks of a kiss that goes beyond all physical kissing with the lips of the body. Such a kiss is, in fact, nothing other than a meeting of two spirits. "In a kiss', he writes, "two spirits meet, mingle, and become one; and as a result, there arises in the mind a wonderful feeling of delight that awakens and binds together the love of them that kiss" (Aelred, p. 673).

Following a contemporary custom which looked on perfection as a ladder rising up towards the spiritualization of matter (the Pauline movement from flesh to spirit), he divides the kiss into three ascending stages of consciousness or awareness. According to the different kinds of union "there is a kiss of the body, a kiss of the spirit and a kiss of the mind. The kiss of the body is made by the impress of the lips; the kiss of the spirit by the union of hearts; the kiss of the mind by the infusion of grace into the soul through the Spirit of God." (Aelred, ibid.). Then he describes three types of union, beginning with the bodily kiss:

> Hence the bodily kiss is not to be given or accepted except for certain and just reasons; for example, as a sign of reconciliation when enemies become friends. Or it may be given as a sign of peace, as those who are about to receive Holy Communion in church express interior peace by an exterior kiss. It may be given as a sign of love, as between bride and bridegroom; or as it is given and received by friends after a long separation. It can be given as a sign of Catholic unity, as is done when one welcomes a guest. But just as many people, for the purpose of indulging their sensuality or cruelty, misuse water, fire, iron, food and air, all of which are good in themselves, so also perverse and low-minded men endeavour to conceal their crimes even with this good gesture which the natural law established to express the affections we have described. (Aelred, ibid.)

After this sound advice about the bodily kiss, Aelred goes on to speak about the kiss of the spirit, exchanged between friends. This is a meeting of minds and an ecstasy of spirit. Going beyond anything bodily, it is an act of the most intense intimacy, bringing in its train overflowing joy:

> The kiss of the spirit is the special prerogative of friends who are bound by a covenant of friendship. It is given and received not by the touching of the mouth but by the union of hearts, not by the union of lips but by the mingling of spirits. Here the Spirit of God makes everything chaste, and by his participation infuses a celestial relish. This kiss I call the kiss of Christ, which however he does not give by his own mouth, but by the mouth of another. For the two friends he creates such a sacred emotion that they feel as if they are two souls in one body, and they say with the prophet: "behold how good and pleasant it is for brethren to dwell together as one."   (Aelred, ibid.)

In an earlier chapter of this book I spoke of a communal *samadhi* or prayer of quiet that can exist between people who love one another deeply. It is easy to see how such union could rise to moments of intense intimacy such as those of which Aelred speaks. For here in moments of ecstatic indwelling and enlightenment the friends become one while remaining themselves.

In the above stage, the risen Christ is present since he is at the core of the two persons who meet and in him they are united. But Aelred's third stage goes on even further to a meeting with Christ himself. This, it is interesting to note, is only achieved after rigorous purification, "when all earthly affections have been mastered and when all earthly desires have been lulled to sleep". Here are his words:

> When, therefore, the mind has become accustomed to this kiss and recognizes that all this sweetness comes from Christ it says as if musing to itself: "Oh, if only he himself would come." And with this it aspires to the kiss of the mind, and cries out with ardent desire, "Let him kiss me with the kiss of his mouth." So when all earthly affections

have been mastered and when all earthly desires have been lulled to sleep, the mind finds delight in the kiss of only Christ, rests in his embrace, exulting and saying: "His left hand is under my head; his right hand shall embrace me."

(Aelred, ibid.)

Aelred, then, sees friendship as a way to Christ. One is reminded of the Chinese *tao* and the Hindu *ways* that lead to enlightenment. Aelred here adds another way, a beautiful way and one that is totally in harmony with, or an expression of, the gospel; namely, the way of friendship. Obviously this is not a way to Christ divorced from his members, as though one jettisoned human friendship when one reached the goal. Rather is it a discovery of the true personality of the friend while Christ is present as a third partner in their love.

Writing in the Hellenistic tradition, Aelred borrows freely from Cicero who, in turn, is rooted in Aristotle. But beneath the veneer of Hellenism his real inspiration comes from the Bible and its story of the Covenant. Let me say a word about this here.

The thunder and flashing lightning of Sinai herald a new era in interpersonal relations, as Moses wends his way up the mountain, enters the cloud of unknowing and speaks to Yahweh face to face as a man might speak to his friend. Here is the grand seal on a divine intimacy which goes back to Abraham and even to the early chapters of Genesis. Moses, the friend of Yahweh, now mediates a covenant which is nothing less than a marriage between the bride and the bridegroom, a bond of friendship between Israel and Yahweh, a link between man and God. It is the archetype and model of human marriage and of any other friendship, such as that between David and Jonathan, who made a solemn covenant because each loved the other "as his own soul" (1 Samuel 18:3). And what a friendship that was! What pathos echoes through David's dirge for the dead Jonathan:

> I am distressed for you, my brother Jonathan;
> very pleasant have you been to me;
> your love to me was wonderful,
> passing the love of women.

(2 Samuel 1:26)

And the love of David and Jonathan is an integral part of their love for Yahweh and their role in salvation history.

Ideally speaking, friendship partakes of the characteristics of the Covenant. It is a deep commitment to another person, reaching its peak-point in a readiness to die: "Greater love has no man than this, that a man lay down his life for his friends" (John 15:13). It is a mutual commitment: I love you, and you return my love, just as the New Covenant will say, "We love [God], because he first loved us" (1 John 4:19). Again, it is a free commitment and the Bible stresses that covenant love can never be forced. What pathos fills the words of Revelation: "Behold, I stand at the door and knock; if any one hears my voice and opens the door, I will come in to him and eat with him, and he with me" (Revelation 3:20). Here we strike the note of freedom. We can knock all day on someone's door; Christ himself can knock all day on someone's door; but if the other chooses to keep that door closed, no one can enter. We are free to accept or reject friendship. I can draft all the covenants I like, but if the other does not respond I am powerless. Yahweh himself cannot — because he will not — break into the heart of a man who is reluctant to open. Friendship is a meeting of persons who dwell in one another as Jesus dwells in the Father and the Father in him. Finally, the partners in the covenant must be faithful, just as Yahweh is faithful to his people, even when they desert him to play the harlot in Egypt. The steadfast love of Yahweh is the supreme model of human fidelity.

And the friendship of Aelred is based on this covenant. What makes it peculiarly mystical is the intuitive depth at which it is enacted in Christ. Going beyond thoughts and concepts and images to reach the inner core of another, it creates a bond, a mutual fidelity, a union in Christ that ordinary friendship does not know.

Aelred wrote for, and about, his fellow monks. But the doctrine he evolved is capable of much broader application. It is even relevant in the turbulent area of man-woman relationships which become more and more critical in the cultural revolution that characterizes our day. With institutional marriage in process of transformation, with all kinds of experiments (wise and otherwise) being attempted, with the increasing desire of married couples to be friends and intimates, not just sexual partners – in this environment, Aelred may have a message for modern man and modern woman. The presupposition is that they are open to mysticism through love and faith and meditation and non-attachment. For this will develop their interior senses, leading them through those stages that culminate in the kiss of Christ, a situation where Christ is somehow present in their love as the Spirit is present in the love of the Father for the Son. And sexual intercourse, being an expression of, and way to, this deeper union of mind and heart, becomes fully human and spiritually creative.

For meditation in all the great religions leads to remarkable control of sexuality. Not that sexual power diminishes with depth in meditation. On the contrary, the non-attachment that accompanies such depth penetrates to the subliminal caverns of psychic life, liberating men and women from the unconscious fears and traumatic anxieties that sometimes cause impotence, frigidity, lack of pleasure and reluctance to give oneself physically to another. In this sense, meditation, far from weakening, may liberate one's sexual energy; and this is one of the claims of Yoga. But together with this liberation come a power and a self-mastery (and this is chastity) which enables people to express their love sexually when it is appropriate to do so and to refrain from physical expression when circumstances so demand. And to do so in such a way that their love, rooted at the deep core of their being, never grows cold. Though Aelred had nothing like this in mind, his principles might well lead to a mysticism of marriage.

Yet another area in which Aelred's doctrine could be relevant is that of personal love between celibate men and women who are vowed to continence and chastity. The history of Christian monasticism contains many instances of such relationships; and there is no scarcity of men and women mystics who loved one another chastely, tenderly and radically. This is all the more remarkable when one reflects that the religious climate in which these holy celibates lived was geared to keep unmarried men and women segregated in all circumstances. Grilles and grates, enclosures and canonical censures were established to thwart any man-woman union outside marriage and to keep the sexes apart. But the mystics have always shown remarkable facility for beating the institution and transcending the cultural taboos of their day. They are the people who, with a smile and a song, really enjoy life; they are the people who lend energy to the thrust of life, dynamically leading the human family into the future. And so we find an Aelred-like friendship existing between St Teresa and St John of the Cross who were lifted up in a common ecstasy, she on one side of the convent grille and he on the other.

I do not vouch for the authenticity of the story I will now quote, though I myself have no objections to taking it literally. Even if spurious, it gives some indication of what pious hagiographers thought about friendship between the mystics:

> It is related that on Trinity Sunday the two saints were conversing, separated by the convent grille, and that as St John held forth in burning language about the mystery which the Church celebrates that day, the heavens appeared to open, and their two souls, united in this sublime contemplation, soared upwards to the supreme Good, a glimpse of which had been vouchsafed to them. Whilst they were thus rapt in ecstasy, Sister Beatrice of Jesus, the portress, came to give a message to the prioress. She knocked; no one answered. She opened the door, and beheld the two saints lifted up into the air in ecstasy; St John holding on to the chair, vainly attempting to struggle with the force which impelled him upwards, St Teresa still on her knees, and also miraculously raised above the ground. News of the wondrous sight spread rapidly through the convent, and many came to witness it. The saint, interrogated afterwards by her daughters, answered: "That is what comes of talking with Father John. Not only does he fall into an ecstasy, but he carries others away with him!"
>
> (Lovat, p. 377)

What a sense of humour Teresa had – and how human! For the above (if it contains a germ of truth) was no more than a climactic moment in a close creative friendship of two extra-ordinary mystics, working together, freely exchanging ideas – while she darned his socks. This was a warm relationship – mystical and creative, yet totally celibate. Probably the great productivity of the two mystics had something to do with their mystical love and understanding. This is the opinion of a leading scholar in Carmelite studies who points out that neither could have reached their immense stature as spiritual writers without this friendship; and he believes that their incredible doctrinal achevement has its roots in their mutual cooperation and love.[1]

To the modern person, however, the puzzling feature of relationships like that of Teresa and John is their radical celibacy: the fact that both partners retained the highest ideals of chastity. A commingling of minds and hearts between two people separated by a lattice-work grille. Is this a Platonic rejection of the body?

While such relationships are rooted in a special charism that not everyone possesses, I do not believe that they contradict the laws of human psychology or that they put an intolerable strain on human nature. Nor are they Platonic. On this point I would like to quote some observations of Viktor Frankl about a deep spiritual love that exists (or, more correctly, can exist) at the core of man's being. Physical sexuality, he maintains, is an expression of this love; but it is not the only expression. And this love can grow and develop without commingling of bodies. Here is what he says:

> Loving represents a coming to relationship with another as a spiritual being. The close connection with spiritual aspects of the partner is the ultimate attainable form of partnership. The lover is no longer aroused in his own physical being, nor stirred in his own emotionality, but moved to the depths of his spiritual core, moved by the partner's spiritual core. Love, then, is an entering into a direct relationship with the personality of the beloved . . . The lover's gaze looks through the physical and psychic dress to the spiritual core, looks to the core of the other's being. He is no longer interested in an alluring physical "type" or attractive temperament; he is concerned with the person, with the partner as unique, irreplaceable and incomparable. (Frankl, p. 108)

[1] See E. W. Trueman Dicken, *Ephemerides Carmeliticae*, vol. XXI (1970).

For Frankl, then, all true love is enacted at the deep core of the being opened up through meditation (though not only through meditation) and as such is a mystical experience. But he is not precisely advocating celibacy, for he continues:

> All this, of course, is not to say that love has no desire to "embody" itself. But it is independent of the body to the extent that it does not need the body. Even in love between the sexes the body, the sexual element, is not primary; it is not an end in itself, but a means of expression. Love as such can exist without it. Where sexuality is possible, love will desire and seek it; but where renunciation is called for, love will not necessarily cool or die ... True love in and for itself needs the body neither for arousal nor for fulfilment, though it makes use of the body for both. (Frankl, p. 112)

At our present stage of evolution the men and women who go beyond the erotic and emotional to reach the spiritual core of another are probably few in number. And perhaps only the mystics (or those who aspire to mysticism) are capable of doing so. Yet the possibility is there. And the mystics are the greatest friends. If they are a married couple, they may express their love through sexual intercourse; if they are celibate, they practise restraint and renunciation. But in either case their love can be warm and growing and creative.

In this whole area, some of the richest and most challenging ideas flow from the pen of Teilhard de Chardin.[1] Radically dedicated to celibacy, he yet had the most intimate spiritual relationships with both men and women friends; and he experienced in the depth of his being the creativity that is unleashed by such encounters. As always, he sees friendship and spiritual love in their cosmic setting. Woman leads man out of his cramping isolation, pointing the way to a universal love that encompasses mankind and the whole

---

[1] See, for example, *Human Energy,* translated by J. M. Cohen (Collins, London, 1969, and Harcourt, Brace, Jovanovich, New York, 1970), pp. 32–4, 72–6, 128–30, 144–55; *The Evolution of Chastity; The Phenomenon of Man,* translated by Bernard Wall (Collins, London, and Harper, New York, 1959), pp. 264–8.

universe, leading on to God. Moreover, man-woman love is the force that builds the cosmos and stimulates the thrust of life towards ever more fullness of being. Teilhard willingly admits that his most cherished ideas came to birth under feminine influence with its tender inspiration.

Casting his mind back millions of years, Teilhard sees the history of the universe as the development of an ever-evolving love. First, in inanimate matter, this love is not more than the interplay of molecular forces. With the birth of life and the growth of the biosphere, love is directed towards reproduction; but with the appearance of man, the reproductive function is accompanied by another dimension, a spiritual and personal dimension: now the couple build or create one another in a mutual complementarity. Indeed, as the human race evolves and develops, the reproductive function assumes a less important role. Matter is spiritualized; love is spiritualized; and in the course of time sexuality in the man will be satisfied by pure femininity.

In other words we have a human race evolving towards virginity which, far from being a denial of love, will be a magnificent expression of love of another kind. For Teilhard the greatness of woman is less in her physical maternity (important and beautiful though this is) than in her spiritual fecundity; and the man-woman relationship, particularly in its celibate form, unleashes the greatest energy in the universe. This is the force that carries forward the thrust of life towards Omega, the personal centre of attraction, the ultimate point of convergence, the magnetic source of love from which nothing can separate us. In the final stage of unification in Omega, men will neither marry nor be given in marriage, "but are like angels in heaven" (Mark 12:25).

Assuredly Teilhard's thought has its limitations.[1] Apart from the the fact that it is written almost exclusively from the man's viewpoint, there is the additional fact that it just sounds fantastic.

---

[1] Though Teilhard's thought has its limitations, he never compromises the traditional morality. I say this because it has been suggested that he was trying to justify sexual intercourse in a life dedicated to celibacy. This is nonsense and an utter travesty of his thought. He was trying to elaborate a theory of celibate love which, without being Platonic, would go beyond physical sex to the highest point in the spiritualization of matter.

He himself admits this, saying that nine-tenths of mankind will consider him a naive fool to entertain such outlandish ideas. But, he goes on, it is only because men attempted the impossible that we are able to fly and to travel in outer space. So why not attempt the impossible in human relations? Besides, few things are impossible if we have faith in man attracted by the ennobling call of Omega. Again, one might question his assumption that the man-woman relationship is the peak-point of evolution and the highest expression of human friendship. This is a claim which he does not adequately substantiate.

But an even greater limitation is the fact that in *The Evolution of Chastity* Teilhard asked the wrong question. Setting out to justify the celibate life, he presumed that virginity is superior to marriage and attempted to explain why this should be. As if the value of celibacy rested on its superiority to marriage. Surely it would have been better to place the two vocations side by side as parallel functions in the mystical body of Christ. This he could have done without jeopardizing his central insight; namely, that the celibates are men and women who feel the attraction of the divine centre drawing them to itself more acutely than the sexual attraction that might prematurely draw them together. This sense of vocation, which alone will justify celibacy (as it alone will explain marriage), is really the key to his thinking. But as often happens with pioneers, his conceptualization and articulation fall short of his intuition.

If Teilhard is correct, mystical friendship will become a common phenomenon in the future. What was the exceptional privilege of a few will become the way of many. This is a remarkable prediction. If true, it proves again that the mystics are in the vanguard of evolution, challenging mankind to move forward to greater maturity and fullness of being. It points to the mystery and the richness and the wonder of one who loves "the mountains, the solitary wooded valleys, strange islands . . . silent music".

15

Friendship – the cosmic dimension

In the last chapter I referred to the Teilhardian observation that woman leads man out of his isolation. This she does by teaching him how to love. Through her he learns what it means to be loved and to love; and such an experience is ultimately "ecstatic". It carries him beyond the barriers of self into a wider world where he meets his truest love, who is "the mountains, the solitary wooded valleys, strange islands . . . silent music". Woman leads man to an enlightenment wherein he loses his little self to find his true self, the universe and God.

Probably all this is true of any love, not just that of man and woman. It is sometimes said that love is an exploration, a going out of self in quest of the mystery of the other; and in this search one goes endlessly on and on and on. For just as in the ascent of Mount Carmel one never comes face to face with God (the veil of faith is always there), so in the journey into the core of another, one never reaches the end. Mystery always remains – and, indeed, this very mystery is the enticing force that draws us on. Again, in the ascent of Mount Carmel one must never stop climbing; one must never be seduced by the beautiful flowers nor terrified by the wild beasts; one must leave all to find the treasure in an endless and anguishing purification. And in the same way, in the search for another one must never be seduced by secondary things; the peripheral joys, the sensual fascination, the ecstatic delights of intimacy. All this joy of friendship is good, exquisitely good; but one who clings to it refuses to grow.

The great enemy is absorption. Two people absorbed in one another are closed to the greater vibrations of the universe and the cosmic Christ. Settling down on a plateau, they will never scale the heights unless they break out of this closed cirnuit into the realm of cosmic creativity where they will build both the universe and one another. By renouncing absorption they find union which, while differentiating, renders one luminous to the other.

In true friendship, then, we find a movement away from absorption towards universality, away from self-centredness towards cosmicfication. Here is a strange combination of affection and detachment, of sincere personal love for another and limitless personal love for the universe, of deep emotional attachment without self-centred clinging. And just as in the ascent of Mount Carmel one sometimes gets ecstatic glimpses of the summit, so, in the journey into the dark being of another, one may get fleeting glimpses of that other's personal core. These glimpses are momentary and passing; they are cosmic experiences of God, because God is the centre of the other's being. If the mystics see the universe in a grain of sand, what must they see in the personal core of another?

All this is found in Aelred, at least in embryo. His third stage is a meeting with "only Christ" – that is, with Christ inseparable from the universe and mankind and his Father. At the same time I believe that in this point Aelred's articulation, like that of Teilhard, falls short of his intuition. A cursory reading of his words might suggest that in the discovery of Christ (the kiss of "only Christ") the human friend, so to speak, falls out of the picture and Christ alone remains. If Aelred means this he would make friendship a *means* rather than a *way*. But I cannot think this was his intention. Rather did he mean that Christ is present as a third party towards whom the gaze of the friends is drawn while they remain closely united one to another – "where two or three are gathered in my name, there am I" (Matthew 18:20). This is how Christ entered into the friendship of the two disciples going to Emmaus. He suddenly was present as a third person who had been walking with them all the time but only now appeared in visible form. The same is true of all the resurrection appearances of Christ: he is suddenly present as *another* in the midst of friends. Then their attention, no longer absorbed in one another, is drawn towards "only Christ". They are still united, closely united, but the pull of the divine centre is now so strong that it annihilates all tendency to absorption in one another, drawing their gaze towards itself. This was the situation of John and Teresa.

Liberated from absorption in one another, they were united in a common gaze upon Christ.

And, of course, even this third stage is not the end of the friendship journey. The goal will only be reached with the *parousia*. This Aelred makes clear:

> In this way, beginning with the love with which he has embraced his friend, and rising up to the love with which he embraces Christ, he will with great happiness enjoy the delight of the friendship of friendships, awaiting the fullness of time . . . when this friendship, to which in this life we admit only a few, will be extended to all and by all will be extended to God, since God will be All in all.
>
> (Aelred, p. 702)

Here we find in Aelred an admirable combination of idealism and realism. Idealism because his is a vision of friendship leading to Omega and to an ultimate loving intimacy with all men. Yet he is realistic enough to see that such a happy consummation can only take place in "the fullness of time". After all, man at his present evolutionary stage does not have the emotional wherewithal to be the *friend* of everybody. What he can do, however, is *love* everybody – or more correctly, anybody. And it is towards this universal love that friendship moves when absorption has lost its grip.

The New Testament has good things to say about all this. First of all there is the mysterious friendship of Jesus with his twelve disciples. He has called them servants and then, at the end, he calls them friends. Something like this transition from discipleship and subordination to friendship and equality is found also in Buddhism. Once enlightened, the disciple is on a par with his master, because now he has received all that the master has to give. And in some similar way, in the last hours of his life, Jesus raises the status of these twelve men from discipleship to friendship. At the last supper he says:

> No longer do I call you servants, for the servant does not know what his master is doing; but I have called you

friends, for all that I have heard from my Father I have made
known to you. (John 15:15)

No longer servants but friends, because he has opened his heart; he
has laid bare his soul; he has told them everything. And now there is
laid at their disposal what Paul vividly calls "the unsearchable
riches of Christ" (Ephesians 3:8)

What Jesus has revealed to them is not just a collection of
parables and teachings but his very self – for this is the word he has
heard from the Father. And the more they enter into the deepest self
of Christ, the more cosmic will they become. Because in the
revelation of himself Jesus reveals the Father – "He who has seen
me has seen the Father" (John 14:9). He also reveals the human
race, which is his body; and he reveals the world, which was made
by him even when it knew him not. That is why this friendship,
which begins a few hours before his death, will never end.

In this whole matter we are strikingly confronted with the
mysteriously cosmic dimension not only of Jesus but of any man. I
once heard a Zen master, speaking to a group of Buddhists and
Christians, say that the great enlightenment of Jesus was expressed
in his word: "Before Abraham was, I am" (John 8:58). This Zen
master believed that here the "I" of Jesus was not the little empirical
ego, the illusory self that Buddhism rejects. Rather was it the "I" of
the universe that came surging up from the depth of his being in an
ecstatic moment of awakening. While the master's faith obviously
differed from mine, I felt that he was giving to Christians a new and
valuable insight into the fact that the person of Christ is the eternal
Word of the Father, cosmic and all-inclusive.

However this may be, the friendship of the disciples with their
Lord became increasingly cosmic. The Church fathers loved to
quote the words of Jesus: "It is to your advantage that I go away"
(John 16:7); and they would comment that by his departure and the
ensuing separation Jesus was liberating the disciples from excess
absorption, leading them on to the cosmic dimension of his risen
existence. They might well have added that in all friendship
separation plays an important role in leading friends away from
absorption to an even greater universality.

The same evolutionary development is found in Paul. His letters show a growing intimacy with Christ, together with a growing thrust towards cosmification, reaching a climax in the later epistles where Paul enjoys the closest union with a risen Jesus who is co-extensive with the universe. Paul cannot adequately express his own experience (who could express such an experience?) but he speaks of the *secret* of Christ, hidden from all ages and only now made known (Colossians 1:26). There is a gradual revelation through the ages of a Christ who has been present in the heart of matter long before he is born as man in Israel. It is as though the incarnation of Christ is in some embryonic way contemporaneous with the birth of the universe. The Harvard astronomer Harlow Shapely put it well when he said, "In the beginning was the word and the word was hydrogen gas." He later protested that this remark was neither blasphemous nor facetious. What he meant was that the Word was somehow incarnate from the beginning in the very heart of matter. This, of course, is the Teilhardian approach to St Paul; and it fits in well with what we are saying here.

For as the Word was incarnate in hydrogen gas, so now in a more unique and personal way is it incarnate in the grand totality of the universe. This is the cosmic Christ, the secret now revealed and constantly being revealed as the universe moves towards the point of convergence where Omega stands triumphant. And Paul, who grasped the unsearchable riches of Christ, knew that friendship with him is friendship with the all.

It seems to me that Paul's friendship with Christ is a model or archetype of human friendships. These, too, have a cosmic dimension because (in the faith of the Christian and in the interpretation of Aelred) friendship with anyone is ultimately friendship with Christ, just as to give a cup of water to anyone is to give a cup of water to Christ. This Christ who is the friend or to whom one gives the cup of water is cosmic, one with the Father and one with mankind. About the precise nature of this mysterious union of Christ with the all, however, little can be said; for this is an area that lies in the darkness of the cloud of unknowing. Here, perhaps, it is enough to recall once more the Teilhardian principle that union differentiates – to such an extent that the more a person becomes Christ the more he becomes himself. And that is why friendship with the other never excludes friendship with Christ, as friendship with Christ cannot exclude the other.

So the truest friendship leads to a universal love, a love of the cosmos and its mysterious source and of all men. Aelred comes to the love of God through the love of man: John of the Cross comes to the love of man through the love of God. Both end in the same place. In either case there is only one love, as is clear in the fourth gospel. "That they may all be one; even as thou, Father, art in me, and I in thee, that they also may be in us, so that the world may believe . . ." (John 17:21). Christ and the Spirit and the Father and the human race are caught up in one mysterious but all-embracing love. There are not two loves, but only one.

And this love is the highest form of human energy. It is the lifeforce as well as the ultimate goal towards which the universe is straining and striving. As we look at the world today, the greatest problem is not air pollution, nor population explosion, nor sexual revolution, nor cultural change. The greatest problem is the imperfection of our love; that is to say, our lack of mysticism. And the people who carry forward the thrust of evolution are the mystics. They are the vanguard, ecstatically pointing towards the future.

EPILOGUE

16

Convergence

Almost fifty years ago, Alfred North Whitehead, commenting on the dwindling influence of Christianity and Buddhism, attributed their decline to a refusal to dialogue. "The decay of Christianity and Buddhism as determinative influences in modern thought", he wrote, "is partly due to the fact that each religion has unduly sheltered itself from the other. The self-sufficient pedantry of learning and the confidence of ignorant zealots have combined to shut up each religion in its own forms of thoughts. Instead of looking to each other for deeper meanings, they have remained self-satisfied and unfertilized. Both have suffered from the rise of the third tradition, which is science, because neither of them had retained the requisite flexibility of adaptation" (Whitehead, pp. 146, 140ff).

A good deal has happened since Whitehead penned these lines; and in the course of this book I have tried to say that Christianity and Buddhism are at last beginning to talk, to dialogue, to help one another: a process of cross-fertilization has now begun. Moreover, a Christian-Buddhist dialogue with science is under way, with scholars and researchers showing profound interest in the meditation and mysticism of Buddhist and Christian cultures. Where this three-cornered dialogue will end, no one can say. But it may well be a breakthrough in human history. It may be one of the most significant happenings of our day.

This is not the first experience of dialogue either for Christianity or for Buddhism. In the West a historic encounter took place when Christianity, basically a Jewish religion, met up with Hellenism and took into itself Greek thought-patterns and insights. This was an enrichment. And now, in the twentieth century, Christianity, conscious of its Jewish origins and maintaining its Hellenistic heritage, faces the indescribable wealth of the Eastern religions. How will she react? Where are we going? These are fascinating questions. For new vistas will now be opened; Western complacency will sustain new shocks; Western religion will be further liberated from age-old cultural and religious taboos. All in all, something new will be born.

In this book I have tried to stress what the great religions have in common. They share the same quest for wisdom, the same sense of man's existential situation and need of salvation, the same belief in man's dignity and value, the same basic attempt to solve man's deeper problems. I have also tried to say that science shares in the quest for wisdom; and in a rapidly converging world, where people and nations are coming together with unprecedented velocity, we need one another. We cannot survive unless we unite to build the earth and mould the human family into a single community. The world needs the Hindu experience of God gathered through many, many centuries of meditation and search. This is the experience of God immanent in nature, in the depth of being, at the core of the human soul. But, side by side with this, the world needs also the great Hebrew experience of the transcendent Yahweh who guides and loves while living beyond the reach of human thought or image. Again, the world needs the Buddhist unrelenting thirst for a wisdom which brings release and salvation through enlightenment. And the world cannot be deaf to the revelation of Jesus who, uniting in his person the transcendent and the immanent, speaks of God as no man ever spoke. And, finally, the world cannot survive without the scientist's untiring quest for truth, his work for human progress and for the betterment of man.

This is a far cry from saying that all these systems are the same. Far from being the same, they manifest a pluralism that is excitingly beautiful. They show us different ways, or *tao*, which lead to supreme wisdom. The word *tao* has fascinated me all through this book; and it is very relevant here. There are many paths to the summit of Mount Fuji, say the Japanese; and there are many religions that lead to something or someone who lies in impenetrable darkness beyond the cloud of unknowing. But unlike the paths of Fuji, the religions need one another. There are, moreover, many ways within each religious tradition. What a variety of ways exists in Mahayana Buddhism alone! And within Christianity, too, I have pointed to the ways of meditation, of purification and of friendship. But perhaps we could ask if there is anything common to all these ways. I believe there is.

In the Christian way the basic experience or enlightenment to which all the paths lead is that of being loved by God. This is the theme of the First Epistle of St John with its ever-recurring theme, "We love, *because he first loved us*" (1 John 4:19). The author keeps reminding us that God took the initiative, that it was not my idea to love God, but rather that my love is the answer to a call or invitation. In other words, the first thing in Christianity is not my love for God and other people, but my belief that the world is loved by God. "God is love"; and from this everything else follows. "God so loved the world that he gave his only Son . . ." (John 3:16). From belief in God's love comes a sense of security, an unshakable faith that (in the words of Julian of Norwich) "all will be well, and all will be well, and all manner of thing will be well". It may look all wrong; but all will be well.

The basic enlightenment of the Old Testament has much in common with this. Here the stress is on the fidelity of God to his Covenant. God is faithful; he will not let you down; he will love in spite of everything. "I have loved you with an everlasting love" (Jeremiah 31:3). And like a theme song through the pages of the Old Testament run the words, "Fear not, for I am with you." These are the words spoken to Moses and to Isaiah and to Jeremiah. The name is called (and how that name penetrates to the core of the being) and then the assurance given that all will be well. Things may be difficult; they may seem impossible; but I will be with you and nothing will harm you. And so again comes the sense of security, the great unshakable faith that "all will be well, and all will be well, and all manner of thing will be well".

In Hinduism, particularly in the *Gita*, we find the same stress on being loved, together with the joy and confidence released through such a conviction. Pure Land Buddhism, too, is based on the merciful love of Amida. Zen, it is true, does not speak in terms of being loved by God, since it says nothing about God at all. But enlightenment is accompanied by joy, a sense of security, the belief that "all will be well, and all will be well, and all manner of thing will be well".

In all these religions we have a common faith that is basically human. It is a faith in the future; it is faith like that of the mother who, clutching her child in her arms in the midst of earthquake, or flood or pestilence or war, tells him that all will be well. "Fear not, for I am with you." Viewed superficially, all is far from well; the situation may even call for despair; death may be imminent. But she has a true intuition that all will somehow be well. This is the intuition to which successful transactional analysis should lead: the belief that "I'm OK and you're OK". It is something that cannot be proved by reasoning and syllogism. In the last analysis I must make an act of faith. And the scientist, it seems to me, must have this faith too. He must have faith in man and in the future of the human race. Without such faith why make the effort? Why make the effort, unless I believe that thanks to this research "all will be well, and all will be well, and all manner of thing will be well"?

This is the faith in man of which the poet spoke when he said that "hope springs eternal in the human breast". It is something common to the various ways. All must finally believe in man.

Perhaps we can also say that the great religions share a belief in a common destiny. It is as though one Spirit, filling and animating the universe, is driving us towards a point of convergence, a common point of intersection, where Buddhist and Christian, Hindu and Jew will meet. This point of convergence (call it Omega or what you will) may lie in the far, far distant future. We cannot see it; we cannot delineate it; but we are sure that it is there, even when we have no blueprint or construction model. I think that in interfaith dialogue we sometimes get a fleeting glimpse or foretaste of this ultimate union toward which we are tending – moments when Buddhists and Christians experience that they are one. Yet in this very dialogue, facing an uncertain future, we feel the need of guidelines to point out the way. During one dialogue which I myself attended a Japanese professor remarked good-humouredly that we all feel danger – cultural and religious danger to the values we cherish. He articulated the unexpressed senitments of many. So let me tentatively suggest some guidelines.

First of all there is the fact that at our present stage of evolution we are on different, if intertwining, paths; and all the great religions wish to be faithful to their past and to their origins. We know that in the modern world fidelity to the past and to history is one of the great desires of individuals and of nations. There is no greater dread than that of losing one's religious and cultural heritage. Nor is this unreasonable. If (as psychoanalysis keeps reminding us) the individual is conditioned by his history, if the past is present within him, constantly pushing him on and influencing his conduct, the same is true of nations and of blocks of nations and of whole cultures. No man and no nation can deny the past without peril to psychological, cultural and religious life. That is why people must ordinarily remain in their own religious tradition unless conversion to another is the outgrowth of the past. The point of intersection and convergence has not yet arrived.

And to preserve the good things of the past, the great religions can be uncompromising without jeopardizing the harmony of dialogue. I myself feel this in regard to Christianity. If it is to be true to its New Testament roots, if it is to be honest in its dialogue with other religions, it has to be faithful to its founder – to the man, the carpenter, Jesus of Nazareth who, Christians believe, rose from the dead. To water down the divine Sonship of the historical Jesus with suggestions that we talk only about the *logos* or the cosmic Christ in the name of ecumenism is, it seems to me, unfair to the Buddhists, the Hindus, the Jews, the scientists with whom we dialogue. For Christianity is built on the belief that the *logos* "emptied himself", became a very poor man, and lives now as the cosmic Christ. This is the peculiar contribution which Christianity makes to the world; and without it, what would Christianity have to offer?

The first guideline, then, is fidelity to the past. But this alone is not enough. The great religions must also march into the future in accordance with the inexorable law of progress, of change, of evolution. Paradoxical though it sounds, in order to be faithful to the past we must be detached from this very past to face the future with a readiness to change. Only in this way can we make progress along the path which leads to Omega.

Finally, it should be remembered that the evolutionary process is not automatic. It must be carried forward by men and women in an ongoing dialogue with one another and with the world. This book has been written in the belief that meditation is a key factor in this dialogue and in the march forward of humanity. For the meditator or the mystic, going beyond thoughts and concepts and images to a deeper level of awareness, finds himself in an ever growing union with the universe and with others – a union which is enacted at the core of his being. And when he enters into dialogue with others who also are meditators or mystics, both may find themselves in a remarkable harmony, even when their conceptual systems and symbols differ radically. They may find that they are dwelling in one another, sharing a common vision as they move towards a common future. This vision cannot be conceptualized. It is certain with the certainty of faith; but it is also obscure because of this very faith.

But the mystic is more particularly the builder of the future because he loves. Throughout this book I have insisted that in the last analysis meditation is a love affair and that love is the most powerful energy in the universe. It is love that builds the earth and carries forward the thrust of evolution. It is love that brings together the great traditions in a union which cross-fertilizes even when it differentiates. It is love that leads them on towards Omega, the point of convergence, which is also "the mountains, the solitary wooded valleys, strange islands . . . silent music".

GLOSSARY OF WORDS USED
IN THE TEXT

agape (Greek), love: used in the New Testament to designate the special reality of Christian love, whose source is the Spirit. It refers in the first place to God's love for men, but also to the love of Christians for one another and for God.

anatta (Pali), *muga* (Japanese), non-self; *anatta doctrine* is the Buddhist teaching that there is no permanent self.

bodhisattva (Sanskrit): in Buddhism, an enlightened person dedicated to helping others reach liberation. He represents the last stage before that of supremely enlightened, fully perfected Buddhahood.

chakras (Sanskrit): centres of energy in the human body. In Hindu tradition there are seven such centres, located, (1) at the base of the spine; (2) at the base of the male genital organ; (3) in the lumbar region; (4) in the cardiac region; (5) in the laryngeal region; (6) between the eyebrows; (7) at the top of the head. In Tantric Buddhism there are only four centres, situated in the umbilical, cardiac, laryngeal regions, and the cerebral plexus.

dokusan (Japanese): in Zen Buddhism, a private interview with the *roshi* for spiritual direction.

eschaton (Greek), the last day: in biblical theology *eschaton* refers to the consummation of history when the risen Christ will return for judgement.

guru (Sanskrit), teacher, venerable one: in Eastern tradition, a *guru* is a religious master or a spiritual director.

Hesychasm: a method of prayer in the Oriental Christian Church that depended on control of the physical faculties, and concentration on the *Jesus Prayer* to achieve peace of soul and union with God. Originally a monastic practice, it was popularized in the thirteenth and fourteenth centuries.

imprimatur (latin), literally, "let it be printed": in the Roman Catholic Church, this word was the official sign of permission for a book to be printed. It was, therefore, the mark of orthodoxy in Catholic books prior to the Second Vatican Council (1962–65)

jiriki (Japanese), self-reliance.

kairos (Greek), time, the right season. In Greek philosophy *kairos* was used to designate a critical period or moment of decision. The *kairos* in Scripture is the time of salvation which God has chosen and decreed to offer the fullness of grace in Jesus Christ. It is therefore also the critical moment in which the final judgement begins.

Kannon (Japanese), also *Kwannon*, and in Sanskrit, *Avalokiteshvara: Kannon*, meaning "the great compassionate one", is the Buddhist saint (*bodhisattva*) of universal love who plays a central role in the devotional practices of all Buddhist sects.

koan (Japanese), paradoxical problem pointing to ultimate truth. It is meaningless to the rational intellect and can only be solved by awakening a deeper level of the mind, beyond discursive thought.

kyrios (Greek), lord or ruler. *Kyrios* was used in the Septuagint as a translation of the divine name, *Yahweh*. In New Testament times, the Early Church used it as a title of praise and adoration for the risen Jesus. By calling the risen Jesus, *Kyrios* (the Lord), the Church acknowledged him to be God.

Logos (Greek), word. *Logos* is the title given in John 1:1–14 and 1 John 1 to Jesus as the Son of God. The Latin translated it as *Verbum* and in English it is "the Word". In biblical theology *Logos* is used for Jesus Christ, the Word made flesh.

makyo (Japanese), *maya* (Sanskrit), illusion or ignorance of the true nature of things. Specifically, *makyo* sometimes refers to the hallucinatory phenomena one may experience at a certain period in the practice of *zazen*.

mandala (Sanskrit), circle, assemblage or picture. In Tantric Buddhism, the *mandala* is a sacred symbol full of cosmic significance.

mantra (Sanskrit), prayer or hymn. The *mantra* in Tantric Huddhism and in other Eastern traditions is a sacred word given by the master to the disciple at the time of initiation. When the disciple's mind is properly attuned, the inner vibrations of this word-symbol, together with its associations in his mind, are said to lead to mind-expansion. One such sacred word is "Om".

miccha samadhi (Pali), *mithya samadhi* (Sanskrit), a state of one-pointed-ness (*samadhi*) about the wrong thing. It is roughly equivalent to false mysticism.

nirvana (Sanskrit), literally, extinction (of individual existence); from *nirva*, to be extinguished or blown out. In Buddhism, *nirvana* is the highest mystical experience of changelessness, inner peace and freedom, attained through the extinction of the self. It denotes a return to the Buddha nature after the dissolution of the physical body; a state of perfect bliss and freedom, beyond life and death.

noosphere, literally, the realm of the mind (Greek, *nous*). Teilhard de Chardin used *noosphere* in a particular way to designate the realm or sphere which encloses human thought and love. He likened it to the biosphere in which all living things are in contact and, interaction with each other. The *noosphere* is superimposed on the biosphere, and comprises all psychosocial and cultural changes, all artistic and scientific achievements, in short, all human achievements and values.

Omega (Greek): *Omega* is the last letter in the Greek alphabet. Teilhard de Chardin used this word in two particular contexts: (1) to signify the end point or term of the natural evolution of mankind and the cosmos; the apex of the convergent social and spiritual development on earth; (2) for God, as a pre-existent, transcendent and immanent superperson who is the loving and lovable and omnipresent activating centre, source and goal of noogenesis. For Teilhard, *Omega* was the risen Christ as depicted by St Paul and St John.

parousia (Greek): In biblical theology, a term used to designate Christ's second coming at the end of history. Its approximate meaning is "saving presence" or "arrival".

pleroma (Greek), literally, that which fills up; a fullness or completeness. In biblical theology, the *pleroma* if the fullness of divine excellence and powers which will be complete at the *parousia*.

prajna (Sanskrit), supreme knowledge or wisdom.

Rinzai (Japanese): one of the two prominent Zen sects in Japan. The other is *Soto*.

roshi (Japanese), Zen master.

samadhi (Sanskrit), *san'mai* (Japanese): in a broad sense *samadhi* refers to a state of heightened and expanded awareness beyond conceptual thought. In this book it is used in this sense, to denote an intense yet effortless concentration, reaching a state of one-pointedness, peace and equilibrium.

samurai (Japanese), a warrior: the *samurai* were the military aristocracy of feudal Japan. *Samurai* also refers to the individual knights or warriors of this social caste. They had the power of life and death over commoners. Their special privileges were abolished with the fall of feudalism in 1871.

sapientia (Latin), wisdom.

satori (Japanese), the experience of enlightenment, i.e., self-realization, opening the mind's eye, awakening to one's true nature and hence to the nature of existence.

sesshin (Japanese): in Zen Buddhism, *sesshin* is a kind of monastic retreat (usually of seven days) devoted principally to long periods of *zazen* in a concentrated and intense effort to achieve enlightenment.

siddhis (Sanskrit), literally, perfections: in Eastern meditation *siddhis* are parapsychological powers (for example, clairvoyance or telepathy) which one may acquire at a certain stage of meditation.

silentium mysticum (Latin), mystical silence. This term is used in Christian mystical theology to denote a state of quiet beyond conceptual thought in which the spirit rests in a sense of God's presence.

Soto (Japanese): one of the two prominent sects of Zen Buddhism in Japan. The other is *Rinzai*.

sutra (Sanskrit): the Buddhist scriptures containing dialogues and sermons attributed to the Buddha.

swami (Hindu), *svamin* (Sanskrit), lord, master, king. In Hindu tradition, *swami* is a title (like "Reverend") given to a religious teacher.

tao (Chinese), literally, a road, a way; figuratively, the course of nature, the absolute, the cosmic order. Thus it means also truth, or right conduct.

zazen (Japanese), sitting in Zen meditation.

BOOKS AND ARTICLES QUOTED
IN THE TEXT

Aelredi, Beati, Abbatis Rievallensis, *opera Omnia* (Editio Migne, Paris, 1855).

Burtt, E.A. (editor), *The Teachings of the Compassionate Buddha* (The New American Library, New York, 1955).

Chang, Garma, *The Practice of Zen* (Harper & Row, New York, 1970).

Francis de Sales, St, *Introduction to the Devout Life*, translated and edited by John K. Ryan (Harper Brothers, New York, 1949).

Frankl, Viktor E., *The Doctor and the Soul* (Alfred A. Knopf, New York, 1955).

Green, Elmer, "Conference on Voluntary Control of Internal States", in *Psychologia* 12:107–8 (1969).

——*Psychophysiological Training for Creativity* (Research Department, The Menninger Foundation, Topeka, Kansas, 1971).

——"Voluntary Control of Internal States: Psychological and Physiological", in *Journal of Transpersonal Psychology*, vol. II, no.1 (1970).

——"On the Meaning of Transpersonal", in *Journal of Transpersonal Psychology*, vol.3, no. 1 (1971).

——*Biofeedback for Mind-Body Self-Regulation* (Research Department, The Menninger Foundation, Topeka, Kansas, 1971).

——*Preliminary Report on Voluntary Control Project: Swami Rama* (The Menninger Foundation, Topeka, Kansas, 1970).

Guibert, Joseph de, *The Theology of the Spiritual Life* (Sheed & Ward, New York and London, 1953 and 1954).

Hirai, Tomio, *The Psychophysiology of Zen* (Igaku Shoin, Tokyo, 1974).

Ignatius of Loyola, St, *The Spiritual Exercises of St Ignatius*, translated by Anthony Mottola, introduction by Robert Gleason, SJ (Doubleday, New York, 1963).

John of the Cross, St, *The Collected Works of St John of the Cross*, translated by Kieran Kavanaugh, OCD, and Otilio Rodriguez, OCD (Institute of Carmelite Studies, Washington, DC, 1973).

Johnston, William, (editor) *The Cloud of Unknowing and the Book of Privy Counselling* (Doubleday, New York, 1973).

——*The Still Point* (Harper & Row Perennial Library, New York, 1971).

Lovat, Lady Alice, *The Life of St Teresa* (Herbert & Daniel, London, 1911).

Naranjo, Claudio, and Ornstein, Robert, *On the Psychology of Meditation* (Viking Press, New York, 1971).

Poulain, Auguste, *Des Grâces d'Oraison* (Paris, 1901).

Segal, Julius, (editor) *Mental Health Program Reports* – 5 (National Institute of Mental Health, Rockville, Md, 1971).

Tart, Charles, (editor), *Altered States of Consciousness* (John Wiley, New York, 1969).

Teresa of Avila, St, *The Life of Saint Teresa of Avila* by herself, translated by J. M. Cohen (Penguin Books, Harmondsworth and Baltimore, Md., 1957).

——*The Interior Castle,* translated by E. Allison Peers (Doubleday, New York, 1961).

——*The Way of Perfection*, translated by E. Allison Peers (Doubleday, New York, 1964).

Wapnick, Kenneth, ("Mysticism and Schizophrenia", in *Journal of Transpersonal Psychology*, vol.1, no.2 (1969).

Weide, Thomas, "Council Grove IV – Toward a Science Concerned with Ultimates", in *Journal of Transpersonal Psychology*, vol. 6, no. 1 (1972).

Whitehead, Alfred N., *Religion in the Making* (Cambridge University Press, Cambridge, 1926, and World Publishing Company, New York, 1954). (Page references are given for both editions.)

INDEX

Abraham, 66, 136, 165, 176
absorption, liberation from, 173–4, 175, 176
activity, 92–4, 97
acupuncture, 115
Aelred of Rievaulx, St, 162–5, 166–7, 174–5, 177
Albertus Magnus, St, 48
alpha blocking, 38–9, 40, 41
alpha brainwaves, 31, 35, 37–40, 41, 42, 45, 60, 88, 116, 123; evil, 103; high-amplitude, 38, 59, 117, 120, 124; producers of, 38, 124; and visualization, 65–6
alpha-theta train, 40–1, 44, 45, 46–7, 65
Amida Buddha, 62, 65, 183
Ananias, 110
Angela of Foligno, 51
Aquinas, St Thomas, 48, 62, 70–1, 88
archery, 18, 120
Aristotle, 26, 88, 165
aspirations, repetition of, 62
astronauts, 52, 142
Augustine, St, 28, 62, 71
aureole, 76n
Aurobindo, Sri, 52
awakening, 91–2

Bacon, Roger, 48
Basil, St, 156
Bede, the Venerable, 48
Berger, Hans, 34
Bergson, Henri, 62, 68, 88, 162
beta brainwaves, 35, 37, 40, 41, 45, 88, 89; filter theory, 60–1; passage to alpha, 60
Bhagavad Gita, 120, 183
Bible, 28, 67, 70, 103, 165, 166
biofeedback, 15, 21, 36, 37, 47, 52, 123, 141; machines, 34, 37, 39, 47, 119
blood-pressure, 117, 119, 136
bodhisattva, 35, 64, 147
body, cosmic dimension, 142–4
body-control, 116, 118–19, 121
Book of Privy Counselling, 102n, 103, 104, 128
Boros, Ladislaus, 81
brain, 90, 124
brainwaves, 30, 34–6, 44–5, 48, 52; and hypnagogic imagery, 44–6, 59. *See* alpha, beta, delta, theta
breathing, 50, 59, 61, 91–2, 126, 143
Bridget, St, 51
Brosse, Thérèse, 115
Buber, Martin, 72
Buddha, 28, 62, 65–6, 134–5
Buddhism, 96–7, 134–5, 183; Amida, 62, 65, 183; and awakening to mystical life, 73–4; detachment in, 139–40; dialogue with Christianity, 28–9, 31, 53, 139–40, 144, 176, 181, 184–5; and ecstasy, 83; eight-fold path, 133, 134; and Epistle to the Romans, 135–6; *Fire Sermon*, 134; *Four Noble Truths*, 133, 136; Mahayana, 183; meditation in, 33; and non-attachment, 155–6; Pure Land, 62, 183; and transition from discipleship to friendship, 175. *See* Zen

calligraphy, 120
cancer, 120
Carmelites, 122
Carthusians, 39, 122
celibacy, 33, 117; and marriage, 172; and personal love, 167, 168, 169, 170, 171

chakras, 107

chastity, 167, 169, 172

child: natural, 41n, 131, 155; Parent and, 124–5, 127, 128, 131, 154–5

Christ, 28, 60, 182; cosmic, 84, 95–6, 127, 137, 146, 147–8, 177, 185; experience of cosmic body of, 144; and friendship, 166; friendship with disciples, 175–6; the great healer, 137–8; kiss of, 164–5, 167, 174; love of, 42–3, 129, 137; meditation and humanity of, 94; and meditation, true and false, 109; as Omega, 148–9; revelation of self to disciples, 176; and reward of faith, 83; risen, 96, 131, 136, 137, 148; temptations, 105; total, 147–8; and transforming union, 77–8; universal, 94, 137, 146; visualization by St Teresa, 66; = wisdom, 33; Zen master on, 176

Christianity: dialogue with Buddhism, 28–9, 31, 53, 144, 176, 181, 184–5; encounter with other religion, 52, 181–2, 185; *koan* in, 64–5; love of God basic experience, 183; *mandala* in, 64; and *mantra*, 62–4; and meditation, 17–18, 21–2

Christology, 146, 148

Cicero, 165

Cistercians, 39

click experiment, 41, 155

Cloud of Unknowing, The, 28, 42–3, 65, 97, 102, 104

compassion, Buddhist, 92

concentration, passive, 118, 121

conceptualization, rejection of, 61–3, 140–1

consciousness: adaptive and maladaptive, 108; altered states of, 26, 30, 59, 69, 72, 142; conferences on states, 23–4, 26–7, 49; discriminating and nondiscriminating, 87, 88–90; expanded states of, 59, 69, 100, 142; intuitive, 61–2; limitation of rational, 62–4, mysticism and research in, 49–52; of natural

child, 41, 41n; neurophysiology, 31; new, 142; new science of, 23–33, 34, 48; premature entry into higher states of, 100; undifferentiated, 87, 88, 89, 91; Zen and Christian contemplative, 43; Zen and Yoga, 43–4

contemplation, 59; "acquired", 62; and alpha brainwaves, 38–40; call of God's love in Christian, 126–7; highest form of activity, 97, and passive energy, 120–1; signs for entrance into depths, 102–4; therapeutic consequences of Christian, 126, 128; urge towards, 103–4

convergence, point of, 184, 185, 186. *See* Omega

conversion, 103

Copernicus, Nicholas, 48

Covenant, the, 165–6

creativity, 46–7

cross, glorying in the, 138–9

crucifix, 64

dancing, 69

darshan, 121

David, 80, 165–6

death, 79–80, 141; gateway to the resurrection, 138, 139–40, 141

delta brainwaves, 36, 37n, 116

detachment, 42, 138, 139, 140, 155–6. *See* non-attachment

Devil, 105–6

dialogue: Buddhist-Christian, 28–9, 31, 53, 144, 176, 181, 184; between Christianity and other religions, 185; meditation key factor, 186; mysticism, 54–5

Dionysius the Areopagite, 51

discernment, 108–9

Dogen, 52

drugs, 52, 130, 159; action on restrictive filters, 60–1; addiction, 101, 128; experimentation with, 30, 48; meditation and abandonment of, 117, 123, 125

duality, 88, 89, 92

ecstasy, 49, 72, 131, 168; and death, 79, 84; foreshadowing of resurrection, 84–5; as mystic stage of consciousness, 75–9; Poulain on, 50–2, 75–7; simple, 76

Einstein, Albert, 27

electroencephalograph, 34–5, 40–1, 42, 43, 101, 103, 117, 120; and biofeedback, 36–7, 47

empathy, 156, 162

energy: bioplasmic, 97; passive, 97, 118, 119, 120, 121–2; spiritual, 122

enlightenment, 63–4, 92, 131; Buddhism and, 134; love way to, 70–2; stimuli, 45; through activity, 92–4

evil spirits, 106–7, 127–8

evolution: and cosmic healing process, 148–9; forwarding by mysticism, 97, 186

faith: and Buddhism, 134; in the future, 184; liberation by, 135; therapeutic consequences, 130–1

fall, the, 136

fasting, 69

fathers of the Church, 28, 33, 60, 176

Faustus, Dr, 105–6

filter theory, 60–1

flight of the spirit, 76

flower arrangement, 18, 120

forgiveness, 130

Frankl, Viktor E., 83, 126, 133, 169–70

Friends, Society of, 17

friendship: and absorption, 173–5; cosmic dimension of, 173–5, 176–7; and the Covenant, 165–6; mystical, 167–70, 172; presence of Christ in, 174–5, 177–8; way to Christ, 165

Galileo, 48

Gandhi, Mahatma, 147

Gertrude, St, 51

Gnosticism, 93, 109

God: and detachment, 140; the Father, 97, 131, 144, 160, 166, 176, 177, 178; fidelity to covenant, 183; fixing of mind on, 65; and love, 70, 167; love for man and world, 126–7, 129, 183; self-communication to man, 54

grace, 53, 54, 68, 99, 129

Green, Elmer, 24, 44–5, 46, 50, 66, 106–7, 116, 124

Greene, Graham, 84

Gregorian chant, 64

Gregory of Nazianzen, St, 156

Guibert, J. de, 77–8

gurus, 39

hallucination, 106

Hammarskjöld, Dag, 72, 147

Harris, Thomas, 41n, 124n, 129

healing: and Buddhism, 139–40; in Christianity, 136–40; cosmic, 144–9

Heidegger, Martin, 133

Heraclitus, 88

Hesychasm, 17

Hinduism, 122, 182, 183; and stages of human life, 81

Hirai, Tomio, 34, 40–2, 43, 50, 123, 155

Holy Spirit, *see* Spirit

Huxley, Aldous, 100

hyperphysics, 96

hypnagogic imagery, 44–6, 59, 65, 66, 100

hypnosis, 30, 118, 158, 159

Iago, 103

Ignatius of Loyola, St, 93, 109–10

incarnationalism, 92, 93, 94, 109, 110

indwelling, 156, 157, 159–61, 164

inner space, 23, 48, 72; dangers of journey into, 99–100, 104–11

interior senses, 66–8, 72, 162, 167

intimacy, 153–5, 156–7; "forced", 158–9; necessity for faith and love, 157, 159, 160–1

Isaiah, 80, 129, 145–5, 148, 183

James, William, 23

Jeremiah, 183

Jesus Prayer, 17

jiriki, 53
John, St, 70, 84, 96, 109, 183
John of the Cross, St, 71, 77, 80, 85,
    91–2, 97, 99, 103, 108, 123, 128,
    140, 178; mystical friendship with
    St Teresa, 168–9, 174–5; works,
    102n
John XXIII, Pope, 147
Jonathan, 165–6
Judaism, 32–3, 182
judo, 120
Julian of Norwich, 183
Jung, C. G., 27, 81, 100, 101, 126

Kama Sutra, 32
Kamiya, Joseph, 38–9, 40, 50, 65
Kannon (bodhisattva), 64, 66
Kekulé, August, 46
King, Martin Luther, 72
Kipling, Rudyard, 115
kiss, 163–5, 167
Kitaro, Nishida, 90
koan, 18, 64–5, 72, 102, 156; use by St
    Paul, 91
Koran, 28
kundalini, 115

Lawrence, D. H., 161
levitation, 76n, 79, 168
life-force, 115
ligature, 75, 79
litanies, 63
locution, 66–7, 100
logos, 185. *See* Word
logotherapy, 133
lotus posture, 118, 121
love: and the contemplative, 41–3;
    covenant, 166; ecstatic, 89; evolu-
    tion, 171; and healing and building
    of universe, 146–7; highest form of
    human energy, 146, 171, 178, 186;
    and loss of self, 173; and medita-
    tion, 32–3, 72, 126–8, 129, 170,
    186; and mysticism, 52–3, 97, 147–
    8; and sex, 32; spiritual, 169–70;
    therapeutic consequences, 125–6,
    129–31; way to enlightenment, 69–
    72

LSD, 23

McLuhan, M., 18
Maharishi Mahesh Yogi, 15
man, faith in, 184
mandala, 64, 71, 72, 156
Manichaeanism, 107
mantra, 156; repetition of, 17, 62–4,
    72, 126
marriage: and mysticism, 166–7;
    spiritual, 77, 93, 95; and virginity,
    172
Mary the Virgin, 67
Mary Magdalen, 60
May, Rollo, 135
meditation, 15–18, 23, 33, 49, 116–
    17, 125, 136, 140–1, 183; in activity
    92–4; agnostic, 19–21; and alpha
    producers, 37–8; cosmic implica-
    tions, 142–4; forces unleashed by,
    27–8, 97, 99; fruits of Christian,
    109; healing power, 119–20, 123–
    31, 132, 141; and interior senses,
    66–8, 72, 162; and intimacy, 153–4,
    155–60; as love affair, 32–3, 72,
    126–7, 128–9, 186; "merging" in
    secular, 157–9; and motivation for
    living, 126; physiological benefits,
    116–20; and rational thinking, 61–
    2; and scientific research, 34–5, 36–
    44, 46–7, 50; secular, 19–21, 33;
    and sexuality, 167; and true love,
    170; "vertical", 18, 155
memory, 124–5, 127, 128–9, 130–31,
    154–5
merging, 157–60
Merton, Thomas, 72
mescalin, 23
metaphysics, 26
migraine, 119, 136
mind: -control, 16, 21, 47; dangers of
    descent into deeper realms, 99–
    101, 106–7, 110–11; healing, 123–31
Mohammed, 27, 28
monasticism and mystical friendship,
    167–9; and science, 48–9
monism, 88
Monroe, Marilyn, 42

Moses, 60, 85, 165, 183
Mount Carmel, ascent of, 173, 174
mysticism, 22, 30, 32, 72, 178; and building of the future, 186; and dialogue, 54–5; and discriminating and non-discriminating consciousness, 89–90; and energy of love, 97–8; and healing of the universe, 145–8; Poulain's "descriptive", 49–53; and psychic exploration, 99–100; religious dimension, 52–4; and schizophrenia, 100–1; as science, 31, 48–9; speculative theologians' approach, 53–4; true and false, 72, 107–9

name-calling, 41–2
Neoplatonism, 93
neurophysiology, 29–30, 47, 54
neurosis, 123–4, 132
Nicolas of Cusa, 48
nirvana, 81, 93, 136, 140, 147
Nixon, Richard, 42, 43
non-attachment, 153–7, 159, 161, 167
noosphere, 21
nothingness, 68–9, 86

Oedipus conflict, 136
Omega Point, 26–7, 133, 148–9, 171–2, 177, 184, 186
original sin, 135, 136
Othello, 103
ox symbolism, 86, 126

Parmenides, 88
parousia, 128, 175
Paul, St, 28, 33, 82, 84, 95, 132, 147, 176; and Christ's love, 137, 149; and cosmic Christ, 95–6, 137, 176–7; on cosmic dimensions of body, 143–4; and cosmic suffering, 146; Damascus encounter, 91, 110; on death and resurrection, 137–9; Epistle to the Romans, 135–6; existential struggle, 136–7; on flight of spirit, 76; and interior senses, 66; intimacy and friendship

with Christ, 156, 176–7; on love of God, 128, 129; and theta imagery, 46
Pentecostal groups, 17
physiological changes, 117–20
planetization, 142, 153
Plato, 88
pleroma, 148
posture, body, 143; lotus, 118, 121
Poulain, Auguste, 49–53, 54, 67–8, 72, 100; on mystic states of consciousness, 73, 74–7, 86, 93
prajna, 33, 134
prayer, 18, 53, 93, 94, 97, 109; contemplative, 25; discursive, 62, 95, 103; group, 121, 164; of quiet, 30, 59, 64, 67, 70, 73–4, 75, 131, 164; as relationship of love, 91, 102; of union, 74–5
Prime Mover, 26, 148–9
projections, 124–5, 127–8, 130, 154–5, 156
prophets of Israel, 66
psychic explorer, 99–100
psychic power, misuse of, 105–6
psychoanalysis, 29, 48, 52, 125, 185
psychology, 29–30, 47, 123, 153, 154
psychophysiology, 29, 54, 76n, 101, 123, 125
psychosomatic medicine, 118
psychosomatic sickness, 115
purification, 154–5, 161, 183

Quakers, *see* Friends, Society of

Rama, Swami, 116, 118
Ramakrishna, 28, 52, 72
rapture, 76
reality: flight from, 100; meditation and, 92–3, 94
religions: challenge of meditation movement, 21–2; common elements in great, 182; and evolutionary progress, 185–6; and faith in the future, 184; fidelity to the past, 185; and science, 27–8, 29, 31, 33, 48, 160; shared belief in common destiny, 184

resurrection, 95–6, 137–9, 140, 141, 143, 146
return to the market-place, 77, 87, 90, 92, 94, 97, 98
Rinzai, see Zen
roshi, 39
Ruysbroeck, Jan van, 51
Sales, St Francis de, 156
samadhi, 29, 30, 33, 59, 70, 131, 155; communal, 164; entering into, 62–5, 74; and false mysticism, 108; of pure evil, 103; *See* prayer of quiet
san'mai, 59, 61. *See samadhi*
Sartre, J.-P., 133
Satan, 106
satori, 30, 32, 120
schizophrenia, 30, 100–1, 128
Schultz, Johannes, 118
science: and altered states of consciousness, 23–4, 25–6; attitude to meditation, 25–6, 28–9, 97, 99; and building of cosmos, 147; dialogue with religion, 26–7, 28–9, 31–2, 33, 181; and faith in the future, 184; and passive energy, 122; quest for truth, 182; rift between religion and, 48; and technology, 32
Segal, Julius, 44, 116, 119, 124
self: ecstasy = relinquishing of, 79; great enemy in Buddhism, 136; liberation of true, 131; loss of, 70, 71, 91, 142
sesshin, 17, 83, 117
sex: control by meditation, 167; and spiritual love, 169–70; technique of, 32
Shapely, Harlow, 177
sickness: attitude of science, 141; man's basic, 133–8, 140; of universe, 144–5, 146–7
siddhis, 105
silence, mystical, 59–60, 61, 65, 69; initiation into, 101–2
sleep, "yogic", 116
Socrates, 27, 147
solitude, 103
Song of Solomon, 102, 163
Soto, see Zen

Southwell, Robert, 71
Spirit, the: and awakening of contemplative love, 102, 103, 104; and Christian contemplation, 127–8; discernment of, 108, 109, 163, 164; meditation and action of, 69; passive energy vehicle for, 121–2; uprising of, 81–2; wind of, 143
spiritualization: human, 81, 84; of matter and love, 171, 171n
Stalin, J., 42, 43
suffering: Buddhism and man's existential, 134; and healing of universe, 146–7, 148; morbid doctrine of, 139, science and, 141
sutras, 28, 33, 64
Suzuki, Dr, 78
swami, 39, 45, 116, 118

tao, 20, 165, 182
Tart, Charles, 25, 38, 39, 157–9
tea ceremony, 18, 120
technology, 32
Teilhard de Chardin, P., 24, 62, 68, 88, 153, 173; and cosmic Christ, 95–6, 97; on direction of evolution, 148–9; *Evolution of Chastity*, 172; on love, 71, 89, 160, 170–1. *See* Omega Point, "union differentiates", virginity
Teresa of Avila, St, 28, 50–2, 60, 68, 70, 72, 93–5, 101, 109, 110; comparison with schizophrenic, 100–1; on humanity of Christ, 94–6; *Interior Castle*, 73, 75, 93–4, 95; and interior senses, 66–8, 162; on joy and fear in ecstasy, 79; mystical friendship with St John of the Cross, 168–9, 174; on rapture, 76–7
therapy: and love, 126, 127–31; meditational, 115–20, 123–31
theta brainwaves, 35–7, 45, 116; and visualization, 65. *See*, alpha-theta train
thought: and detachment, 140–1; discursive, 103, 104, 121, 125; part in mystical life, 104
Tillich, Paul, 129

Torah, 33
transactional analysis, 124, 129, 154, 184
Troisfontaines, Roger, 81n

ultimates, 26
union: "differentiates", 71, 89, 160–1; transforming, 77, 89
unity, 88–91, 92
universe: breathing, 91, 92; and cosmic influence, 142–3; sickness, 144–7
Upanishads, 27

Vatican Council II, 30
virginity, superiority of, 171–2
visions, 49, 51
visualization, 16, 65–6
volition, passive, 119–20, 121

Wapnick, Kenneth, 100–1
way: of friendship, 165, 183; man's need for, 20, *See tao*
Whitehead, A. N., 88, 181
wisdom, 32, 33, 182
woman, 170–1, 173
Word, the, 92, 177

Yahweh, 33, 48, 60, 66, 67, 85, 129, 165, 166, 182

Yoga, 15, 116, 118; and alpha consciousness, 38, 39; and body-control, 116–17, 118–19, 121; consciousness, 30, 43–4; and liberation of sexual energy, 167; role of *chakras*, 107
yogis, 44, 61, 115–16

zazen, 41, 123, 135
Zen, 19, 62, 120, 122, 135, 183; and alpha consciousness, 35, 38, 39, 40–2, 117; Christian, 17; consciousness, 30, 43–4; deeply restful state, 117–18; and detachment, 140–1; dialogue with Christianity, 28–9, 31, 176; and ecstasy, 78–9, 83; and final consummation, 84; habitual state of *samadhi*, 74; jettisoning of conceptualization, 61, 62; master "sits" for universe, 97, 142, 145; and non-discriminating consciouness, 87, 89; "prayer of the unconsciousness made conscious", 25; psychophysiology of, 123; and rationality, 90; and "return to the market-place", 77, 87, 89–90, 92–3, 94, 97, 98; *Rinzai*, 30; and sickness, 30, *Soto*, 30, 61; stages in breathing, 91; stimulus technique for enlightenment, 45. *See* Buddhism, *samadhi*

THE WOUNDED STAG

For
Juan Diego
and
The Woman
he loves

CONTENTS

1 The desert   213

2 Christian mysticism   223

3 Moses the mystic   233

4 Presence and absence (1)   243

5 Presence and absence (2)   251

6 Conflict (1)   258

7 Conflict (2)   266

8 Covenant and conversion   274

9 Jesus mysticism   286

10 Eucharistic mysticism (1)   293

11 Eucharistic mysticism (2)   302

12 Mysticism and life   312

13 Mysticism and poverty   321

14 Mysticism and peace   330

15 The woman   344

Epilogue   357

Index   359

"The Wounded Stag
Appears
On the Hill"
St John of the Cross

1

The desert

In the year of Our Lord 1981, when Menachem Begin was Prime Minister in Israel and Anwar Sadat was President of Egypt, I had the privilege of spending six months in Jerusalem. I lived at an institute on the outskirts of the holy city with a motley group of scripture scholars, each of whom pursued his or her biblical project with admirable enthusiasm and devotion. My project (and what a project!) was to study the roots of Christian mysticism. Having spent many years comparing Christian mysticism with its Buddhist counterpart, having searched for similarities and explored common ground, I felt that the time had come to investigate the unique dimension of the Christian experience and to look for its distinctive features. In doing this I wanted to go beyond St John of the Cross and St Teresa of Avila, beyond Meister Eckhart and *The Cloud of Unknowing*, beyond Augustine and Gregory, to the very origins of that mystical prayer which assumes increasing significance in the lives of contemporary men and women.

I suspected that I would find what I wanted in the desert. After all, was it not in the desert that the people of Israel experienced the steadfast love of Yahweh and entered into covenant with Him? Was it not in the desert that the word came to John the Baptist? Was it not in the wilderness that Jesus prayed and fasted before meeting the devil? And the early Christian monks fled from pagan Rome into the rich silence of the desert where they prayed and fasted and bequeathed to us an invaluable treasury of spiritual maxims and mystical counsel.

So I spent considerable time in the desert – in the Judean desert, in the Negev, in Sinai, and finally in the Egyptian desert south of Alexandria. I came to love the Dead Sea. I was fascinated by Jericho and by that monastery perched high on the cliff called "the

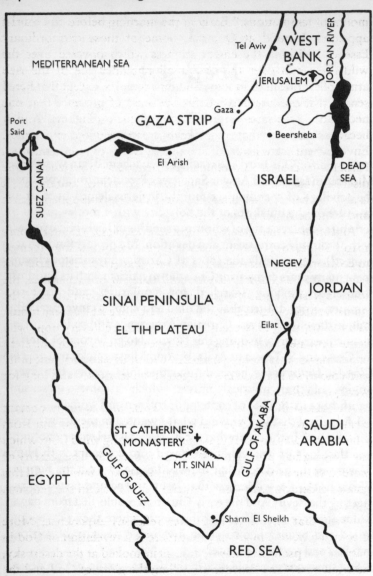

MEDITERRANEAN SEA

WEST BANK

JORDAN RIVER

Tel Aviv

JERUSALEM

Gaza

GAZA STRIP

Port Said

El Arish

Beersheba

ISRAEL

DEAD SEA

SUEZ CANAL

NEGEV

JORDAN

SINAI PENINSULA

EL TIH PLATEAU

Eilat

ST. CATHERINE'S MONASTERY

MT. SINAI

GULF OF AKABA

SAUDI ARABIA

EGYPT

GULF OF SUEZ

Sharm El Sheikh

RED SEA

SINAI: The Great and Terrible Wilderness

mount of temptations." Early in the morning before any tourist appeared, I stood at Qumran, home of those extraordinary Essenes, relishing the empty stillness which hovered over the wilderness and over the sea. It all reminded me of the rich atmosphere one finds in some Buddhist temples, except that here I sensed that obscure and indefinable sense of presence that one necessarily associates with the monotheistic religions. And it became clear to me that environment creates religious experience. Environment can lead to an altered state of consciousness. Perhaps it creates something like mystical experience. One discovers that the vast and empty desert is not only "out there"; it is also "in here." One enters the inner desert. And perhaps Jesus and John the Baptist did just that.

And Sinai – "that great and terrible wilderness" (Deuteronomy 1:19)! There, too, the immensity and the awesome beauty seemed to create religious experience. I had not expected such variety of scenery; and as I saw the miles and miles of brown stones, the towering, shapeless, twisted rocks, and sparkling sand, the nomadic bedouins, I resonated with that fifteenth-century monk, Felix Fabri, who wrote that "every day, indeed every hour, you come into new country, of a different nature, with different conditions of atmosphere and soil, with hills of a different build and colour, so that you are amazed at what you see and long for what you will see next."

And the suffering of the desert. This, too, is an important element in religious experience. By day the merciless sun from which there was no escape; by night the cutting wind from which my sleeping bag provided inadequate protection. The scarcity of water and the separation from everything that is familiar. All this creates a detachment – and detachment is basic in the religious path.

I said that environment creates religious experience. More theologically, one might say that there is a revelation of God in nature. The psalmist knew it; and, as he looked at the desert sky, he cried out: "The heavens are telling the glory of God and the firmament proclaims his handiwork" (Psalms 19:1). Paul knew it and he said that "ever since the creation of the world His invisible nature, namely, his eternal power and deity, has been clearly perceived in the things that have been made" (Romans 1:20). Yes, the vast desert reveals something of God: and it draws us into His all-pervading presence.

II

And yet, when all is said and done, the revelation of God through the great and terrible wilderness is of secondary importance. Something more earth-shaking happened in Sinai. *God spoke*. He spoke to Moses face to face as a man might speak with his friend; and from that moment a remarkable friendship was initiated between Yahweh and the human family. From then until now "the invisible God out of the abundance of His love speaks to men as friends and lives among them,"[1]

But God could have spoken elsewhere. He could have spoken in Belfast or Nagasaki. He could have spoken in Zamboanga or Kalamazoo. He chose the desert. And in subsequent Judeo-Christian tradition the place where God spoke was called the desert. That is why the New Testament sees Jesus in the desert when he goes to a lonely place to pray, or when he climbs the mountain in Galilee, or when he walks by the sea. The Christian writers are not speaking about the physical desert with its sand and rock. For them the desert exists wherever one prays and listens to the word of God. And in our day many people find their desert in the inner city or prison or in hospital or in the plain sufferings of an ordinary life.

III

Together with an Anglican priest friend I visited a Coptic monastery in the desert south of Alexandria. This was a new experience. For whereas Sinai and the wilderness around Jerusalem have a variety of scenery and sometimes a covering of grass which permits the pasture of flocks, this Egyptian desert consisted of sand and sand and more sand. After leaving Cairo we had gone astray, when a group of jovial monks took us into their big safari, drove us through the desert to their monastery, and treated us with royal hospitality. The monastery was like a great ship in the sea of desert, and from the roof I watched the monks like tiny ants walking out into the sand under the blazing sun. "It is our life," one monk said to me; and he explained that their life is one of presence to the desert, presence to God. For the desert is an empty and vast symbol of the unknowable God.

Again, it was an ideal setting for mysticism. The desert leads to a cosmic experience, a kenotic or emptying experience; it leads to the *nada, nada, nada* of those apophatic mystics who emphasize that we know more about what God is *not* than about what He *is*.

Yet the same question haunted me: How does this differ from the mystical experience of the Buddhist or the Hindu? How does it differ from the experience of anyone who enters the vast and lonely desert to relish the emptiness or to enter the fascinating world of supraconceptual silence? What is distinctively Christian about the prayer of these monks?

And then the answer became clear, ridiculously clear. Of course. The monks were constantly reading the Scriptures. They were attentive to the word of God. They sang His praises in liturgy. They gathered to break bread and to celebrate the new covenant in his blood. They prayed to the Virgin Mary to whom their monastery was dedicated. And then they went alone into the desert, the word was ringing in their ears and singing in their hearts. Word and sacrament carried them into the vast and empty inner desert of which the outer desert is but a symbol. Word and sacrament filled the deep, deep caverns of their unconscious minds as they walked or sat silently in those wastes of sand.

IV

Yes, God spoke in the desert. Of course He had appeared to Abraham and revealed His name. "I appeared to Abraham, to Isaac and to Jacob, as God almighty, but by my name the Lord I did not make myself known to them" (Exodus 6:3). After revealing His name to Moses, God spoke through the prophets; and finally He spoke through His only Son. He spoke not only with words but also through mighty deeds. He spoke especially through the life, death, and resurrection of Jesus who is His only-begotten Son.

And God continues to speak. For "God who spoke of old uninterruptedly converses with the Bride of His beloved Son; and the Holy Spirit . . . leads unto all truth those who believe and makes the word of God dwell abundantly in them"[2] God continues to speak powerfully and eloquently. He carries on a conversation with the human family as He carried on a conversation with Moses. *And we hear His voice when we read the Scriptures or hear them read in community.* Listen to the Council:*

> For in the sacred books, the Father who is in heaven meets His children with great love and speaks with them; and the force and power in the word of God is so great that it remains the support and energy of the Church, the strength of faith for her children, the food of the soul, the pure and perennial source of spiritual life.[3]

And elsewhere the same Council quotes St Ambrose: "We speak to Him when we pray; we hear Him when we read the divine sayings."[4]

God not only spoke. He entered into covenant with His people. He called His chosen Moses to the top of the mountain and through him told the people how much He loved them, how He protected them, and He asked for their unconditional love in return. This mutual love of God and people was solemnly sealed in the blood of animals. "And Moses took the blood and threw it upon the people, and said, 'Behold the blood of the covenant which the Lord has made with you in accordance with all these words' " (Exodus 24:8). Christians believe that this covenant was renewed in the blood of Jesus who died and rose for our salvation – "he entered once and for all into the Holy Places, taking not the blood of goats and calves but his own blood, thus securing an eternal redemption" (Hebrews 9:12).

---

*Throughout this book when I speak of "the Council" I mean the Second Vatican Council, 1963–65.

As God continues to speak, so He continues to reenact the covenant. He does so through the Eucharist wherein Christians find nourishment, receive God's love, and love God in return. Listen to the Council speaking of the two tables of word and sacrament:

> The Church has always venerated the divine Scripture just as she venerates the body of the Lord, since from the table of both the word of God and the body of Christ she unceasingly receives and offers to the faithful the bread of life, especially in the sacred liturgy.[5]

In short, Scripture and sacrament nourish the spiritual life of all Christians and of all Christian mystics.

Concretely, the Christian mystics have constantly read the Scriptures and have lived the Scriptures. They quote the word of God on every page they write. This word of Scripture has been their nourishment and their joy. It has carried them into the cloud of unknowing, into the silent darkness where God dwells in inaccessible light. It has pointed the way to the deepest realm of the interior castle. "For the word of God is living and active, sharper than any two-edged sword" (Hebrews 4:12).

Again, the Christian mystics have celebrated the Eucharist. Those who were Catholic have believed in the real presence of Jesus, who is the bread of life. Their interior senses have tasted and relished this bread which, like the manna in the desert, is sweeter than honey. They have felt the indwelling presence of the Lord himself. And the Eucharist has united them with Christians throughout the world.

V

I have spoken of word and sacrament as chief nourishers of the mystical life. Let me now mention one more source of nourishment, namely, the word of God as it lives in the community, particularly as it lives in the masses of the people united with their shepherds. Let me explain.

The living word of Jesus was transmitted to those disciples who lived with him and loved him. They, in turn, passed it on to others, and others to others, and so on. They wrote it down (and this is Scripture) but it also passed on orally. And so it continues to live in the people. It lives actively not only in the hearts of bishops and theologians but also in the masses – in the hearts of the butcher, the baker, and the candlestick-maker. The old theologians expressed this in a number of Latin tags which are profoundly meaningful. *Vox populi: vox Dei*, they said, indicating that the voice of the people is the voice of God. Again, they set great store by the praying church (*ecclesia orans*) claiming that the prayer of the people is a norm of belief; *lex orandi: lex credendi*. Again, they spoke of the *sensus fidelium* (the sense of the faithful) reminding us that the faithful everywhere have a sensitivity to the word and are guided by the Spirit.

And so the mystics remain in touch with this living community and vivify it. They are never isolated – out on a limb – but part of a vibrant tradition from which they get help and guidance and to which they give support. They read the books that this tradition has produced or (for some mystics are illiterate) they receive guidance from representatives of this tradition. However deeply they penetrate into the desert, they are never alone. The support of the Christian community is always with them.

VI

I said I was searching for the roots of Christian mysticism. Now I say unhesitatingly that there are three sources of Christian mystical experience: (1) the Word of God in sacred scripture, (2) the sacraments, particularly the Eucharist, and (3) the Word of God in the community called church.

If, then, you ask for practical advice on how to enter the Christian mystical life, I do not advise you to take the plane to Tel Aviv and the bus to the Judean desert. I do not tell you to travel to Cairo and then to Sinai or to the desert south of Alexandria. I do not tell you to sit in the lotus and breathe from your abdomen. All this is good, very good, but in the end peripheral. Instead I say:

Listen to the word! Read the Scriptures! Read them again and again with faith and love until the word comes to life within you, penetrating the deepest layers of your unconscious.

Again, celebrate the Eucharist! Break bread with the community! Be present to the mystery of faith and partake of the bread of life. This will lead you into that rich inner desert of silence and joy where your life lies hidden with Christ in God. This will lead you to say with Paul: "It is no longer I who live, but Christ lives in me" (Galatians 2:20). This will lead you to cry out with Jesus: "Abba, Father!"

Again, listen to the community. Be part of the community. Get guidance from some representative of the community; read the mystical literature the community has produced. Never get isolated. Never go out on a limb. Community!

VII

I hear you say: "Yes, you are talking about Christian revelation. You are simply saying that Christian mysticism is rooted in the Christian revelation and that this is its unique and special dimension. Fine! Wonderful! I buy all this. But I have a difficulty: If my prayer is filled with Scripture and sacrament will it not be worthy, conceptual, discursive? Where will be the cloud of unknowing, the emptiness, the void, the silence, the altered state of consciousness? Where will be those levels of awareness which I associate with mysticism?"

I hear you. But listen to me. If you constantly receive the Eucharist and if you constantly read the Scriptures with faith, you will find that you are carried into the cloud of unknowing and the silence and the void. You will find that you are carried beyond the words to the Reality, the mysterious Reality, to which the words point. You will find that you are not just understanding the Scriptures, you are also loving them, and understanding them through love. Then the word of God will come to life in you. And this is Christian mysticism. *The Christian mystic is one who lives the Christ-mystery and is transformed by it.* He or she is one who not only knows Jesus but loves Jesus, identifies with Jesus, lives the very life of Jesus, and cries out: "Abba, Father!"

NOTES

1. *Dei Verbum* C.I; *The Documents of Vatican II,* ed. Walter M. Abbott (New York: America Press, 1966), p. 112.
2. ibid, C.2; ibid., p. 116.
3. ibid., C.6; ibid., p. 125.
4. ibid., ibid., p. 127.
5. ibid,; ibid., p. 125.

2

Christian mysticism

I

I have said that I was searching for the roots of Christiam mysticism. And, of course, this brings me up against the awful problem of saying what I mean by the word *mysticism*. In a former book entitled *The Inner Eye of Love*, I tried to say that mysticism is a profoundly human phenomenon appearing in more or less similar form in all the great religions. For every religion has its mystics. Let me briefly summarize what I said there.

There exists in this poor world of ours an unconditional, unrestricted love: a love that goes on and on and on, a love to which there are no limits. Just as the human mind asks questions, questions, questions, so the human heart longs to love and to love and to love. In the Christian view, however, this love is not something one drums up by personal effort. It is called forth by God Who takes the initiative. "We love because He first loved us" (1 John 4:19).

Now love is a powerful lamp, a burning candle. It throws light on its environs and leads to knowledge. This knowledge I call faith: it is the richest wisdom. And as faith penetrates deeper and deeper into the human psyche, it leads to altered states of consciousness and greatly enhanced awareness. It holds sway at the depths of one's being. And now I call it mysticism. I believe that this mysticism is found everywhere and that it exists even in those religions which do not speak of love but which demand a total commitment.

I still hold the view expressed in my former book. However, as my reader will observe, in an effort to find common ground with other religions, I approached the problem from a subjective standpoint. And since the human psyche is everywhere the same, I had no difficulty in finding a common pattern of religious experience. But in this book, which aims at highlighting what is unique and distinctive in Christian mysticism, I want to look also at the objective dimension.

"Objective dimension!" you say. "How can mystical experience have an objective dimension? Surely we call mysticism non-objective prayer precisely because we are so united with God that subject-object distinctions disappear. The mystics say they are immersed in God like a drop of water in the ocean or like the light shining through a pane of glass. And quite apart from the mystics, some philosophers maintain that God is not an object."

I hear you. And first let me concede that much depends on what we mean by the word *object*. If by *object* we mean something "out there," something opposite to me in a dualistic sense, then God is not an object. I can never say, "God is there and I am here," as if I were separated from my Source. For God is the core of my being and the core of all beings. He is closer to me than I am to myself.

But the word *object* can be understood in another way. If I ask questions, I intend something. If I am committed, I am committed to some ideal. If I love, I love some reality. In all these cases I transcend myself, reaching out towards a reality beyond my consciousness. Or again, when I cry out: "Abba, Father!" am I not calling on a Being beyond myself, a Being who can be called *object*?"

As for the mystics, their language is full of paradox. It is true that they talk of an extraordinarily close union. The author of *The Cloud* says that *God is my being* – and that is good theology. But he never says, *I am God*. Other mystics speak constantly of a sense of presence, a sense of absence, a sense of otherness. They call on a God Who is beyond them. Those who were theologians spoke of a substantial union which never happens – because this would mean that we become the substance of God – and of a transforming union which happens in mystical experience and is union through love. All in all, if we are to avoid pantheism, we have to recognize a certain objectivity in mystical experience.

II

Excellent studies have now been done on the origins of the word *mysticism*. The distinguished French scholars, Louis Bouyer, points out that while the words *mystery* and *mystical* were used by the Greeks to describe the rites of their mystery religions, early Christian writers used these words in their own distinct and unique way.[1] Just as the Greek *theos* and the Latin *deus*, which the Greeks and Romans used for their gods and goddesses, were applied by Christians to the God of Abraham and Isaac and Jacob and, in consequence, were totally transformed, so *the church fathers took the noun* mystery *and the adjective* mystical *and applied them to the mystery of Christ, particularly as it appears in St Paul.* Indeed, for the fathers, this Pauline mystery was a key to the understanding of the whole New Testament. It is also the key to the understanding of Christian mysticism. For the object of Christian mysticism is precisely this mystery.

Recall those powerful passages where Paul speaks to the Corinthians about the mystery of Christ, the mystery of the cross – "a stumbling block to Jews and folly to gentiles, but to those who are called, both Jews and Greeks, Christ the power of God and the wisdom of God" (1 Corinthians 1:24). Paul imparts "a secret and hidden wisdom of God, which God desired before the ages for our glorification" (1 Corinthians 2:27). It is a knowledge taught by the Spirit and it is primarily a paradoxical understanding of the death and resurrection of Jesus.

And Colossians and Ephesians speak of the same mystery – "the mystery hidden for ages and generations and now made manifest to his saints" (Colossians 1:26). And this mystery is "Christ in you, the hope of glory" (Colossians 1:27). This is Jesus Christ in whom "the whole fullness of deity dwells bodily" (Colossians 2:9). This is the Jesus Christ whose love is unfathomable, so that Paul prays "that you, being rooted and grounded in love, may have power to comprehend with all the saints what is the breadth and length and height and depth and to know the love of Christ which surpasses knowledge, that you may be filled with all the fullness of God" (Ephesians 3:17–18). Such is the incomprehensible mystery of Christ through whom the Father wishes "to reconcile to himself all things, whether on earth or in heaven, making peace by the blood of his cross" (Colossians 1:20).

And to enter into the mystery of Christ is to approach the Father towards whom Jesus always points, and to cry out: "Abba, Father!" To enter into the mystery of Christ is to enter into the cloud of unknowing where one meets the Father in darkness and speaks to Him as one might speak with a friend. To enter into the mystery of Christ is to enter into the Trinity where, identified with Jesus and filled with the Spirit, I am one with the Father. But why say more? The whole New Testament is a record of mystery: the mystery of Jesus – "But who do you say that I am?" (Mark 16:15). The mystery of the kingdom hidden in parables. The mystery of the Father hidden in Jesus – "He who has seen me has seen the Father" (John 14:9). The mystery of the sending of the Spirit. And the eschatological mystery of the end of time – "In that day you will know that I am in my father and you in me and I in you" (John 14:20). What a series of mysteries! Christianity is basically mystery. And all is contained in the mystery of Christ. One who enters deeply into this mystery enters into mystical experience.

And do not think that to enter the mystery of Christ is to escape from the world. Again I say that the mystery of Christ is centred on his cross. This means that it is the mystery of the poor, the sick, the afflicted, the deranged, the imprisoned, the dying, and all those suffering people with whom Jesus identifies. It is the mystery of the exploited, the manipulated, the terrorized, the oppressed. It is the mystery of nuclear war, of hunger, of injustice, of human anguish. It is the mystery of you and me when we suffer and when we sin. Christian mystical experience, far from flying from the suffering and sinful world, is an entrance into its very heart.

III

And throughout the centuries the mystery of Christ has always been the object of Christian prayer and worship, finding expression in rich and varied symbols. One such symbol is the Sacred Heart of Jesus. Pierced with a lance and pouring blood and water, the heart of Jesus has been a powerful symbol of the interior life of Jesus and of his immense love for the Father and for the human family. Entrance into the heart of Jesus means entrance not only into the mystery of Jesus himself but into the mystery of the Father whom he reveals. It means entrance not only into the suffering of Jesus himself but into the suffering of the whole land which he loves.

As the epigraph of this book I have chosen yet another symbol from St John of the Cross: the wounded stag. In his great poem "The Spiritual Canticle" the saint writes:

> The wounded stag appears on the hill.[2]

And in his commentary the poet tells us that the wounded stag is Jesus himself. He is wounded because we are wounded. He is wounded with love. The Spanish mystic goes on to tell us that it is characteristic of the stag to climb to high places and, when wounded, to race in search of refreshment and cool water. If he hears the cry of his mate and senses that she is wounded, he immediately runs to her to embrace and comfort her. Of Jesus, the wounded stag, St John of the Cross writes:

> Beholding that the bride is wounded with love for Him, He also, because of her moan, is wounded with love for her. Among lovers, the wound of one is a wound for both, and the two have one feeling.[3]

I have chosen this symbol for my epigraph because it shows that all Christian mysticism has its origin not in our love for Jesus but in the mystery of his great love for us. "Greater love has no man than this" (John 15:13).

Put in a nutshell, the mystery of Christ is the mystery of love. It finds powerful expression in the Johannine sentence that "God is love" (1 John 4:16). Or again it finds moving expression in the Johannine statement that "God so loved the world that He gave His only Son . . ." (John 3:16). Christian mysticism is nothing other than an entrance into the baffling mystery of love and the experience of its transforming power.

But where is this mystery of love? What signposts point to it? Where is the path?

IV

With an impressive array of quotations from the church fathers, Bouyer claims that the word *mystical* was used principally in a scriptural and sacramental context. Origen (*c.* 184–253), for example, looks at biblical interpretation as a religious experience and a mystical experience. A fifth-century epistle of St Nilus (died *c.* 430) says that the Eucharist must be approached "not as simple bread but as mystical bread." And Theodoret (*c.* 393–466) calls the moment of communion "the mystical moment in which we receive the body of the Bridegroom."

My reader will observe that Bouyer's studies lead to the very conclusion I reached in the last chapter: *the pillars of Christian mysticism are word and sacrament.* It is precisely by hearing the word and participating in the sacraments, particularly the Eucharist, that I am drawn into the mystery of Christ and into the mystical life. Moreover, word and sacrament form liturgy and community. Mysticism has a strong communal dimension.

V

With Dionysius in the sixth century we find the word *mystical* applied to a very clear-cut phenomenon. In his *Theologia Mystica* Dionysius describes Moses climbing the mountain and entering into the darkness. This Dionysian darkness is what we would now call an altered state of consciousness. It is the state of a mind emptied of discursive and conceptual thinking and remaining silent and empty.

In clearly emphasizing the subjective and psychological dimension of mystical experience, Dionysius was something of an innovator. But he never rejected tradition. His *Theologia Mystica* is profoundly influenced by Gregory of Nyssa's *Life of Moses* and by Origen's *Homilies on the Exodus.* For him the darkness of the cloud of unknowing is nothing other than the mystery of Christ, for "he transposes into the language of his own era the universal reconciliation and restoration in Christ which St Paul preached as 'the mystery.'"[4] Dionysius stands in the full stream of biblical and eucharistic mysticism.

And succeeding ages, while retaining the scriptural and eucharistic dimensions, continued to map out the mystical states of consciousness. This was completely necessary for the spiritual guidance of timid (and less timid) mystics who walked this perilous path. One map describes the journey in terms of the purgative, illuminative, and unitive ways. Yet another, the map of the great Teresa, depicts the interior castle with seven mansions representing seven states of consciousness. A scholastic model speaks of acquired and infused contemplation. Others speak of the way of beginners, proficients, and perfect. The various states of consciousness, however, are not clear-cut. Teresa says that one may roam from mansion to mansion with great freedom.

I have said that these maps were necessary for the guidance of mystics. All the more so since not all mystical states are delectable. Some are filled with anguish and pain; some are turbulent and stormy; some are described in terms of dereliction and abandonment. Some are even dangerous and treacherous and are called "false mysticism" – not because the state itself is false but because it leads in the wrong direction and may bring the hapless mystic to destruction.

Then there was mystical theology. This was supraconceptual knowledge of the mystery. Today we think of theology in rational and scientific terms. But for Dionysius mystical theology is the hidden or secret wisdom found in deep prayer. Indeed, his mystical theology corresponds to what today we call mysticism or mystical experience. And this understanding of mystical theology is found in St John of the Cross. About an updated mystical theology I have spoken elsewhere, maintaining that today we must elaborate a mystical theology which is nothing other than *reflection on mystical experience.*[5]

VI

From what I have said it will be clear that *mysticism* is an orthodox Christian word, traditional, meaningful, and valuable. It will also be clear that mystical experience in its origins is thoroughly

Christian, biblical, sacramental, and communitarian. Some nineteenth-century scholars, however, tried to debunk both the word and the phenomenon. Some Christian scholars saw mysticism as a pagan leprosy, a neoplatonic contamination poisoning the pure and limpid waters of biblical spirituality. Bouyer claims that much of this comes from bad scholarship. "Much verbiage would have been avoided, in this field as in many others, if students had begun by examining the texts, all the texts, in which the word occurs in ancient times, and by seeking, according to the context and not in accordance with *a priori* theories, the meaning of the word."[6]

Contemporary thought is in danger of misunderstanding mysticism in another way. Fascinated by psychology, many people identify mystical experience with the altered state of consciousness, be it ecstasy or trance or some lesser form of inner union. This is a snare. For the fact is that most of these altered states can be reproduced in the laboratory through hypnosis or biofeedback or the use of drugs or psychological techniques. What makes mysticism to be mysticism is not the altered state of consciousness but the unrestricted love, the total commitment, the enlightened faith. *What makes Christian mysticism to be Christian mysticism is the orientation to the mystery of Christ in a scriptural and sacramental context.* Assuredly the radical and loving commitment to Christ in his mysteries ordinarily leads to altered states of consciousness. But these are of secondary importance. Besides, the act of love by which one cries out, "Abba, Father!" can arise at any level of consciousness.

Yet it is good that the study of mystical states of consciousness goes on. Great progress has been made in our day, thanks to modern psychology and to Asian religious experience. I write these lines in the Philippines where I have come in contact with many forms of trance, shamanistic in origin but now thoroughly Christianized. I believe that the ongoing study of such phenomena will help us purify our mystical theology and our understanding of the ways of God.

VII

And so the task confronting Christianity today is to renew its mystical life. Anyone aware of the signs of the times must see a longing for deep prayer, for mystical prayer, throughout the Christian world. If we can see mysticism as a total commitment to the first precept of the Decalogue to love God with one's whole heart and soul and mind and strength; if we can see it as a commitment to the mystery of Christ; if we can see it as a transforming experience whereby one comes to love Christ in the poor and the oppressed and the despised; if we see mysticism as a road, perhaps the only road, to a total and suprarational commitment to peace; then we will realize that mystical experience is at the very core of our Christian life, the path to which all Christians are called.

Let us carry out this mystical renewal in an ecumenical context. This is a field wherein we need collaboration from Christians of all denominations. While it is true that Protestant scholars led the antimystical crusade within Christianity, it is also true that there is profound biblical mysticism within Protestantism. Indeed the lives and writings of some of the reformers are full of mysticism.

Together we can answer the longings of the people for mystical prayer. Together we can dialogue with the great mystics of Asia. This is the way of the future.

I hear you say: "I like what you say about the mystery of Christ as the unique and special dimension of Christian mysticism. This surely rings true. But I still have a question. You have spoken eloquently and written beautifully about dialogue with Buddhism. You have said that we must join with men and women of other faiths in a common search for truth. And now, by stressing the mystery of Christ, you are widening the gap that separates us from these people. How come?"

Far be it from me to do such a thing. I cannot believe that entrance into the mystery of Christ separates me from any human person in the whole wide world. Let me again quote the Council. It is saying that God's grace is at work in all human hearts and that by his Incarnation the Son of God has united himself in some fashion with every man and woman; and then with delicacy and grace it continues:

> For since Christ died for all, and since our ultimate vocation is in fact one, and divine, we ought to believe that the Holy Spirit in a manner known only to God offers to every man and woman the possibility of being associated with this paschal mystery.[7]

Everyone has the possibility of entering into the mystery of Christ. Everyone is loved by the wounded stag. Are we not all – Buddhists, Christians and everyone else – faced with the same mystery hidden from all ages and now revealed through Jesus Christ in the fullness of time?

NOTES

1. See Louis Bouyer, "Myticism: An Essay on the History of the World", in *Understanding Mysticism,* ed. Richard Woods (New York: Doubleday, 1980), pp. 42–55. See also Louis Bouyer, *The Spirituality of the New Testament and the Fathers* (London: Burns and Oates, 1963).
2. "The Spiritual Canticle", Stanza 13, n.9, in *The Collected Works of St John of the Cross,* trans. Kieran Kavanaugh and Otilio Rodriguez (Washington, D.C.: ICS Publications, 1979), p. 411.
3. ibid., 460.
4. Bouyer, "Mysticism: An Essay on the History of the Word".
5. See in my book, *The Inner Eye of Love* (San Francisco: Harper & Row; London: Collins, 1978), ch. 4, "Mystical Theology".
6. Bouyer, "Mysticism: An Essay on the History of the Word".
7. *Gaudium et Spes* C.1, 122: *The Documents of Vatican II,* ed. Walter M. Abbot (New York: American Press, 1966), pp. 221–22.

3

Moses the mystic

I

At 4.30 a.m. on a bitterly cold April morning, we climbed into a big, open safari and headed for Sinai. Sleepy, silent, wrapped in overcoats, balaclava helmets, and a variety of contraptions, we huddled together for protection against the piercing, desert wind. Skirting Jerusalem, our safari went down, down, down that winding road past the inn of the Good Samaritan – down to sea level, below sea level, down to the Dead Sea. And now we began to thaw out, to get rid of those overcoats, and to relish the warm air. Finally, at 'En Gedi we uncorked our flasks and indulged in hot coffee. We were close to the lovers' cave.: "Return, return, O Shulammite, return, return, that we may look upon you" (Song of Songs 6:13).

Beside me sat a young scholar who was writing a commentary on Exodus. I asked him what he thought of Moses the mystic "Moses the mystic!" he gasped. "We've just about reached belief in the historical existence of Moses. Whether he was a Jew or an Egyptian we do not know. Whether there was one exodus or a series of migrations we do not know. What route the Israelites took we do not know. Whether Moses met the real Pharaoh, or some lesser light we do not know. We know so little! How can you talk about Moses the mystic?"

I explained my point: "The church fathers and the desert fathers read Exodus as a story. They read and reread. They heard it proclaimed at liturgy. They relished its words and phrases in their *lectio divina*. And they identified with Moses. With him they climbed the mountain and entered the cloud. With him they spoke to God face to face as one might speak with a friend. And *they found that they were drawn into the mystical life*. In this sense Moses was a mystic."

"I could not quarrel with that," he answered. And we remained friends.

In fact we had touched upon one of the most thorny theological problems of our day, or of any day: How to interpret the Scriptures?

It is now clear to everybody that the historical-critical approach, however valuable, is woefully insufficient. It alone will not put us in touch with the underlying mystery; it alone will not bring us to those eternal realities towards which the Scriptures point; it alone will not enrich our lives with mysticism. How, then, are we to approach and interpret the Scriptures?

About this I have written at length elsewhere and need not repeat myself here.[1] Only let me make two points.

The first is that in addition to the knowledge which comes from science there is a knowledge which comes from love – love for the sacred text, love for the human authors, unrestricted love for the Divine Author. This love leads to involvement, to union, to enlightenment, to conversion of heart. United with the text, I come to live it and to understand it *through life*. This is the knowledge that Aquinas calls *knowledge of connaturality*. It is wonderfully high wisdom. It is mystical wisdom. To compare the knowledge coming from science with the knowledge coming from love is like comparing the light of a candle with the light of the sun. Yet both forms of knowledge are necessary.

My second point is that the Council, calling on an ancient Christian tradition, claims that the new Testament is hidden in the Old and the Old is made manifest in the New. Here are the Council's words:

> God, the inspirer and author of both testaments, wisely arranged that the New Testament be hidden in the Old and the Old be made manifest in the New ... the books of the Old Testament with all their parts, caught up into the proclamation of the gospel, acquire and show forth their full meaning in the New Testament and in turn shed light on it and explain it.[2]

With this in mind we can see how Gregory of Nyssa, Dionysius, and the rest see Moses climbing the mountain as *entering into the* mystery of Christ. We can also see how Christian mystical writers from Augustine to the authors of *The Cloud* and from Origen to Thomas Aquinas have seen Moses as the model of mystical prayer. These authors have seen the cloud of Exodus as a symbol of that supraconceptual obscurity into which the mystic necessarily enters. They have seen all those symbols – the wilderness, the burning bush, the cloud, the pillar of fire, the paschal lamb, the water from the rock, the manna, the golden calf, the tabernacle, the ark of the covenant – as expressing different aspects of the Christ-mystery.

Let me, then, following in the footsteps of those mystical giants, humbly pay tribute to Moses the mystic.

II

The mystical life sometimes begins with an overpowering and unforgettable experience of God's loving presence. Such was the case with the prophets who saw God in an inaugural vision. Such was the case with Paul who met Jesus on the road to Damascus. Such was the case with Moses to whom the angel of the Lord appeared in a flame of fire out of the midst of a bush. God is present, tangibly present. This is the God of Abraham, the God of Isaac, the God of Jacob. This is the transcendent God. But now He is very, very close. Moses takes off his shoes because the ground is holy. "And Moses hid his face, for he was afraid to look at God" (Exodus 3:6).

Ordinary fire consumes and reduces to ashes. But this fire of God's presence destroys nothing. It gives life; and out of the bush Moses hears himself called by name: "Moses, Moses!" He is uniquely loved and specially chosen.

And as Moses has a name, so also has God. "I am who I am"; or "I am" or "I will be what I will be" or "I will cause to be what I will cause to be." Whatever our interpretation, we cannot avoid the note of *presence, loving presence.* "I am presence," says God.

Nor is this presence static. It is a dynamic presence, a guiding presence; and Yahweh subsequently assures Moses: "My presence will go with you and I will give you rest" (Exodus 33:14). This presence guides Moses and the people through the wilderness as a cloud by day and a pillar of fire by night. "And the Lord went before them by day in a pillar of cloud to lead them along the way, and by night in a pillar of fire to give them light, that they might travel by day and by night" (Exodus 13:21). This presence gives courage, joy, self-confidence, energy, power. When Moses stammers and stumbles and balks at the magnitude of the mission, the voice assures him: "But I will be with you . . . " (Exodus 3:12).

Now all this symbolism accurately describes the mystical life of thousands of Christians. Their mystical journey has begun with an obscure sense of presence, a conviction that God is close. He is around me and within me, without being identical with me. And as time goes on, I may reach the conviction (either gradually or in a flash) that I am loved and chosen – that I am called by name as was Moses. Not that my name is audibly called. More often an inner *silent voice* assures me of a deeply personal, loving call. This is a source of great joy and unshakable confidence: it carries an inner authority and I cannot disobey.

Again, this presence of God is dynamic, leading me like the cloud by day and the pillar of fire by night. With this as my guide I no longer reason or think or calculate. Such thinking and calculation would be a subtle snare distracting me from the deeper promptings of the Spirit.

St John of the Cross, writing about the obscure night (which is his cloud), sings out:

> O guiding light!
> O night more lovely than the dawn![3]

And, wonder of wonders, the night guides, with more certainty than the noonday sun, to the union of lover and beloved:

> O night that has united
> The Lover with His beloved,
> Transforming the beloved in her Lover.[4]

How wonderfully the presence of the Lord guides us through the desert of life to the promised land, which is loving union with Him!

Admittedly, the notion of a guiding night is paradoxical. How can the darkness guide? The other symbol, the pillar of fire, is easier to grasp. Interiorized, this pillar of fire becomes *the living flame of love* burning brightly within the breast of the mystic. The mystical life finally consists in fidelity in this inner fire glowing gently in my heart. It tells me what to do and where to go. It guides me unerringly through the desert of life to the promised land where dwells the One I love.

And in all this, the unique dimension of the Judeo-Christian tradition shines forth. Moses himself claims that he and his people are unique precisely because the presence of God goes with them always:

> For how shall it be known that I have found favour in thy sight, I and thy people? Is it not in thy going with us, so that we are distinct, I and thy people, from all other people, that are upon the face of the earth? (Exodus 33:16)

This guiding presence is indeed a distinct characteristic of the Judeo-Christian mystical journey.

III

Central to the mystical life of Moses is his friendship with God. "Thus the Lord used to speak to Moses face to face, as a man speaks with his friend" (Exodus 33:11). To Jew and Gentile it is indeed a mind-boggling thing that the omnipotent God should speak to puny men and women as a friend. Yet the theme of intimacy with God runs all through the Bible, reaching a touching climax with the words of Jesus to his disciples: "You are my friends . . ." (John 15:14).

The intimacy of Moses with God is very real. He complains to Yahweh, argues with Him, pours forth his frustrations, intercedes for the people, makes the audacious request to see the face of God. What intimacy is here! And Moses always prefaces his remarks with the words: "If I have found favour in your sight . . ."; as if to say, "If you really love me, and I know that you do . . ." Think of his anguished struggle with God when, in spite of all those plagues, Pharaoh's heart remained obdurate. Think of that passage in Numbers where Moses identifies with his own femininity, assumes the role of the mother and exclaims:

> Did I conceive all this people? Did I bring them forth, that thou shouldst say to me: "Carry them in your bosom as a nurse carries the suckling child ...?" (Numbers 11:12)

Only close friends talk like that.

And again, the mystical life of numerous Christians can be described in terms of friendship. In her inimitable, homely way, St Teresa can say that "prayer is nothing else than an intimate friendship, a frequent heart-to-heart conversation with him whom we know loves us." And many Christians, following her example, can sit in the presence of God and talk to Him as a friend. Like Moses they speak about their problems, air their frustrations, make audacious petitions, intercede for their families, all the time realizing that they are loved by the friend of friends. Here is a wonderful model of prayer.

"Prayer," you say, "Yes. But is it mystical prayer? Surely mystical prayer is silent, wordless in a cloud of unknowing."

Let me pause a moment. Words can come from various levels of the psyche; and mystical words come from the deepest level of all. While it is true that mystical prayer contains periods of wordlessness, it is also true that there can be mystical dialogue, mystical conversation, rising up from an altered state of consciousness, from those hidden depths where God dwells in inaccessible light. Nor are these words necessarily earth-shaking and ecstatic. They may be simple and quiet like the words of one who speaks face to face with a friend. Such were the words of Moses. Such are the words of innumerable Christian mystics.[5]

IV

As the story of Moses the mystic entered the mystical literature of Christianity, the question was asked: Did Moses see God? In the terminology of the scholastic theologians: Did Moses attain to the beatific vision in this life? Did he see the essence of God? While we can all see God *as He is in creatures,* did Moses see God *as He is in*

Himself? And as the question was asked about Moses, so also it was asked about St Paul. Remember that in The Second Epistle to the Corinthians Paul says that he was caught up to the third heaven – and, indeed, to paradise. Does this mean that Paul also enjoyed the vision of God's essence? And if Moses and Paul saw God, what about the host of other holy men and women, beginning with Elias?

A solid theological tradition, rooted in Exodus itself, states unhesitatingly that Moses did not see God. His audacious prayer to see God's glory meets with a clear-cut refusal:

> I will make all my goodness pass before you and will proclaim before you my name . . . But . . . you cannot see my face; for man shall not see me and live."
>
> (Exodus 33:19–20)

The Lord then comes down in a cloud; Moses is filled with awe as the Lord passes before him; but the face of God he does not see. And this scene finds an echo in the fourth gospel which firmly declares that "no one has ever seen God . . ." (John 1:18). This is clear speaking.

In his excellent study, *Western Mysticism*, Edward Cuthbert Butler, with ample quotations from the fathers, maintains that the tradition that neither Moses nor anyone else sees the face of God is firmly grounded throughout Christian theology. However, the other theory, that Moses and Paul enjoyed a fleeting vision of God, is found in Augustine and Thomas, mighty and prestigious theological giants. Augustine based his claim principally on the text of Numbers that God spoke to Moses "mouth to mouth":

> If there is a prophet among you, I the Lord make myself known to him in a vision, I speak with him in a dream. Not so with my servant Moses . . . With him I speak mouth to mouth, clearly, and not in dark speech; and he beholds the form of the Lord.
>
> (Numbers 12:6)

Edward Cuthbert Butler rightly says that this text (like the others stating that God spoke to Moses face to face) says nothing about the beatific vision. As for Paul, he nowhere claims to have seen God. Butler, claiming that Thomas followed Augustine, concludes:

> In the face of . . . biblical evidence, and of the grave
> philosophical difficulties involved, it may well be thought
> that but for St Augustine's ill-founded speculation,
> accepted and endorsed by St Thomas, the idea of the vision
> of God's essence by any man would not have found a place
> in theological tradition.[6]

Alas, Augustine and Thomas were not familiar with the
historical-critical method. Their ill-founded speculation reminds
us that science plays a vital role in the interpretation of Scripture.

But a problem remains. Granted that Moses did not see God,
what was the nature of his experience?

The old theologians were fascinated by the picture of Moses
entering the darkness. Remember how God came down in a thick
cloud. Sinai was wrapped in smoke. "And the people stood afar
off, while Moses drew near to the thick darkness where God was"
(Exodus 20:21).

In his *Life of Moses*, Gregory of Nyssa, watching Moses enter
the thick darkness, claims that the great leader did have a direct
vision of God. But (paradox of paradoxes) it was a dark vision. It
was a seeing which is not seeing, a knowledge which is ignorance.
Graphically he describes how the mind (the mind of Moses or the
mind of any mystic) travels beyond all sensible seeing, beyond all
imaginative seeing, beyond all understanding and reasoning until
it *sees God in darkness*. Here are his words:

> For leaving behind everything that is observed, not only
> what sense comprehends but also what the intelligence
> thinks it sees, it keeps on penetrating deeper until by the
> intelligence's yearning for understanding it gains access to
> the invisible and the incomprehensible, and then it sees
> God. This is the true knowledge of what is sought; this is
> the seeing that consists in not seeing, because that which is
> sought transcends all knowledge, being separated on all
> sides by incomprehensibility as by a kind of darkness.[7]

Gregory has been called "the father of Christian mysticism" and
this passage was to have immense influence on subsequent
apophatic mysticism and its offspring, the theology of negation.

St John of the Cross follows in the footsteps of Gregory and of Gregory's disciple Dionysius. Put briefly, his doctrine of the darkness is as follows: God is so utterly different from anything or anyone we know, the love of God is so different from anything we have ever experienced, the glory of God is such a dazzling and blinding light, that as we approach God our dazed faculties, unable to endure the sight, are plunged into the most radical darkness. Just as the bat is blinded by the intense light of the sun, so we are blinded by the intense light of God. We do have a vision of God (as Moses had a vision of God) but we see Him in darkness. *We see Him through faith.* St John of the Cross elaborates a profound theology of faith in which he does not hesitate to say that by faith we meet God face to face. And in naked faith this dark vision of God is filled with mystical suffering.

Faith is a dark vision of God. To this I shall return. Here it is enough to watch Moses enter the cloud, recalling that he is followed by a host of mystics who enter the darkness where God resides in light inaccessible.

V

Moses is indeed a rich and many-sided personality. Sometimes he is depicted as a prophet. And a great prophet he was: "And there has not arisen a prophet since in Israel like Moses, whom the Lord knew face to face . . . " (Deuteronomy 34:10). But the prophecy of Moses came out of his mystical experience and was its fruit.

Again, Moses is sometimes called the lawgiver. And a great lawgiver he was – immortalized in marble by Michelangelo. Yet the law came out of his mystical meeting with God.

Again, Moses was the leader of his people, the former of community. But he can weld the people together only because he has met God in mystical prayer.

And through Exodus we see him grow. We see him transfigured. This young Hebrew who killed the Egyptian and hid him in the sand; this young Hebrew who stammered so much that he needed help from Aaron; this young Hebrew is so transformed through mystical encounter that his face shines with a blinding radiance – with the glory of that God Who spoke to him as a friend. "And when Aaron and all the people of Israel saw Moses, behold, the skin of his face shone, and they were afraid to come near him" (Exodus 24:30). Mystical love has transformed not only his mind and heart but his very body and his whole person.

And the mystical experience of Moses was not just his own. It was the experience of the whole people of Israel; for they (in Paul's enigmatic phrase) "were baptized into Moses in the cloud in the sea" (1 Corinthians 10:2). Just as John was the beloved disciple and we are all beloved disciples, so Moses was the friend of God and we are all friends of God. As Moses was the mystic, so we are all called to be mystics. We also can climb the mountain where God will speak to us face to face as one speaks to a friend.

NOTES

1. See in my book. *The Mirror Mind* (New York: Harper & Row; London: Collins, 1981), ch. 5, "The Holy Book".
2. *Dei Verbum*, C.4,16; *The Documents of Vatican II*, ed. Walter M. Abbot (New York: American Press, 1966), p. 122.
3. *The Collected Works of St John of the Cross*, trnas. Kieran Kavanaugh and Otilio Rodriguez (Washington, D.C.: ICS Publications, 1979), 9.
4. Ibid.
5. *The Mirror Mind*, ch. 4 "Words and Silence".
6. Edward Cuthbert Butler, *Western Mysticism* (New York: E.P. Dutton, 1923; London: Constable, 1926), pp. 53, 54.
7. Gregory of Nyssa, *The Life of Moses*, trans. Abraham J. Malherbe and Everett Ferguson (New York: Paulist Press, 1978).

4

Presence and absence (1)

I

I have said that the Book of Exodus is pervaded with the sense of God's presence and can be read as a great treatise on mysticism. I have spoken about Moses the mystic, Moses the friend of God. And now I would like to speak about the sense of presence and absence in the lives of millions of Christians who, following in the footsteps of Moses, have enjoyed friendship with their God.

II

From the earliest times, Christians who wish to come close to God have been urged to walk constantly in His loving presence. We have been urged to reflect that God is everywhere; for He is the great reality in whom we live and move and have our being. Is not this the message of the Book of Psalms which poetically reminds us of the all-pervading presence of God? And then there is the New Testament teaching that the Blessed Trinity dwells deeply in us as in a temple. We know that St Ignatius of Loyola told his disciples to recall the presence of God before entering into prayer; and he advised busy people to pause for a moment during the day to recall that God is close, very close, and that He is dwelling in them. Then there is the holy Carmelite, Brother Lawrence, who taught "the practice of the presence of God" as a key to the inner journey.

As we advance along the path to God, however, there comes a time when the presence of God ceases to be a *practice* and becomes a *given*. It is no longer something I *do* but something that happens. I suddenly, perhaps unexpectedly, become aware that God is here. I become aware of what the mystics call "an obscure sense of presence." It is obscure because it has no clear-cut images or pictures of God. It is memorable and important because it is an altered, new state of consciousness, an enhanced awareness as though I was entering a hitherto unfamiliar world, or as though I was suddenly in possession of a sixth sense.

This experiential sense of God's loving presence is traditionally regarded as the first stage of Christiam mysticism. When it comes over me, I may have a sense of the divine indwelling, a realization that God lives at the very centre of my being. Or it may be a feeling that I am surrounded by God as by a loving atmosphere, that I am plunged in God like a sponge in the ocean. Or it may simply be a sense that God is present in a way I cannot understand; I cannot locate that presence inside or outside or anywhere at all.

This sense of God's presence carries great conviction. Now I need no proof that God exists. I cannot deny it; I cannot deny my own experience; for that experience is self-authenticating. Of course my certainty is subjective. That is to say, it is for me alone. I cannot *prove* God's presence to anyone else. All I can do is bear witness to what has happened to me.

III

This sense of presence may come at any time in life. Not infrequently children experience God's presence, only to forget about it when they grow to adulthood. In adults the same experience is often the outcome of years of discursive and ejaculatory prayer, of reading the Scriptures, and of constant celebration of the Eucharist. Their prayer has become more and more simple, more and more an activity of the heart, till the day comes when they just want to be silent and wordless in the felt presence of God. Now they no longer desire to think; they only want to be.

The sense of God's presence may be accompanied by distractions. It is as though there were two layers in the psyche. At one level the imagination is running wild: at a deeper level I am quietly aware of God's presence. In this state, technically known as *the prayer of quiet,* all good teachers recommend that one remain quietly in God's presence at the depths of one's being, making no effort to chase away the distraction. Don't fight! Let them be! Let them come and go! St Teresa calls the wild and unruly imagination "the fool of the house."

Yet at other times one's faculties may be so held by the divine presence that one seems to be in some kind of ligature, unable to think or pray discursively. This ligature may even lead to ecstasy.

It is important to note that this presence is not static. God is not present in me like still water in a glass. No, no. The presence of God changes me radically, guiding me through the inner desert like the cloud by day and the pillar of fire by night. Of course I may be sitting in seeming passivity; I may seem to be doing nothing at all. I may have scruples that I am wasting my time. But, unknown to myself, growth is taking place. I am being changed like the log transformed into the fire. Put in scriptural terms, the presence of God is effecting in me a profound *metanoia*. "Change your hearts and believe the Gospel," said Jesus; and in the mystical life he himself is changing the heart of stone into a heart of flesh.

But not only is the heart changed by this silent contemplation. A profound change is wrought in the whole person. The body is transformed as was the body of Moses who wore a veil on his face to conceal the radiant beauty and splendour of God's glory. In the same way, the contemplative becomes more and more beautiful, more and more attractive, more and more charming and lovable.

IV

Interestingly enough, some of the most vivid descriptions of mystical experience come from the lips of men and women who have been recalled from the brink of death. Such people often say that, as they slipped towards death, they seemed to enter into a new dimension, into another ground of being, into a state of consciousness where time and space seemed different. The experience was not terrifying because they were greeted by a warm and loving presence, or they experienced an accepting light. They claim that the experience so changed them that they returned to ordinary life liberated from the fear of death and with a new scale of values. What had seemed important was no longer important; what had seemed unimportant had become the very centre of their lives.

Now all this is reminiscent of the talk of the mystics. It is all the more interesting in view of the fact that the old authors claimed that mystical experience is a foretaste of eternal life. What more natural than that this foretaste should come when, faced with death, one stands at the gates of eternity?

V

And this brings me to an issue discussed at length by mystical theologians: Do many people enjoy the loving sense of God's presence? How frequent is the mystical experience?

Some theologians at the beginning of the century claimed that mysticism was a special charismatic gift granted to a privileged few. Others, holding that it was no more than a development of the ordinary grace of baptism, spoke of "the universal vocation to mysticism." Every Christian, they said, is called to be a mystic.

I myself have come to believe in the universal vocation to mysticism for the following reasons.

First, the Council spoke of the universal vocation to holiness, insisting that all the faithful are called to the summit of perfection.[1] Now it is true that the Council did not speak explicitly about mysticism. Nevertheless, if you read the relevant document you see that the Council quite forcefully rejects the medieval notion of an élite called to perfection and a riff-raff called to salvation. Élitism is gone. And as we are all called to holiness, may not all be called to mysticism? And will not this be especially true if the essence of mysticism is nothing other than the unrestricted love, the agape which forms the very core of Christian holiness?

Second, if one holds with Karl Rahner that Christianity is basically presence to transcendent mystery, then the seeds of mystical presence are already in the mind and heart at baptism. And the Christian life consists in being more and more present to the mystery as the mystery is ever more lovingly present to us. Rahner himself seems to draw this conclusion when he claims that the fervent Christian of the future will be a mystic.

My third reason is personal. As my experience of the Christian world deepens, I see that many, many people are called to pray in altered states of consciousness. Here in the Philippines, where I write this book, I see simple people praying silently for hours in the great prayer centres of Quiapo and Baclaran in central Manila – and well-informed people tell me that the poor are indeed blessed with mystical gifts. And what happens here happens throughout the world. This leads me to the conclusion that the Christian spirit open to God moves spontaneously towards mystical states of consciousness. Sometimes people need only a little instruction. They need only be told to use fewer words, to be quiet, to let themselves be drawn into the cloud of unknowing.

It is true, of course, that some committed Christians seem to experience no mysticism during their lives. But we cannot exclude the possibility that for these, mystical experience comes at the time of death. For these the mystical moments of death are a preparation for the most radical, altered state, which is eternal life.

VI

Now let me say a word about the theology of this sense of presence.

Following St Thomas and St John of the Cross, we can distinguish three modes of divine presence: *presence by essence, presence by grace, presence by love.*

Presence by essence is a consequence of ongoing creation: if God were not present, holding it in existence, the universe would immediately fall into nothingness. And the same is true for us. If God were not present, holding us in existence, we would fall into nothingness. *Presence by grace* is a consequence of baptism whereby the Blessed Trinity comes to dwell within our hearts. But we may not be aware of this divine indwelling. *Presence by love* is the existential and experiential sense of presence about which I have been speaking.

Presence through love! Remember I said that altered states of consciousness can be induced by hypnosis, by biofeedback, by drugs. Yogis enter into trance by staring at the flame of a candle or by fixing their gaze on a single point. *The special characteristic of Christian prayer is that altered states of consciousness are induced not by techniques but by love.*

Presence through love! Not my love for God but God's love for me. Or, more correctly, the intense mutual love existing between God and the human person. Usually this love is the fruit of years of toil, but sometimes it comes quite suddenly to those who reach the vineyard at the eleventh hour. It is precisely this love that creates a sense of presence (and later a sense of absence) that leads to ecstasy, that leads to forgetfulness of time, that leads to those altered states of consciousness which forever will be the subject of psychological research.

Love and presence lead to union. Again the scholastics distinguish between an *essential union* with God common to all created things, and a *transforming* union arising from love. I spoke of this when I said that God can be considered as an object. Let me now quote St John of the Cross on how the soul is one with God yet not one with God:

> When God grants this supernatural favour to the soul, so great a union is caused that all the things of both God and the soul become one in participant transformation, and the soul appears to be God more than a soul. Indeed, it is God by participation. Yet truly, its being (even though transformed) is naturally as distinct from God's as it was before, just as the window, although illumined by the ray, has an existence distinct from the ray.[2]

Here, while stressing the most intimate union, the saint avoids any taint of pantheism.

VII

Scholastic theologians spoke of acquired and infused presence, as they spoke of acquired and infused contemplation. Acquired contemplation is found through personal effort with the aid of ordinary grace: infused contemplation is that gift of presence that comes gratuitously and is identified with mysticism. This distinction is based on a psychology which speaks of a twofold knowledge: ordinary knowledge coming through the senses according to the Aristotelian dictum that there is nothing in the intellect which was not previously in the senses (*nihil est in intellectu quod non fuit prius in sensu*); and extraordinary or mystical knowledge directly *infused* by God who now communicates Himself by pure spirit.

I believe that today, when we use a new psychology, this distinction between acquired and infused is no longer useful. We now speak in terms of altered states of consciousness; and it is difficult to maintain that one state is more "infused by God" than the other. Indeed, we know that some people (and this is particularly true in Asia) can enter into trance with the greatest ease. And who can say that this trance-like state is more "infused" than their ordinary, waking consciousness? In other words, to call one state "acquired" and the other "infused" is highly questionable.

And yet we cannot neglect an age-old Christian tradition that God sometimes acts directly on the human soul. Listen to the author of *The Cloud* speaking about grace-filled moments when God works all by Himself:

> Then you will feel little or no constraint, for God will sometimes work in your spirit all by Himself. Yet not always nor for very long but as it seems best to Him. When He does you will rejoice and be happy to let Him do as He wishes.[3]

These are indeed special moments when one exclaims: "This is God! I cannot doubt it! I did nothing to merit this wonderful grace."

Ignatius of Loyola talks about similar experiences and he calls them moments of "consolation without previous cause." For him this consolation is of the greatest importance because here "there can be no deception . . . since it can proceed from God our Lord only."

It should be noted, however, that Ignatius and the author of *The Cloud* are not building up a psychological system in which certain states are caused by God alone. They are speaking of privileged moments when I can have *subjective certainty* that God is present and that I am personally loved by Him.

VIII

I hear you say: "You are speaking about the presence of God. But what about Jesus Christ? Where is he in this obscure sense of presence? Where is the specifically Christian dimension you set out to explore?"

I believe that the obscure sense of presence is part of the religious experience of all the monotheistic religions. However, my Christian faith tells me that when I enter into the cloud of unknowing and experience this obscure sense of presence, I am present to the mystery of Christ – or, rather, that the mystery of Christ is present to me. Not that I have a clear-cut picture of the Risen Jesus. It is rather that I relish the presence of a mystery hidden for ages in God and revealed through Jesus Christ.

NOTES

1. *Lumen Gentium* C.5; *The Documents of Vatican II*, ed. Walter M. Abbot (New York: American Press, 1966), p. 65ff.
2. "The Ascent of Mount Carmel", in *The Collected Works of St John of the Cross,* trans. Kieran Kavanaugh and Ottilio Rodriguez (Washington, D.C.: ICS Publications, 1979), II, 5, p. 117.
3. *The Cloud of Unknowing and The Book of Privy Counselling*, ed. and trans. William Johnston (New York: Doubleday Image Book, 1979), ch. 26, pp. 83–84.

5

Presence and absence (2)

I

I have spoken of God's presence. He is closer to us than we are to ourselves. Above all, He is present to us by love, as we are present to Him by love. But, alas, we do not always feel His all-pervading presence. The masters agree that the mystical path has its hour of abandonment, of desolation, of darkness. These are times when God (though intimately present) seems far, far away, and we cry out: "Where are you, my God? Where have you hidden, Beloved?" Such was the cry of the psalmist who exclaimed: "My God, my God, why hast thou forsaken me?" (Psalm 22:1). And, wonder of wonders, these very words echo on the lips of Jesus: "Lama sabacthani?"

Paul, too, had his times of awful desolation: "We were so utterly, unbearably crushed that we despaired of life itself. Why, we felt we had received the sentences of death . . ." (2 Corinthians 1:8–9). What was biting Paul? What is behind the desolation, the seeming absence of God which we all experience?

One cause of desolation is simply the ordinary pain of living. We human beings cannot forever remain at a high pitch of mystical awareness. We must come down to earth. And when Paul speaks concretely of his desolation he talks about shipwrecks and hunger and thirst and sleeplessness and criticism from the brethren. All this could happen to any of us; and it would knock us into a state of desolation where we ask: Where is God? In other words, to use modern parlance, desolation has an element of humdrum anxiety, depression, insecurity, sadness, melancholy, deflation, and all the negative emotions that are part of human living.

But this is not all. Desolation and darkness belong to, are built into, the mystical process. Let me explain why.

In the mystical life the shadow part of our personality rises to the surface of consciousness. We are confronted with our own seamy side. We get into an altered state of consciousness that is very, very painful. This may take the form of fears, anxieties, neuroses, childhood traumas, hurts and wounds of the past – painful memories of all kinds. Or it may take the form of the seven deadly sins about which I shall speak in the next chapter. All this darkness floats to the surface (or, put in another way, I enter more deeply into an altered state of consciousness where I meet it) and the result is very, very painful. Some people may feel themselves filled with the black, black guilt of an Oedipus who killed his father and married his mother. Oedipus, driven to despair, gouged out his eyes in bitter self-hatred. And the mystic may feel the same despair even when he or she calls with agony on Jesus the saviour. Other people may feel anxiety, scrupulosity, insecurity, doubt. They may experience the unresolved conflicts, the unfinished business of childhood – the tears not shed, the anger never released, the fear not expressed, the curiosity not satisfied. And in all this they feel lost in the storm, until Jesus comes walking on the waters to bring them peace and integration.

Here let me pause to observe that the contemplative process has much in common with psychotherapy. In both cases one is painfully and inescapably brought face to face with one's shadow. But the mystic is healed by calling with faith on Jesus the saviour. Let me further pause to state that psychologists will never understand the human psyche with all its altered states until they look carefully at the mystical journey towards wholeness. But back to my theme.

God is present in all these hurts. He is more present in darkness than in light. He is nearer in time of desolation than in time of consolation. So the concrete advice is: Stay with the darkness. Go through it. Don't run away! And through all this you will grow from childhood to maturity; for your faculties will expand, making you more and more capable of receiving those sublime communications which come from the darkness of God.

All this is the night of the senses.

The night of the spirit is concerned with meaning. Now philosophers and sages keep telling us that we are all symbolic animals and find meaning through symbols. Moreover it is precisely religion which provides the symbols we need for our spiritual nourishment – God our Father, Jesus our saviour, the stories of Scripture, the story of life after death, and so on. And it may happen that as we grow in love, as our minds and hearts expand, our symbols lose meaning. They no longer talk to us about God or about anything. Only one symbol remains: emptiness, darkness, absence. A terrible night is now caused by *loss of meaning*.

One who suffered in this way was Thérèse of Lisieux (1873–1897) about whom I would now like to say a word.

Born into a pious French family, Thérèse from early childhood had no doubt that one day she would leave earth to live forever with God in heaven. "Just as the genius of Christopher Columbus gave him a presentiment of a new world when nobody even thought of such a thing, so also I felt that another land would one day serve me as a permanent dwelling place."[1] But as she matured in spirit (even though she was chronologically very young) this clear belief in another world began to fade. Like Moses she entered into a thick, thick cloud; she entered into the night of faith. Here are her poignant words:

> Then suddenly the fog which surrounds me becomes more dense; it penetrates my soul and envelops it in such a way that it is impossible to discover within it the sweet image of my fatherland; everything has disappeared! When I want to rest my heart fatigued by the darkness which surrounds it by the memory of the luminous country after which I aspire, my torment redoubles; it seems to me that the darkness, borrowing the voice of sinners, says mockingly to me: "You are dreaming about the light, about a fatherland embalmed in the sweetest perfumes; you are dreaming about the eternal possession of the Creator of all these marvels; you believe that one day you will walk out of this fog which surrounds you! Advance, advance; rejoice in death which will give you not what you hope for but a night still more profound, the night of nothingness."[2]

The fog is, of course, the cloud of unknowing. How dark it has become! It is no longer a luminous cloud but a thick night. And

Thérèse writes to her Superior: "Dear Mother, the image I wanted to give you of the darkness that obscures my soul is as imperfect as a sketch is to the model; however, I don't want to write any longer about it; I fear I might blaspheme; I fear even that I have already said too much."[3]

In spite of the darkness, Thérèse continues to write and speak enthusiastically about the love of God and about His mercy. But she herself confesses:

> When I sing of the happiness of heaven and the eternal possession of God, I feel no joy in this, for I sing simply of what *I want to believe.* It is true that at times a very small ray of the sun comes to illumine the darkness, and then the trial ceases *for an instant,* but afterwards the memory of this ray, instead of causing me joy, makes my darkness even more dense.[4]

The italics are not mine, but hers. She felt that she no longer believed in eternal life or in a transcendent God. She felt that at heart she was an atheist.

How do we explain this agonizing state of consciousness of Thérèse We are here faced with mystery. But let me make three observations.

First, there is the paradoxical fact that the very love which in the early stages creates a warm sense of presence eventually creates a gnawing sense of absence. I have already said that love of God is so different from anything we know, so different from what we ordinarily call love, so utterly unfamiliar, that our human faculties, unable to bear the weight, are plunged into thick darkness. Face to face with God. Thérèse was blinded by the excess of light. But, alas, she was unable to understand that the blackness was a dark vision of God.

Second, the symbolism which formerly nourished her life fell to pieces. The Christian story sounded like a fairy tale. She was left with the ultimate archetype: emptiness, nothingness. And *with the loss of symbol came a loss of meaning:* she no longer saw meaning in the great story on which she had built her life.

Third, some unresolved childhood neuroses may have remained in her unconscious mind. We know that in her last months of agony she feared she might destroy herself and asked that sharp instruments not be placed within her reach. We also know that she exhibited some neurotic tendencies in childhood. Some unfinished business may have remained – some vestiges of unresolved conflict. If this is so, the night of sense and the night of spirit came together. And what thick darkness ensued!

But, you say, is this not atheism? Or is it not Buddhism? This blank of nothingness, this total absence of a transcendent God?

It may look that way. But in the psyche of Thérèse there is one important movement which is found neither in atheism nor in Buddhism: a total and unwavering commitment to a transcendent God whom she does not see nor hear nor touch nor feel – a transcendent God who *seems* to be absent or dead. Reasons for belief had fallen away. Yet she claimed that she now made more acts of faith than at any time in her life. Now this faith (that is to say, total commitment) was all the more pure because she believed not because of what she felt, not because of cultural props, not because of beautiful symbolism, not because it felt good to believe, not because theologians proved God's existence, not because she felt the sweet and mystical sense of God's presence. She believed because she believed. She believed God for God. And this is pure faith. It was of this faith that the Johannine Jesus spoke when he gently chided Thomas: "Blessed are those who have not seen and yet believed" (John 20:29).

III

I have spoken of presence and absence. But the goal is vision.

Deep in the heart of every man and woman lies the desire to see God. To this desire Moses gave expression when he audaciously asked to see the face of Yahweh. To this desire the psalmist gives expression when he longs for God as the hart longs for flowing streams or as the parched earth longs for water. So great is the human longing for God. And in the mystical life this longing becomes a gaping wound, a wound of love, the wound of one who loves God but cannot see Him.

To this desire St John of the Cross gives expression when he sings in "The Spiritual Canticle":

Reveal Your presence and may the vision of Your beauty
be my death.

Presence here means vision; and the saint is longing, longing for the vision of God. Yet he knows that he cannot see God in this life (yes, in testimony of this he quotes the words of Yahweh to Moses) and so the only way to see God is through death.

Two visions bring death he says. One is the vision of the fabulous and venomous reptile called the basilisk which, hatched by a serpent from a cock's egg, slays by its breath or look. The other is the vision of the beauty of God. And for this second vision he would undergo a thousand deaths.

Here, then, St John of the Cross follows the theological opinion which states that no one sees God in this life. What we can have here below is a dark, dark vision of God. "For the likeness between faith and God is so close that no other difference exists than that between believing in God and seeing him."[5] That the elect see God was taught by Pope Benedict XII in the Constitution *Benedictus Deus* of 1336: "The souls of the blessed in heaven have an intuitive and direct vision of the divine essence without the intermediary of any previously known creature. The divine essence manifests itself directly and openly in perfect clarity. The souls of the blessed enjoy it continually and will enjoy it forever. Such is eternal life." St John of the Cross, no mean theologian, was undoubtedly familiar with this document.

And so the longing for the vision of God in eternity becomes a raging fire. Nothing on the face of the earth will now satisfy the mystic longing. Any sense of presence, any vision, any locution, any rapture, any mystical experience whatsoever is no more than a foretaste of the beatifying vision of God.

IV

I hear you say: "Presence and absence! Wonderful! But are not these mystics engaged in a pious and loving ego-trip, far, far from the immense problems of our troubled century? What about nuclear war? What about pollution of the atmosphere? What about starvation and oppression and torture?"

Let me explain. Every step of the way, the mystics are close not only to God but to the whole human family. Even (indeed especially) in those dark nights of seeming despair when God seems absent and hell lies open — even then they are very, very close to us.

For the fact is that our modern world is in a dark night. And the evils of hunger and war and oppression are symptoms of an even deeper evil: rejection of God and deliberate choice of darkness. Many, many people are without faith, without hope, without love, lost in a morass of despair, wandering in the night, lost in this world — and who knows if they will be lost in another?

And in their dark nights the mystics go through hell, not for themselves but for the world. They taste the very despair their contemporaries taste; they resonate with the agony of those who believe that God is really dead. They are like Jesus in Gethsemane; they cry out: "Lama sabacthani!" And their unwavering faith is a light to a faithless world.

To us their lives may look irrelevant. They themselves may feel totally irrelevant — that is part of their darkness. But they are at the centre of the titanic struggle for the salvation of the world. They are a beacon to all of us. Through them we are saved.

NOTES

1. *Story of a Soul,* trans. John Clarke, O.C.D. (Washington, D.C.: ICS Publications, 1975), p. 213).
2. ibid.
3. ibid.
4. ibid., p.214.
5. "The Ascent of Mount Carmel", in *The Collected Works of St John of the Cross,* trans. Kieran Kavanaugh and Otilio Rodriguez (Washington, D.C.: ICS Publications, 1979), bk.II, ch. 9, p. 213.

6

Conflict (1)

I

I spoke of the desert as a place of prayer wherein one experiences the presence of God. And so it is. But paradoxically the desert is also the place of temptation wherein one meets the devil. Indeed, thousands of holy men and women, following in the footsteps of Jesus, have retired to the wilderness precisely to meet Satan and to conquer him in bloody or unbloody conflict.

On one of my trips I became acutely aware of the diabolical dimension of the great and terrible wilderness. Whereas Jerusalem is filled with places of worship, the desert south of 'En Gedi seemed not only empty but profoundly godless. From Sedom to Eilat and from Nueiba to Sharm es Sheikh I found no synagogue, no church, no mosque, no temple. Certainly the wandering bedouin have their place of prayer; but I did not see it. Where was God? We were warned to sleep out in the open away from rocks or clumps of grass where poisonous snakes and venomous scorpions lurked threateningly. Where was God? It is not surprising, I reflected, that holy people overcome with hunger and thirst, exhausted and weakened by the merciless heat and the piercing cold should find themselves face to face with Satan.

For when one enters the desert (whether real or metaphorical) without books and magazines, without radio and television, when one's senses are no longer bombarded by all the junk to which we are ordinarily exposed, when the top layers of our psyche are swept clean and bare and empty – then the deeper layers of the psyche rise to the surface. The inner demons lift up their ugly faces. The snakes and scorpions which were dormant or hard at work in the unconscious now raise their venomous heads and slither into the conscious mind. And we are face to face with the devil.

II

I said that holy men and women went into the desert precisely to meet Satan.

"How terrible!" you say. "How morbid! Why should anyone want to meet Satan? Surely we should spend our lives avoiding him."

One moment. The desert fathers claimed that it was much better to meet the devil than not to meet the devil. For he is always at work; and *he is never more dangerous than when he conceals himself*. So bring him out of the darkness into the light. Face him squarely and, trusting in God, you will conquer, "for he who is in you is greater than he who is in the world" (1 John 4:4).

Besides, there is an inevitability about temptation and darkness and conflict. All this is a necessary and valuable part of human life. "No temptation: no salvation," said the fathers. Temptation is a glorious time of opportunity. When you limp away like Jacob, realizing your own brokenness and failure, crying out: "Lord, be merciful to me a sinner!"; when you throw yourself on God's mercy knowing that you yourself are a powerless, burnt-out case – then your salvation is at hand.

And there is the additional fact that unless you conquer Satan in the desert you cannot safely go into the field of action. Only when he had won the battle in the desert did Jesus embark upon his public ministry. Only after spending the night in prayer on the mountain did he choose his disciples. Only after the agony in Gethsemane did he face his passion with tranquillity and courage. And many of his followers have had a similar experience. Their desert victory was the very condition of their action. Yes, while retreat to the desert may look like an escape, it is in fact a facing up to the real problems of life: it is a necessary prelude to Christian action.

And this traditional doctrine fits harmoniously with much modern psychology. Just as the desert fathers said it was good to face the devil, so wise old Jung insists that it is good and salutary – even necessary for growth – to face one's shadow and to confront one's inner demons. For we all have our shadow and our demons. No one is exempt. And the Pharisee who said he was not like the rest of men was very, very wrong. Who is without his or her fears, neuroses, anxieties? Who is untouched by those demons called the seven deadly sins: pride, covetousness, lust, gluttony, envy, anger, and sloth? Alas, alas, for the darkness in all of us!

And as long as they lurk in the unconscious, these fears, anxieties, angers, and lusts can tyrannize us – they can be compulsive, they can create havoc of all kinds. That is why any self-respecting psychologist will say: "Don't avoid them! Go through them! Bring them into the light and face them fairly and squarely. Only then will you be able to handle them."

More easily said than done. Fearing the darkness, we flee from our unconscious. Is it not more pleasant to play tennis or drink beer or watch television? But we cannot run away forever. Sooner or later the circumstances of life or a divine call or both will force us to face our unconscious. And when we do so with fortitude and courage, lo and behold, we discover that the unconscious is our friend. Yes, even the shadow can be our friend, leading us to the centre of our soul where God lives in light inaccessible.

III

I said that we are confronted with grimacing monsters of anxiety or fear or gluttony or lust or whatever. Let me here select for consideration one of these monsters which is particularly active in our day: the demon of anger leading to hatred and violence.

Psychologists give us lots of good advice about how to handle our anger, hostility, aggression. Generally, they will say that we should recognize our feelings, get in touch with them and accept them. Only in this way can we lead a rich emotional life.

When anger arises in the heart from the frustration of not getting what we want, then the worst possible thing is to deny it, repress it, pretend it is not there. "I'm not angry. Ha! Ha!" For this is to ram it into the unconscious where it will fester, causing acute depression or exploding in some unforeseen way. Much better, then, to recognize it and tell your friends about it. In short, learn to live with your shadowy demon and to accept him or her.

Now all this makes sense. And I have often told people to sit with their anger. Sit in the lotus! Get in touch with it! Accept it!

Having said this, however, it is also true that this is psychology for a bourgeois society. Talk to someone born in Belfast or Beirut or Johannesburg. Talk to someone who has seen his or her father humiliated by the police in the early hours of the morning. Talk to someone who has been imprisoned for a crime he or she did not commit. Talk to people who have suffered crushing injustice and tell me what they say. You will see that real anger cannot be handled by psychology alone, but only through profound healing, authentic conversion, mystical transformation.

Paul was well aware of this. I do not say that his problem was anger, but it was some kindred emotion; and Paul laments: "For I do not do what I want, but I do the very thing I hate . . . So then it is no longer I that do it, but sin which dwells within me" (Romans 7:15, 17). What a struggle went on in the breast of Paul! And he was acutely aware of his need for a saviour. "Wretched man that I am! Who will deliver me from this body of death? Thanks be to God through Jesus Christ our Lord" (Romans 7:25).

Paul is aware of two laws: the law of God in his inmost self and another law in his members. But, thanks to the grace of Jesus, it is the law of God that triumphs. "For the law of the Spirit of life in Christ Jesus has set me free from the law of sin and death" (Romans 8:2).

If, then, you would follow Paul, and if you feel drawn to contemplation, I would urge you to sit quietly in the presence of God and in the cloud of unknowing. Get in touch with your anger. Let it surface, while you remain with your deep, true self where you meet God. The storm may be terrible; you may find it intolerable to sit; all hell may break loose inside you. But remain with it; don't give up; and finally you will cry triumphantly with Paul: "The law of the Spirit of life in Christ Jesus has set me free from the law of sin and death" (Romans 8:2).

In this process, the first step is acceptance, integration, interior peace and calm. This solves the problem of fragmentation and inner division. But it is not enough. Terrorist and establishment alike have integrated anger, only to direct it with cold-blooded hatred to destructive ends. Much more is asked of the Christian. He or she must go beyond inner peace to an interiorization of the

Sermon on the Mount: "But I say to you that hear, love your enemies, do good to those who hate you . . ." (Luke 6:27). He or she must come to see the working of God even in the quagmire of injustice. And no psychology will help us do that but only the love of God in Christ Jesus our Lord. Only through profound conversion of heart, the gift of the Spirit, only through mystical transformation do we come to live the Gospel existentially.

Now the Gospel does not tell us to annihilate our anger (Jesus did not annihilate his) nor does it tell us to ram it into the unconscious. Rather must we transform it (or, more correctly, let God transform it) into a seeking of the kingdom of God and His justice. And, when this is done, destructive anger becomes just anger. It becomes the anger of a Mahatma Gandhi, a Martin Luther King, a Dorothy Day, a Thomas Merton, a Lech Walesa. Now it is the just anger of people who have harnessed all their energies in the service of the oppressed. In them *the demon of anger has become a friend*. Overpowering and uncontrollable anger has become an enlightened passion for justice. But this has only happened (let me repeat it) through a profound conversion of heart which is nothing less than mystical. "Thanks be to God through Jesus Christ our Lord!"

And what I say of anger is equally true of the other deadly sins. They can be transformed into their opposites. The demons become our friends.

IV

But let me return to the children of Israel.

Their wandering in the desert was filled with temptation. And Paul sternly warns the Corinthians not to be like them since "God was not pleased; for they were overthrown in the wilderness" (1 Corinthians 10:5). But why was God not pleased? What was their sin?

At first one might say that their main sin was that they grumbled and complained. The desert was too much for them and they longed for the fleshpots of Egypt – the fish, the cucumbers, the leeks, the onions, and the garlic:

Would that we had died in the land of Egypt! Or would
that we had died in the wilderness! Why does the Lord
bring us into the land, to fall by the sword? Our wives and
our little ones will become a prey; would it not be better for
us to go back to Egypt?   (Numbers 14:2–3)

They indeed grumbled. But the grumbling and discontent led to a
more serious sin: doubt, lack of faith. They doubted Moses; they
doubted themselves; they doubted their call. And finally, when
Moses climbed the mountain, they doubted God and persuaded
Aaron to make a golden calf. That is why they were destroyed by
serpents and twenty-three thousand fell in a single day.

Their grumbling was an expression of what we now call
anxiety. They were anxious about their future, about their
wives and little ones. And anxiety led them to turn away from
God.

We know that the demon of anxiety is one of the most insidious
monsters in the modern psyche. Apart from conscious anxiety
about yesterday and tomorrow, there is that unconscious anxiety
which can become compulsive, driving people to alcohol, to
drugs, to inordinate sex, to compulsive craving for power, and
even to self-destruction. It can drive people to manipulate and
exploit others, not from hatred, but from a desire to prove
themselves and to allay their inner fears. And it can drive out faith.
Consumed by anxiety, we cannot believe that God loves and
protects us; we act as though all depended upon ourselves; we are
practical atheists. hence the Gospel constantly attributes anxiety
to lack of faith: "Why are you anxious . . . O men of little faith?"
(Matthew 6:28).

You ask: "Must we cast out this demon? Or can he or she also
become a friend?"

Psychologists tell us that anxiety is an inescapable part of
human living and that it will be with us to the end. Nevertheless, I
believe that this demon is gradually transformed through
persevering contemplative prayer. When we learn *to sit with our
anxiety*, agonizing though this may be; when we allow it to come
to the surface of consciousness; when we learn to get in touch with
it and accept it; when we get in touch with the deeper law of the

Spirit of Life in Christ Jesus – then our salvation will come through the gift of profound conversion of heart.

For contemplative prayer brings an ongoing liberation. As destructive anger becomes just anger, so destructive anxiety becomes compassionate concern for ourselves and for others. This is the concern of the good angels (if I may borrow from St Francis de Sales), who watch over us with tender care but never lose their peace. Once again, a demon has become a friend.

V

The mystical life can be described as a journey into the depths of one's being, a journey to the true self and through the true self to God, Who is the centre. Down, down I go through alternate layers of light and darkness, meeting all the slimy monsters and frightening demons that inhabit the subliminal world. And if I progress far enough, I meet not only my own little monsters: I meet the monsters of the human race. I meet the root causes of war, oppression, torture, hunger, terrorism. I meet hatred, despair, injustice, atheism, darkness, I meet archetypal evil. And, horror of horrors, I meet it in myself.

"In myself?" you say. "How can that be? How can the evils of the world be in poor little me? How can I be responsible for massacres of innocent people, for torture, for oppression of the poor?"

Alas, we are all responsible. For we all share in the collective unconscious of the human family. We are not isolated monads but members of a species, members of a living and conscious body.

Most of us are not in touch with this collective unconscious. We are far too superficial for that. So, when things go wrong, we point an accusing finger at princes and politicians or at terroristts and revolutionaries. But mystics who enter deeply into the inner desert meet archetypal evil and, with God's grace, they conquer it. Some then enter the world of politics or economics or law or whatever – and their influence is crucial. Others help the destitute poor or the underprivileged or the handicapped. Others feel that their vocation is just to pray and suffer for the salvation of the world. But whatever they do, they are the true social workers and they change our world.

7

Conflict (2)

I

The synoptic gospels tell us that Jesus was led by the Spirit into the wilderness to be tempted by the devil. For forty days and forty nights he fasted and then, when he was hungry, he came face to face with evil.

Victorious, Jesus returns in the power of the Spirit to the world of people and to his public ministry. So great is his power that the people exclaim: "With authority he commands even the unclean spirits, and they obey him" (Mark 1:27). And at the end of his life Jesus can say confidently: "Now shall the ruler of the world be cast out" (John 12:31). And of Satan he can say clearly: "He has no power over me" (John 14:30).

Yet temptation was woven into the very texture of Jesus' life. St Luke tells us that the evil one "departed from him until an opportune time" (Luke 4:13), as if to say that Satan was constantly looking for opportunities to overthrow him. And Jesus was often troubled in spirit with a trouble that reached a great climax in Gethsemane.

The temptations of Jesus, however, were different from those I outlined in the last chapters. Whereas our temptations come mainly (but not exclusively) from inner demons, the offspring of original sin, Jesus had no original sin. He met objective evil. He met the implacable enemy of human nature who can never become our friend because he is irrevocably committed to destruction.

II

In order to understand the traditional doctrine of temptation it is necessary to say a word about the mystical understanding of the human psyche.

The old authors based their psychology on Plato and Aristotle, making necessary additions and modifications. One such addition was their doctrine of the apex or centre of the soul – the citadel of the soul, the deepest part of the human person, the place where the human meets the divine. This was the mysterious area of primordial commitment, the sovereign point of the spirit which can be touched only by God. Hidden and secret, it was concealed even from Satan who could not enter *unless invited to do so by a pact whereby one committed oneself totally to evil.*

Today we grasp at some similar centre when we speak of the mystery of the human person or of the true self or of identity, or when we talk about the fundamental option. We say that this deep self is only discovered gradually. Frequently it is uncovered through the suffering of analysis which brings joy, because I am liberated from the superego, and pain, because I discover not who I was told to be, not what the law commands me to be, but who I really am. Again, the paths of mysticism and psychoanalysis cross! But let me return to mystical psychology.

The psyche is divided into sense and spirit. Ordinarily Satan (who cannot get to the centre without a clear invitation) takes his stand at the gateway between sense and spirit. He may have stood here when he invited Jesus to turn the stones into bread.

But besides sense and the deep, deep centre, there is an in-between area of spirit to which the evil one has access. St John of the Cross speaks of shattering encounters with evil which proceed "nakedly from spirit to spirit"; and he says that "the horror the evil spirit causes . . . if he reaches the spiritual part is unbearable."[1] So violent is this encounter that the person would die if it lasted for long:

> This consternation is greater suffering than any other torment in this life. Since this horrendous communication proceeds from spirit to spirit manifestly and somewhat

incorporeally, it in a way transcends all sensory pain. This spiritual suffering does not last long, for if it did, the soul would depart from the body due to this violent communication.[2]

Only enlightened mystics who have reached a high degree of spiritual maturity are capable of encountering evil in this frightening way.

Let me here pause to add that as one can horrendously meet evil at this deep and spiritual level, so one can joyfully meet good at the same level – and this is a powerful enlightenment. *Spirit meets spirit.* Surely there was something of this in the encounter of Mary and Elizabeth when both were filled with the Holy Spirit and Mary raised her voice to cry: *"Magnificat!"* Surely there was something of this at the meeting of Magdalen with Jesus when he said: "Mary" and she exclaimed: "Rabboni." Here is the great mysticism of interpersonal encounter. But let me return to Jesus and the evil one.

One of his temptations takes the form of a mystical experience – though not of a horrendous and frightening nature. Luke tells us that "the devil took him up and showed him all the kingdoms of the world in a moment of time" (Luke 4:5). This must have been a flash of light akin to that which some people have at the time of death when they momentarily see their whole lives in a panoramic vision. In the same way Jesus, in a split second, sees all the kingdoms of the world. What a mystical experience!

And for the Christian who believes that Jesus was the Incarnate Word it is indeed mind-boggling to reflect that *he was so human as to undergo a mystical experience under the influence of Satan.* Yet Luke says just that.

And St John of the Cross talks constantly about diabolical interference in the mystical life. So much so, that he is extremely wary of all kinds of enlightenments, raptures, voices, visions, ecstasies, and the like. Assuredly the evil one can do no harm to one who, unmasking him as did Jesus, turns to God. But one who accepts such mystical experiences and acts on them is a pitifully deceived false mystic.

Surely there is here a vital lesson for contemporary men and women. So many seekers, dabbling in Asian mysticism or in drugs or in the occult, have big enlightenments and beautiful illuminations. And they like to tell their friends or to contribute articles to magazines. Let them reflect carefully that Jesus had a big illumination caused by Satan. Let them reflect that the mystical path is full of danger and that discernment is of cardinal importance.

III

The direction of the temptation is even more stunning. Satan promises Jesus authority over the whole world on one condition:

> If you, then, will worship me, it shall be yours. (Luke 4:7)

Is it possible that the Son of God should be invited to worship evil? Is it possible that the all-holy one should be tempted to make a total commitment to evil? Luke seems to say precisely this.

And if Jesus is asked to make a total commitment to evil, can we doubt that the same temptation has come to his followers through the ages? At the very peak-point of the mystical life, when they were in touch with their true selves and the deepest level of spirit, they have been tempted to choose evil. The desert fathers say grimly that the devils rejoice more in the fall of such a sublime mystic than in the destruction of thousands of lesser lights.

St Ignatius points to this in his *Spiritual Exercises* when he asks the retreatant to reflect on the sin of the angels and on the sin of Adam. According to the theology of his time, these were sins not of human weakness but of deliberate choice – a choice made in total liberty and without pressure from the passions.

Let me pause again to observe that we here find one of the unique characteristics of Judeo-Christian mysticism. At the very peak-point of the mystical life, when one is in touch with the true self, one is still capable of evil and, indeed, of the greatest evil. I see nothing quite like this in Hinduism or in Buddhism.

And if consummate mystics have been tempted to make a total commitment to evil, how much more the small fry! Indeed, this is the only real temptation in human life and to yield to it is the only real sin. Isolated acts of pride, covetousness, lust, gluttony, envy, anger, and sloth – these are not tragedies. They are part of human living. Christian tradition has consistently taught that no one is free from original sin; and if one promptly rises from the mire, isolated sins can be a distinct advantage on the path to God. The real tragedy is when people are drawn to change their direction, to commit themselves to evil, to change their very identity (for our identity is constituted by that to which we are committed) and to surrender the very apex of their soul to evil. This is the ultimate temptation; this is to choose hell.

Let me put it in another way. As faith is commitment to God, so sin in its radical form is commitment to evil. All lesser temptations are dangerous only in so far as they lead to this. Concretely, this definitive sin could take the form of a total commitment to any of the seven deadly sins. And this finally is a commitment to the definitive destruction of oneself and others. Just as the first commandment is to love God, oneself and one's neighbour, so the final sin is to commit oneself to hate God, to hate self, and to hate one's neighbour.

"Hate God?" you say. "Why should anyone hate God?"

It sounds strange, but deep in the human heart is a tendency to forget God, to hate God, to reject God, to put oneself in God's place. *Non serviam!* "I will not serve!" The old authors called it pride and, alas, it is very much alive today. Moreover the person who hates God hates self and the whole universe – for God is not separate from His world.

Yes, the fact is that the great struggle in human life is for the apex or citadel of the soul, the deep, deep centre where we make our fundamental option and our ultimate commitment either to good or to evil. When a person committed to evil changes this commitment and with it his or her horizon, this is called conversion. When a person committed to good turns toward evil, this is called sin.

Again you ask: "Why do we sin? Why do we blind ourselves to the true light? How is it possible for the human person deliberately to choose evil? How come evil even exists – if it does exist?"

These are questions which have baffled theologians since

Augustine and before. They speak of the mystery of iniquity: *mysterium iniquitatis*. And it is indeed a sobering mystery.

IV

I spoke of how consummate mystics can be invited to choose evil. Ordinarily, however, temptation is a long process and the aim of the tempter is to deceive and draw us along the path to evil. Remember how Paul tells the Corinthians that Satan disguises himself as an angel of light, and he writes:

> But I am afraid that as the serpent deceived Eve by his cunning, your thoughts will be led astray from a sincere and pure devotion to Christ. (2 Corinthians 11:3)

The serpent! Temptation is primarily deceit by a crafty enemy. And how deceitful evil can be! One of the most subtle temptations of Jesus comes from his best friend. Remember how Peter, dismayed at the thought of the passion and death of Jesus, exclaims: "God forbid, Lord! This shall never happen to you" (Matthew 16:22); and Jesus with unwonted severity confronts him: "Get behind me, Satan! You are a hindrance to me; for you are not on the side of God, but of men" (Matthew 16:23). Unwittingly, and under the guise of compassion, Peter was doing the work of Satan, trying to deflect Jesus from his sublime vocation to suffer and die.

No spiritual writer has unmasked the process of deception with more psychological insight than St Ignatius. He would have us constantly reflect on the inner movements, examine our consciousness and detect not only any movement towards sin but also the movements which lead to anxiety, fear, commotion, loss of peace. For in one who would travel the path to God, as the great goods are peace and joy and the other fruits of the spirit, so the greatest evils after sin are turmoil and anxiety leading to loss of faith, loss of hope, loss of charity, and change of commitment.

When it comes to outlining the actual process, St Ignatius is clear. The path of Satan is one of riches, honour, pride, leading to all other evils. The path of Jesus, on the other hand, is one of poverty, insults, humility, leading to all good.

But even as I write, I hear your exasperated voice: "Your whole thesis is individualistic and self-centred. What has it to do with the world torn assunder with social problems? Surely the great sins of today are the sins of nations, not those of individuals."

I agree. But my thesis is not individualistic. While it is true that the centre of the soul is intensely personal and that sin is finally a personal choice, still the paths of Ignatius are eminently relevant not only for individuals but also for societies. Let me explain.

We know that the great problem of today is nuclear war. We also know that if there is a nuclear war (which God forbid) it will be fought *for money, for oil, for petrodollars*. For it is no secret that when, in a given society, a significant number of people are totally committed to economic progress, when they are willing to sell arms to all and sundry for money, when they are then committed to their own and their country's affluence and prestige – then they forget God or put themselves in the place of God. And from this stems all evil, including nuclear war. This is the inexorable path described by Ignatius.

We also know that if a significant number of people are willing to renounce affluence, if they care little about prestige and all about justice, if they empty themselves in a *kenosis* like Jesus – then they can save the world. And this again is the Ignatian path.

Commitment to a poverty that leads to kenosis, far from being individualistic, is the greatest service one can render to today's world.

V

All this may sound sombre. Indeed the stakes are high. Yet the New Testament is vibrantly optimistic: "Be of good cheer. I have overcome the world" (John 16:33). The wounded stag appears on the hill and by his wounds we are healed and saved. Through his blood we triumph in every temptation. Anyone who calls on the name of Jesus will be victorious "because if you confess with your lips that Jesus is Lord and believe in your heart that God raised him from the dead, you will be saved" (Romans 10:9). Hence the words which bring salvation are: "Jesus is Lord."

Finally, let me cite an ancient and new Catholic belief that we are always safe in the company of the Virgin Mary. Tradition tells us that the demons fly from her in horror lest they be crushed by the heel which pressed upon the serpent's head. When the children of Israel carried the ark of the covenant into battle they were always victorious. And Mary is the ark of the covenant in the New Dispensation.

NOTES

1. "The Dark Night", in *The Collected Works of St John of the Cross,* trans. Kieran Kavanaugh and Otilio Rodriguez (Washington, D.C.: ICS Publications, 1979), bk. II, ch. 23, 1–5.
2. ibid., 1.9.

8

Covenant and conversion

I

Following the cloud by day and the pillar of fire by night, Moses and the people travelled through the great and terrible wilderness to Mount Sinai – to Horeb, to the mountain of God. And our little band of scholars, following in their footsteps, came to the holy mountain.

We climbed Gebel Musa and enjoyed the breathtaking view from its ethereal summit. Whether or not Moses climbed this mountain nobody knows. An ancient tradition claims that the nearby Gebel Serba is the genuine article. Be that as it may, our journey was no less politically tense than that of Moses and his people. The Israelis were withdrawing by stages from Sinai in accordance with the agreement of Camp David, and we passed checkpoint after checkpoint as we crossed that desolate border into Egypt.

At the foot of the mountain stands the ancient monastery of St Catherine. Founded as a shrine by Empress Helena in 327, becoming a combination of monastery and fortress in 530, it is one of the oldest continously occupied buildings in the whole world. But the monks value their obscurity and we had little chance to talk with them. Further down is the great, broad plain where the children of Israel supposedly camped and watched their great leader wend his lonely way up the mountain to meet God in a thick cloud amidst peals of thunder and flashes of lightning.

II

With the covenant we are at the heart of Judeo-Christian religious experience. Moses is the mediator of this covenant as Jesus will be the mediator of a new covenant. In both cases the binding force is love. God has loved His people. He has led them out of Egypt. He has carried them on eagles' wings and brought them to Himself. His love has been steadfast and unfailing. And in return the people are summoned to an unrestricted, unconditional love. The powerful words of Deuteronomy echo through the centuries and continue to ring vibrantly in the ears of contemporary men and women:

> Hear, O Israel; the Lord our God is one Lord; and you shall love the Lord your God with all your heart, and with all your soul, and with all your might.
>
> (Deuteronomy 6:4,5)

Here God asks for a total love, an unrestricted love, a love that goes on and on and on, a love that cannot not lead to altered states of consciousness, to inner revolution, to the most profound mystical experience. When we are faithful to the covenant, when we receive God's love and respond with all our heart and with all our soul and with all our might, then we undergo *metanoia* or conversion or change of heart. This is the transformation, the revolution in consciousness, the death and resurrection which is at the very heart of the Christian mystical life. It is an experience which is at once personal and communal. Moses entered the cloud alone but the people shared his experience when they cried: "All that the Lord has spoken we will do" (Exodus 19:8). In Paul's enigmatic phrase, "they were baptized into Moses in the cloud and in the sea" (1 Corinthians 10:2).

III

The covenant, far from being a superhuman call, is a way of becoming fully alive, a way of becoming fully human. And likewise metanoia, even in its deepest and most mystical form, is a completely human experience. In fact the way to metanoia can be described in terms of fidelity to the transcendental precepts which reflect the basic dynamism of the human Spirit: *Be atttentive, be intelligent, be reasonable, be responsible, be in love.* As is clear, the covenant is concerned with the last of these: *Be in love*. But (and this is important) a close look at the covenant reveals an even more fundamental and challenging transcendental precept:

Accept love
or
Be loved
or
Let yourself be loved

This precept is basic to Exodus and Deuteronomy and the Psalms, where we hear constantly of the great things God has done for His people, of the great love He has manifested for them. It stands out beautifully in Deutero-Isaiah where Yahweh tells his people: "You are precious in my eyes and honoured, and I love you" (Isaiah 43:4). It is the message of the First Epistle of St John: "In this is love, not that we loved God but that he loved us . . . " (1 John 4:10). And the same epistle says: "We love because he first loved us" (1 John 4:10).

From this it becomes clear that the great challenge of the Christian life is to receive love, to open our hearts to the one who knocks, to accept him into the very depths of our being.

Nor is this easy. We all know that human nature is perversely full of paradox. On the one hand we long for love. The deepest longing of the human heart is for love – for human love and divine love. On the other hand we fight against the very love we long for; we shut it out; we slam the door so that even God cannot enter.

And so we poor humans must learn to be loved. One way of doing this is through meditation on the Scriptures. We can take a phrase like "We love because he first loved us" or "You are precious in my eyes . . . I love you." We can take one such phrase and turn it over and over in our mind and heart. We relish it. We savour it. We let it talk to us. *We live it*. And one day we shout out: "We love because He first loved us! Now I see. Now I understand. I never realized this until now. *Eureka!* I am loved. I am precious in His eyes and He loves me."

Or another way is simply to ask God to love us: "Give me your love and your grace, for this is enough for me."

Or again we may learn to open our hearts to human love. For never let us forget that authentic human love is God's love made incarnate. So accept the love which comes your way. If you think that nobody loves you, this is probably because you are unconsciously warding off love. You just are not taking it in. Accept it with gratitude and you will experience joy.

To accept love, then, if the first step in fulfilling the covenant; it is the first step towards metanoia.

IV

And now I hear you say: "But why is human nature so perverse? Why do we refuse love? Why do we shut out the very thing we want? How explain this?"

Fallen nature is full of mystery and contradiction. Alas, deep down in all of us is a tendency to hate ourselves and to destroy ourselves. Sometimes this stems from an unconscious sense of guilt, unconscious desire for self-punishment and self-flagellation. Whatever the cause, some people have an acute sense of their own radical unlovableness. They have the "I'm not OK" syndrome. They feel deeply, "It just isn't possible that anyone, including God, could possibly love me." And this paralyzes them, making them reject love. Such people must learn to love themselves; and one way to do this is to accept the love of God and the love of people in the way I have just described.

Besides, in all of us there is a fear of intimacy and a fear of love. You see, just as human love unites us with a human person, so divine love unites us with God and with the universe and with everyone – it unites us with the totality. And something inside us fights against this. "I want my independence. I want to build my own kingdom. I will not serve. I will not submit to love." This is the deadly sin of pride which strikes roots in all of us.

And there is one more point. Receiving love seems wonderfully consoling. What greater joy than to accept the immense love of God?

Yes and no. St John of the Cross tells us that as we come close to God we discover that He is like night to the soul. The love of God is very different from any other love we know or experience. It is so unfamiliar, so strange, so powerful, so unconditional that it blinds our faculties and plunges us into painful darkness. Sometimes God's love is like nothingness, emptiness, blackness. Small wonder that we fly in panic from the hound of heaven.

Yes, love blinds us, consumes us, devours us. But the pain is accompanied by joy. And as we learn to become like little children, as we learn to empty ourselves, as we learn to open the door and keep it open so that God and people can enter, then we come to experience that we are loved and that we are lovable. We are lovable because we were created in the image of God; we are lovable because we were redeemed by Jesus Christ. Redemption has made us lovable, even more lovable than if we had never sinned.

Such is the theory. It is through meditation and, above all, through covenant mysticism that this theory becomes life. Through deep meditation we discover the true self and, entering into a new state of consciousness, we realize existentially with great joy that we are indeed loved.

V

Accepting love, we return it not only to God but to people – to everyone we meet without exception. "If God so loved us, we also ought to love one another . . . " (1 John 4:11). There seems to be a psychological law that authentic love cannot remain locked up within the human heart. It rebounds to the one who loves us. And if this lover identifies with all men and women (as does Jesus) then his love ricochets from us to all men and women. If this lover identifies in a special way with the poor and the suffering and the oppressed (as does Jesus) then his love ricochets from us to the poor and the suffering and the oppressed.

Indeed, the covenantal love found in metanoia penetrates all human relationships – love of husband and wife, love of parents and children, love between friends, love in community, love for the church, love for country, love for the world. All these loves are caught up in the mystical love of the covenant. They share in the Christian mystical experience.

VI

Most of what I have said about metanoia and covenant love applies to the old and the new covenant. Now let me say a word about the metanoia which is specifically Christian.

The New Testament constantly refers back to Deuteronomy telling us that the first commandment is to love God with our whole heart and soul and mind and strength. And at the Last Supper, as the new Moses, Jesus mediates another commandment in his own blood. As Moses had sprinkled the blood of animals on the altar and on the people, thus uniting God and humanity, so Jesus will shed his own blood, reconciling the human family with God our Father. "Drink of it all of you; for this is my blood of the covenant, which is poured out for many for the forgiveness of sins" (Matthew 26:28).

This new covenant is renewed in the Eucharist when we gather to break bread and to celebrate the great event that has saved us:

Christ has died
Christ has risen
Christ will come again

It is not surprising, then, that from the earliest times the Eucharist, the new covenant in his blood, has been the principal source of Christian religious experience and of Christian mystical experience. Participating in this sacrament we receive the love of Jesus into the depths of our being; we eat his body and drink his blood; united with him we offer ourselves to the Father: "Abba, Father!"

Such is the new covenant. Now let me point to the principal characteristics of the metanoia it engenders.

First, it is a change of heart whereby we commit ourselves totally to Jesus, the Risen Lord. Now we realize that he loves us immensely for the wounded stag has appeared on the hill. And filled with love and wounded with love we cry out with Paul: "What shall I do, Lord" (Acts of Apostles 20:10). Jesus, in turn, leads us to the Father. Remember how he prayed to his Father "that the love with which thou has loved me may be in them, and I in them" (John 17:26). This means that the Spirit is in us and Jesus is in us. And so, one with Jesus and filled with the Spirit, we cry out: "Abba, Father!"

Second, Christian metanoia is a change of heart whereby we commit ourselves totally to the gospel. "Repent, and believe in the gospel" (Mark 1:15). This does not mean that we make a commitment to scriptural exegesis. It does not mean that we make a commitment to a mere understanding of the gospel. It means that *we make a commitment to live the gospel* – not to live it in the world of Corinth or Philippi or Rome or Alexandria, but to live it in our modern world with its turmoil and anguish, with its poverty and oppression, with its glittering scientific achievements and its dismal social failures.

Third, Christian metanoia is a change of heart whereby we commit ourselves to the community. Here the community is the church. Not the church in a narrow, sectarian sense of that word. The Council gave us a new vision of the church as the community of the disciples of Jesus united among themselves and united with Jews, Moslems, Hindus, Buddhists. This is a church which feels united with all men and women of good will, even those who are atheist or agnostic. To love the church is to love the whole world: to be committed to the church is to be committed to the world. Listen to the words of the Council:

> All men and women are called to be part of this catholic unity of the People of God ... And there belong to it or are related to it in various ways, the Catholic faithful as well as all who believe in Christ, and indeed the whole of humankind. For all are called to salvation by the grace of God.[1]

To love the church is to love the whole of humankind.

VII

In the Christian life the initial metanoia is baptism which, for Paul, is the experience of death and rebirth. "Do you not know that all of us who have been baptized into Christ Jesus were baptized into his death? We were buried therefore with him by baptism into death, so that as Christ was raised from the dead ... we too might walk in newness of life" (Romans 6:3, 4).

When we think of baptism we usually think of the ritual pouring of water; but Paul is talking here of the great spiritual experience underlying the pouring of water. Probably he is thinking of his own mystical experience on the road to Damascus where he died a great death and "suffered the loss of all things" (Philippians 3:8) in order to rise to newness of life. For Paul this was clearly a painful experience followed by great joy.

And the same holds true for metanoia in our lives. Ordinarily it is preceded by suffering, by shock, by pain, by death. We hit rock bottom before rising with ecstatic joy.

But baptism is no more than a beginning. Metanoia is an ongoing process extending throughout life and reaching a mighty climax in death. Paul vividly compares himself to a runner in the Isthmian games. He has not arrived at the goal: he has not yet made the grade; he is still imperfect. "Brethren, I do not consider that I have made it my own; but one thing I do, forgetting what lies behind and straining forward to what lies ahead, I press on towards the goal for the prize of the upward call of God in Christ Jesus" (Philippians 3:13, 14).

The process! Like Paul we are all on the way. Like Paul we have our blind spots, our unconverted areas, our unregenerate dimension. It is indeed strange to see how people can be totally converted to the gospel in some areas and radically blind in others. How shocking to see people filled with compassion and advocating war! We raise our hands in horror but we do the same ourselves. We see the speck in the eye of others but miss the log in our own.

But as the process of accepting love and loving goes on, it brings a change of consciousness whereby the heart of stone becomes a heart of flesh. Ordinarily this is a gradual process accompanied by occasional flashes of insight, by falls and retrogression and stupidities and mistakes. The great challenge is to remain open to love, to remain open to change, to remain open to growth.

Sometimes (perhaps three or four times in a lifetime) metanoia may take the form of a great upheaval, an inner revolution, a violent shock through which one painfully yet joyfully acquires a new vision and sets out a new path. These are times of crisis when one realizes that this life of love is an awful risk, leading us to a place we do not know by a path we know not.

VIII

From all that has been said it will be clear that metanoia is the very core and centre of Christian prayer and of Christian mysticism. Meditation which does not lead to metanoia cannot be called Christian. It may bring us to wonderful altered states of consciousness; it may leave us refreshed, rested, and relaxed; it may bring us to trance and ecstasy; it may enhance our human potential a hundredfold. But if it does not bring fidelity to the covenant of love, it cannot be called Christian. On this point St Teresa of Avila is enlightening. She speaks of rapture and ecstasy and ligature and various states of consciousness in the lower mansions of the soul; but when she comes to the seventh and last mansion she speaks almost exclusively about love of neighbour. "Beloved, if God so loved us, we also ought to love one another" (1 John 4:11).

You say: "But what kind of metanoia is called for in our day? You have said we must live the gospel in this modern world and not in Corinth or in Philippi. What are you getting at?"

First of all, let me say that we live at a turning point in human history; we are in the throes of what Karl Jaspers called *an axial age*. We are faced with the alternatives of destroying ourselves in a nuclear holocaust or advancing to a new anthropological stage — to a new stage in evolution. In these critical circumstances, our first duty is to get in touch with the new age in which we live, to see the signs of the times, to resonate with the problems of contemporary men and women. We cannot do this without a profound conversion of heart that will take us out of one world and into another. This is the conversion, the renewal, the updating, the aggiornamento to which the Council called all Christians – and not only all Christians but all men and women. Alas, so many committed Christians continue to live in a world that no longer exists and to operate through structures that have long since died. It is this that makes them irrelevant. Let us open our hearts to the new global consciousness that is emerging everywhere. Let us read the gospel in our new historical setting. If we do so, we will find that this gospel takes on a new splendour and a new meaning – a wealth of meaning that the biblical authors themselves could not have foreseen. And if we strive to be faithful to the covenant we will likewise discover that the covenant takes on a new and startling meaning in this new world which is painfully coming to birth.

And in this basic conversion to the modern world we will find ample guidance in the Second Vatican Council, in numerous statements of the World Council of Churches, in those prophetic voices that are raised in different continents throughout the world. These summon us to a change of heart and a revolution in consciousness without which the human family may well perish. About this inner revolution I will speak more in detail as this book develops. Here let me mention certain specific areas where the covenant takes on new and lustrous meaning in a new world.

1. Fidelity to the covenant in our world will bring a conversion to peace. If we have experienced God's love for us and if this has led us to love the world, we cannot but recoil from the prospect of war and long for peace. We will recoil not only from war but from any kind of violence whether it be the institutionalized violence of established governments or the revolutionary violence of terrorists. Moreover, conversion of heart will enable us to pay the price, to make the sacrifices which peace demands – if necessary to change our life-style, to cut down on luxuries, to share with others. If we really want peace we may have to die and to suffer the loss of all things as did Paul on the road to Damascus. "Blessed are the peacemakers . . ." takes on a new splendour in our day.

2. Fidelity to the covenant will bring a conversion to the poor. If we have experienced God's love for us and if we want to

respond according to the spirit of the gospel, we will love in a special way the poor, the afflicted, the exploited, the underprivileged, the hungry. But (and again this is the crux) conversion of heart alone will enable us to pay the price and to make the sacrifices – to lower our standard of living, to share with the poor, to fight against a system which exploits and terrorizes and oppresses the third world. If we want to love the poor we may have to suffer the loss of everything as did Paul. "Blessed are the poor . . ." takes on a new splendour in our day.

3. Fidelity to the covenant will bring a conversion to those who do not share our religious convictions. It will lead us to love not only Christians of various denominations but also Jews, Moslems, Hindus, Buddhists. Thoroughgoing conversion alone will enable us to rise above the narrow sectarianism which has caused horrible wars and continues to divide our contemporary world.

4. Fidelity to the covenant will bring conversion to woman and those feminine values without which we cannot build a just and peaceful society. For Christians, I myself associate this with a conversion to the Virgin Mary and a renewed realization of her role in the mystical life.

5. Fidelity to the covenant will bring conversion to our contemporary world. Let us now listen to prophetic voices wherever they are. Let us repent of our failure to appreciate the scientific achievements and the prophetic insights of so many thinkers who built our modern world.

IX

I have spoken of our need for conversion. Now let me quote two prophets of our century. This first is a scientist. Here are the words of Albert Einstein:

> We must never relax our efforts to arouse in the people of the world, and especially in governments, an awareness of the unprecedented disaster which they are absolutely certain to bring upon themselves unless there is a

fundamental change in their attitude towards one another as well as in their concept of the future. The unleased power of the atom has changed everything except our way of thinking.

To change our way of thinking and to change our hearts. This is the challenge.

My second prophet is a religious leader. Pope Paul, addressing the General Assembly of the United Nations in 1965, spoke as follows:

> The hour has struck for our *conversion*, for personal transformation, for interior renewal. We must get used to thinking of man in a new way; and in a new way of man's life in common; with a new manner too of conceiving the paths of history and the destiny of the world, according to the words of St Paul: "You must be clothed in the new self, which is created in God's image, justified and sanctified through the truth" (Ephesians 4:23). The hour has struck for a halt, a moment of recollection, of reflection, almost of prayer. A moment to think anew of our common origin, our history, our common destiny. Today as never before, in our era so marked by human progress, there is need for an appeal to the moral conscience of man.

The hour has indeed struck for a change of heart, for a revolution in consciousness, for a renewed and mystical conversion to the covenant.

NOTE

1. *Lumen Gentium* C.2, 13; *The Documents of Vatican II*, ed. Walter M. Abbot (New York: American Press, 1966), p. 32.

9

Jesus mysticism

I

I started this book with a search for the unique dimension of Christian mysticism. Having spent many years in a comparative study of Buddhism and Christianity, I wanted to see what was special and unique about the mystical experience of Christians. And I found something very distinctive in the sense of presence, the felt sense of presence of a loving and transcendent God whom I call Father. This is a God Who is not only transcendent but also immanent because He dwells in the depths of my being.

However, the sense of a transcendent God is not uniquely Christian. While in Jerusalem I had the privilege and the joy of praying side by side with Jews at the Western Wall of the Temple. And as we swayed to and fro, calling on God and reciting the psalms, I became acutely aware of my kinship with Jews and our sense of a common Father. Again, in Cairo I prayed in mosques, touching the ground with my forehead, and again I realized that Moslems have a profound and reverent sense of God's transcendent presence. Yes, Jews, Moslems, Christians, we acknowledge the same God; we sense the same loving presence; we are all children of Abraham.

What is uniquely Christian, then, is not the sense of God's presence but involvement with Jesus Christ, the Risen Lord. The fervent Christian is led into a mystical relationship with Jesus, a relationship which, beginning with presence, leads to union and on to identification. And then, one with Jesus in the Spirit, he or she cried out: "Abba, Father!"

Let me now say something about this mystical relationship with Jesus.

II

This mystical relationship with Jesus is, of course, based on the New Covenant in his blood. The starting point is his love for me – "he loved me and gave himself for me" (Galations 2:20). He is the good shepherd who lays down his life for his sheep; he is the servant of Yahweh who was wounded for our sins and bruised for our iniquity; he is the wounded stag who is wounded because we are wounded. A deep realization of his love leads to a sense of presence, *an obscure yet tangible sense of presence. And this in turn leads* to that union whereby I become one with him and call upon the Father.

A realization of his loving presence also leads to friendship, a friendship rooted in that last discourse where the beloved disciple lay close to the breast of Jesus and heard him say: "You are my friends . . . No longer do I call you servants . . . but I have called you friends . . ." (John 15:14, 15).

Friendship with Jesus has played a central part in the lives of thousands of Christian mystics who have experienced Jesus walking beside them as he walked beside the disciples going to Emmaus, or who have experienced him living in them as he lived in Paul. With Peter they have said: "Yes, Lord; you know that I love you" (John 21:16). They have spoken to the Lord about their hopes and fears, about their plans and projects, about their successes and failures, about their joys and sorrows. They have realized that he is the friend of friends, the faithful one who will not let them down. They have realized that this is the friendship in which all other friendships are rooted.

Intimacy with Jesus has also been central to the lives of thousands, even millions, of simple Christians who have knelt before him asking for daily bread and for help in their difficulties.

But now I hear you again. You ask about social problems and nuclear war. You complain that this Jesus-and-I spirituality is a cop-out, a flight from the urgent problems of our explosive world.

Well, it could be a cop-out. But properly understood this prayer has a profoundly social dimension. For if my friendship is authentic, I will be concerned not only with my problems but also with his. And we know that Jesus is concerned with the poor, the sick, the oppressed, the downtrodden, the underprivileged, the despised. Not only is he concerned with them; he identifies with them. If we want to be his friend, we must also be their friend. If we want to be his friend, we must open our hearts to his presence in the vast world of suffering and injustice and oppression. Friendship with Jesus is friendship with the world.

III

Let me here pause to say that this loving involvement with Jesus, the Risen Lord, is the very essence not only of Christian mysticism but of the Christian life. This needs to be said. Alas and alack, so many Christians think that the Christian life consists in keeping the rules. Or they think that faith consists of subscribing to the correct formula. How far they are from the gospel and from the kingdom! How Paul would have torn his hair, if he had hair!

It is good to reflect that the Council spoke of faith as a total commitment to God who reveals that it deliberately got away from the idea that faith means assent to a series of propositions.[1] When this commitment is made in a radical way it leads to an altered state of consciousness which is truly mystical.

And do not think that I am throwing church law out the window. It surely has its place. I only say that to make law the centre of the Christian life is contrary to the gospel, where total commitment to Jesus beyond any rule or law is the one thing necessary.

IV

I hear you say: "Intimacy with Jesus! Friendship with the Risen Lord! This is beautiful and beautifully Christian. But is it mysticism? Surely mysticism means entering the void, the cloud of unknowing, the emptiness, the darkness, the nothingness; whereas the prayer you describe is full of words, thoughts, images, pictures, emotions. How can this be mysticism?"

Let me first describe this prayer. One may pour forth one's

heart to the Lord in words. Or one may repeat some form of the Jesus prayer or whatever. But eventually this leads to a silence whereby one rests in his loving presence without words. And in this silence there may be no picture, no thoughts, but only a simple sense of presence, of love, of union. Indeed, if you ask someone who prays like this, "What does Jesus look like?" the person cannot answer because he or she has no mental picture of Jesus but only a rich feeling that Jesus is lovingly and peacefully present – perhaps like warmth or light. Here there is an altered state of consciousness. Here there is mysticism.

But apart from this, I must say something sharp and direct: You don't understand the void! Many people don't understand the void. They have no experience; and they think that the void or the cloud means blotting out all images, getting rid of thought, making one's mind a blank – becoming a zombie!

Now this is not the void. In Zen, for example, one can enter the void while listening to the sound of the waterfall or watching the falling peach blossom or looking at the murmuring stream or atttending to the flow of one's breath. *The void is constituted by detachment, nonattachment, nonclinging – not by blotting things out.* In the void I do not cling to thought; but I may think. I do not cling to words; but I may use words; I do not cling to pictures but I may have mental pictures. In short, the void is not an annihilation of thinking and feeling and imagining (if it were that, Christians would rightly reject it) but a purification of all these.

St Teresa of Avila entered into the void and she saw Jesus therein. I believe the two disciples going to Emmaus entered into the void, into an altered state of consciousness, when they talked to Jesus and later said: "Did not our hearts burn within us while he talked to us on the road, while he opened to us the scriptures" (Luke 24:32). The void is no mere negation (even though it is often described in negative terms) but a state of consciousness full of spiritual wealth.

V

In Christian tradition, as Moses was the great mystic of the Old Testament, Mary of Bethany was the great mystic of the New. From the time of Augustine and before, Mary sitting at the feet of Jesus was the model of the mystics. Great was her love for Jesus; even greater was his love for her. Here we have intimacy; here we have union; here we have mysticism.

The author of *The Cloud*, highlighting this famous scene, writes of Mary:

> Neither did she notice our Lord's human bearing, the beauty of his mortal body, or the sweetness of his human voice and conversation . . . But she forgot all this and was totally absorbed in the highest wisdom of God concealed in the obscurity of his humanity.[2]

Now let me here be frank. While I love and admire the author of *The Cloud*, the above statement does not make me happy. The author implies that Mary forgot the humanity of Jesus and was preoccupied with his divinity. Here I detect a neoplatonic flight from the body (we know that the English author belonged to the Dionysian tradition) and a certain fear of the senses. Perhaps the author feared an erotic interpretation of this beautiful scene.

How different is the approach of St Teresa of Avila! She never wants to forget the humanity of Jesus, however deep her mystical experience; and *for her this is possible because of her doctrine of interior senses*. Nor is this just her doctine; it is found in a whole tradition going right back to Origen who speaks of "the heavenly sensuality of those experienced in prayer."

This doctrine is found preeminently in St Ignatius who loves to introduce us to a world of inner seeing, hearing, smelling, touching, tasting, savouring. This is no world of pure spirit. It is a world of flesh and blood, albeit of transformed, transfigured flesh and blood. Ignatius loved the *Anima Christi* wherein the inner senses shine forth brilliantly, even shockingly. "Blood of Christ, inebriate me" runs the prayer; as though one were to cry:

> "Blood of Christ, make me drunk!"

And it goes on:

"Hide me within thy wounds!"

Surely these words have no meaning outside a mystical world of transfigured sensation.[3]

Joined to this, Ignatius had a strong sense of history. After his conversion he wanted to go to the Holy Land. He wanted to see the place where Jesus Christ lived and died. He was aware of the most minute details. And when he asks us to kneel at the foot of the cross to be inebriated with the blood of Christ and to hide within his wounds, Ignatius is keenly aware that *this crucifixion really happened*. What a combination of history and mysticism! What a sense of the reality of the Incarnation!

Let me add a word. I write these pages in the Philippines at a small village outside Manila. Around me I have seen simple people touching and kissing statues of Our Lord. I have seen them rubbing the statue with their handkerchiefs and then rubbing the same handkerchiefs all over their bodies and the bodies of their children. I know that this shocks some visitors. But to me it is profoundly Christian, and it even contains an element of mysticism – mysticism of the senses. The people are immersing themselves in the humanity of Jesus. The sense of touch is deeply significant for them. Blood of Christ inebriate me! Hide me within thy wounds!

VI

The church fathers loved to quote the words of Paul: "But put on the Lord Jesus . . ." (Romans 13:14). Here Paul is asking us to put on Jesus as we put on a garment – to be clothed with him. And later authors ask to be naked of self and clothed with Christ.

And being clothed with him we identify with him in his death and resurrection. Union with Jesus is not something static but a living out of the Pauline ideal "that I may share his suffering, becoming like him in his death that if possible I may attain the resurrection from the dead" (Philippians 3:10, 11). And in Romans Paul writes: "If we have died with Christ, we believe that we shall also live with him" (Romans 6:8). And in Galatians: "I have been crucified with Christ . . ." (Galatians 2:20).

As the eyes of Jesus were always fixed on the Father, so are the eyes of one who says: "It is no longer I who live but Christ who lives in me" (Galatians 2:20). And so, as friendship develops it leads to identification with the one we love. Identified with Jesus and filled with the Spirit, we cry out: "Abba, Father!" Now we have entered with Jesus into the inner life of the Trinity. Here is the apex of Christian mysticism.

VII

Christianity, then, is intensely human and intensely incarnational. Paul, great mystic that he was, tells the Corinthians that he "decided to know nothing . . . except Jesus Christ and him crucified" (1 Corinthians 2:2). John, the mystical eagle, soars to heaven with his eyes fixed on Jesus: for in Jesus he sees the Father. Francis of Assisi, Ignatius of Loyola, Teresa of Avila — they all soar to heaven not by forgetting Jesus but through him, with him, and in him.

For this human Jesus born of the Virgin Mary is also divine. He invites us to share in his divinity, to become children of God, to enter the very life of the Trinity, where with him and in the Spirit we cry out: "Abba, Father!"

I said that the word *mysticism* was originally associated with mystery. And what mystery is more sublime than this?

NOTES

1. *Dei Verbum* C.1, 5; *The Documents of Vatican II*, ed. Walter M. Abbott (New York: American Press, 1966), p. 113.
2. *The Cloud of Unknowing and the Book of Privy Counselling*, ed. and trans. William Johnston (New York: Doubleday Image Books, 1973), ch. 17, p. 71.
3. For a development of this theme, see my *The Mirror Mind* (San Francisco: Harper & Row; London: William Collins, 1981), ch. 6.

10

Eucharistic mysticism (1)

I

I have said that in Christian mysticism one may not deliberately forget the humanity of Christ: we cannot sidestep the Incarnation. If we do, we may eventually forget not only the humanity of Jesus but everyone's humanity, including our own. We may find ourselves forgetting the Jesus who is in the poor and the sick and the oppressed. We may forget the whole social dimension of Christianity in favour of a vague, cosmic religion of pure spirit which tries to go directly to the godhead.

"I see this in theory," you say. "But I am perplexed. Are you trying to push me back to the old discursive prayer with its images and pictures of Jesus? Besides, where is this humanity of Jesus? Where can I find him?"

Here we get some help from the Council. Speaking about the work of redemption, it outlines the modes on which Christ is present:

> To accomplish so great a work, Christ is always present in His Church, especially in her liturgical celebrations. He is present in the sacrifice of the Mass, not only in the person of His minister, "the same one now offering, through the ministry of priests, who formerly offered Himself on the cross," but especially under the Eucharistic species. By His power He is present in the sacraments, so that when a man baptizes it is really Christ Himself who baptizes. He is present, finally, when the Church prays and sings, for He promised: "Where two or three are gathered together for my sake there am I in the midst of them. (Mattthew 18:20).[1]

Now draw the practical conclusion from the above. Jesus is present in the Eucharist. He is present when you read the Bible, including the Old Testament. He is present in the community where two or three are gathered in his name. He is also present (though the Council, speaking in a luturgical context, does not here mention the fact) in the hungry, the thirsty, the naked, the imprisoned. You may have no picture of him. You may not be able to describe him. You may say in astonishment: "Lord when did we see thee hungry and feed thee, or thirsty and give thee drink?" (Matthew 25:37). You may recognize his presence only through naked faith. But believe that he is really there. *As his presence is mystery, so an experienced grasp of his presence is mysticism.*

In this chapter I would like to reflect on his presence in the Eucharist. I believe that this is a real presence. The Eucharist is a symbol but it is also the reality: it is a symbol which contains the reality. One thing is sure: Christians have always believed that it is the body of Christ – not just his soul, not just his divinity, but also his body.

II

Let me begin with the primitive Christian community. Whatever definition one gives to mysticism, it is impossible to deny that the first disciples underwent profound mystical experience. It all began when Jesus was crucified. This was their dark, dark night, when their grief and depression knew no bounds and they were brought to the brink of despair. But as the mother who was in travail is flooded with ecstatic joy at the birth of her child, so the sorrow of Calvary turned into the overwhelming joy of the resurrection and the ascension, reaching a great climax at pentecost. In all this, the disciples were filled with the unrestricted love that goes on and on and on. Their consciousness was expanded when suddenly they recognized him in the breaking of bread or standing by the sea. Their experience needed no proof for it was total and self-authenticating. Above all, through this series of shocks they underwent profound conversion of heart. Transformed and changed out of all recognition they fearlessly proclaimed the good news. Who can doubt that the earliest Christian experience was intensely mystical?

At the Last Supper, his farewell meal, Jesus had taken bread and blessed and broke it saying, "This is my body which is given for you. Do this in remembrance of me." And likewise the cup after supper saying, "This cup which is poured out for you is the new covenant in my blood" (Luke 22:19, 20). At that time Jesus, foreseeing Calvary, accepted his death as the offering of himself to the Father for the redemption of the world. Now, after his ascension, his disciples, faithful to his word, gathered together to break bread and to remember that saving event. When I say "remember" I do not mean that they recalled something that happened in the past but that *they made the event present*. This was the remembering which brought Christ in his redemptive act into their very midst so that subsequent generations would speak of "the real presence," would believe that the bread and wine are changed into the body and blood of Christ, and would chant the anamnesis:

> When we eat this bread
> And drink this cup
> We proclaim your death, Lord Jesus,
> Until you come in glory.

I said the Christians gathered for the breaking of bread. They also told the story of Jesus and later this story became the New Testament. And it was the combination of word and sacrament and loving community that created the mystical experience, a mystical experience of the individual and of the group.

And in all this let me again underline the historical dimension of Christian mysticism. The Christian community did not, and does not, bring about a repetition of what happened on Calvary. "For we know that Christ being raised from the dead will never die again; death no longer has dominion over him" (Romans 6:9). What happened in history once and for all enters into our place and our time – and it will do so until the Parousia, or Second Coming. Such is the incarnational and historical dimension of the Christian mystical experience.

But, alas, human nature is not always geared to mysticism. Already in the early days, the meal in Corinth became rowdy and unmystical. Paul scolds his spiritual children vigorously: "When you meet together it is not the Lord's supper you eat. For in eating, each one goes ahead with his own meal, and one is hungry and another is drunk" (1 Corinthians 11:20, 21). And then, recalling the night on which Jesus was betrayed, Paul insists on the reverence with which one should eat and drink, lest one profane the body and blood of the Lord.

And through the centuries the Christian community has remembered-and-made-present the mystery of Christ. At times this had been, and still is, a powerful mystical experience. At other times, as in Corinth, "each one goes ahead with his own meal, and one is hungry and another is drunk." And so it will be until be comes in glory.

III

"But now you upset all my ideas," you say. "You turn me upside down! I thought of my mysticism as a very spiritual experience: you say it is incarnational and you even associate it with eating! I thought of mysticism as outside time and space: you focus on an event which took place at a specific time in a specific place. I thought of mysticism as intensely individual and solitary: you associate it with a community. You shock me!"

I hear what you say. As I write this book I realize more and more that Christian mysticism is indeed unique. But let me make a few points of explanation.

First of all, a mysticism of eating is not foreign to Asia. Think of the aesthetic and spiritual dimension of the Chinese cuisine. Think of the Japanese tea ceremony. Westerners in the seventeenth century were astonished and amused that Japanese should develop an art and a spirituality of drinking tea.

And in the Jewish tradition also we find a mysticism of the meal. I myself had some experience of this when I was invited to share a paschal meal with some Jewish friends in Jerusalem. The father blessed his children; he read Exodus and explained it to them while they cheerfully asked questions. We drank our four glasses of wine and enjoyed a family meal. Then I realized existentially that eating can be a religious experience. I got an inkling into that paschal meal at which Jesus instituted the Eucharist.

Again, at Qumran, I visited the ruins of the Essenes' dining room with the lectern where a monk read the Bible to the assembled community. Then I recalled how in the Christian monastic tradition also the refectory was a holy place, a place of silence where the Scriptures were read while the community ate. And, interestingly enough, something similar is found in Buddhist monasticism.

Eating, ordinary eating, is sacred for two reasons. First, because it is a celebration of death and life. The fruits of the earth die in order to come to life within us and as part of us. Second, the meal is sacred because it is a sign and a pledge of the friendship and love that exists between those who eat together.

It is not surprising, then, that Jesus should carry out a large part of his public ministry at meals. It is not surprising to see him feed the five thousand. It is surprising, but beautifully surprising, to see him eat with tax collectors and sinners. The meals about which we read in the gospel all point to that supreme banquet where Jesus says: "I am the bread of life" (John 6:48) and, "Truly, truly, I say to you, unless you eat the flesh of the Son of man and drink his blood, you have no life in you" (John 6:53).

And so we celebrate the mystical banquet: "Your fathers ate the manna in the wilderness, and they died. This is the bread which comes down from heaven, that a man may eat of it and not die" (John 6:49, 50). For many Christians the moments after receiving the Eucharist are profoundly mystical. They savour and taste the bread of life; they become aware of the extraordinary union of love that exists between themselves and their Lord. With Paul they cry: "It is no longer I who live, but Christ who lives in me . . ." (Galatians 2:20). Now they know that their true life lies hidden with Christ in God. Now they can say: "For me to live is Christ, and to die is gain" (Philippians 1:21). Now they feel that they are being transformed so that Jesus comes to see through their eyes, to hear through their ears, to bless through their hands, to love through their hearts. I here spell out in words what they feel; but the actual experience may be one of total silence, an intensely felt presence, a loving union, a mystical ecstasy.

IV

The Eucharist has both a personal and community dimension. And today we feel drawn more and more to emphasize the community dimension, to emphasize with Paul that "because there is one bread, we who are many are one body, for we all partake of the one bread" (1 Corinthians 10:17), to stress with John that Jesus is the true vine and we the branches.

In fact the Eucharist has always been the key to Christian community, since it forms a bond which is far beyond the natural love of human beings one for another – or perhaps it is more correct to say that it transforms the natural love of human beings one for another. This has been particularly evident in monastic and religious life where "the community liturgy" has been the key to everything. Through the community liturgy a real mysticism of interpersonal relations has slowly developed. And when I say a real mysticism I do not mean that communities have always enjoyed a rich sense of God's loving presence. From what I have said in this book it will be clear that absence, abandonment, anxiety, depression, struggle, failure, and dark night are built into mysticism. And this holds true not only for the individual but also for communities.

We know that whole communities pass collectively through dark and harrowing nights. If they then knew what was happening! If they then knew that their darkness and suffering is a very real experience of God's presence! If they knew this, they might pass triumphantly through death to resurrection, as the apostolic community passed through the anguish of Calvary to the joy of Pentecost.

Here I speak of community mysticism in monastic life. Until our day this eucharistic mysticism of community has been little developed in lay communities and in married life. But we are now in an age of the laity, an age when we know that all Christians are called to holiness and to mysticism; and the time has come for us to investigate and to live out a eucharistic mysticism of lay community and of family life. This is surely one of the great challenges of our day.

And let me add one word. Aquinas describes beautifully how

the Eucharist is the centre of Christian sacramental life – all the sacraments, he says, point towards it. I myself always had difficulty in seeing how the sacrament of matrimony points towards the Eucharist. Only now do I get some inkling. For the Eucharist is the body of Christ and, properly understood, it will lead us to a whole theology of the body and even of sexuality. Moreover, the Eucharist is the key to community; and what community is more vital in human life than the family?

V

For from the rising of the sun to its setting my name is great among the nations, and in every place incense is offered to my name, and a pure offering; for my name is great among the nations, says the Lord of hosts.   (Malachi 1:11).

The church fathers loved to quote the above words from the prophet Malachi, applying them to the eucharistic sacrifice which from East to West is always offered to the Father for the redemption of the world. At any given moment the great event of salvation is somewhere remembered-and-made-present; and the faithful have been encouraged to pause for a moment in a busy day to unite themselves with this earthshaking event.

In the early days the Eucharist was reserved after the celebration to be brought to the sick and dying. And today we still have the beautiful word *viaticum* meaning "food for the journey," the journey of death. Christians, moreover, were permitted to retain the sacred species in their homes for this purpose.

From this there naturally developed the custom of revering and honouring and adoring the Eucharist, though this custom became widespread only from the ninth century. Then came the feast of *Corpus Christi* (the Body of Christ) with eucharistic processions and prayer before the Blessed Sacrament. About this I shall speak at greater length in the next chapter. Here only let me say that reservation of the sacrament gave a great incentive to Christian prayer and Christian mysticism.

Yes, I hear what you say. You have read that this medieval eucharistic piety was too individualistic, that it separated the body of Christ from the liturgical celebration, that it encouraged a static devotion to Jesus while overlooking *the event* which is the very core of his redemptive work.

There is some truth in all this. However, it simply reminds us that misunderstanding and abuses always creep into religious life and that reformation is always needed. For eucharistic piety *need not* be individualistic, as I have repeatedly pointed out. And it *need not* neglect the great event of our salvation. For whenever one looks at the tabernacle wherein the sacred species are reserved, one can recite the anamnesis: "Christ has died; Christ has risen: Christ will come again." In other words, one can recall the whole mystery of Christ, not just his static and individual presence.

Let us not forget that prayer before the tabernacle has nourished the spiritual life of millions of Christians. Even today if you visit a church in Manila or Belfast, in Tokyo or Hong Kong, you will find people kneeling in silent prayer. Often this is prayer of petition; or it is thanksgiving; or it is that familiarity with Jesus that I described in the last chapter. Sometimes people recite the rosary, recalling the mystery of Christ in the company of the Virgin Mary; sometimes they use no words but relish and taste that the Lord is sweet. This is indeed a prayer of the people, of the masses of the people.

"But," you say, "is it scriptural? Is it found in the New Testament?"

To this I answer that as there is a development of doctrine within Christianity, so there is development of religious experience. No sensible theologian thinks that we should preach to modern New York or Tokyo exactly what Paul taught to Corinth. Everybody knows that doctrines develop and change and are adapted as they enter new cultures and as, under the guidance of the Spirit, the community gets new insights. If we were to maintain that people today should pray and sing and celebrate liturgy as did the early Christians, we would get bogged down in a biblical fundamentalism: we would lose the richness which Christianity possesses precisely because of its universality, its openness to all cultures, its willingness to make progress and to develop.

Obviously we need norms to test the validity of later developments and adaptations. Let us recall (and let theologians recall) the old theological adage, *lex orandi: lex credendi:* the way of praying is a norm of faith. The word of God is found not only in the Scriptures but also in the living faith and worship of the masses of the people in union with their shepherds.

VI

But does the eucharistic community isolate Christians? Does it separate us from the world community of Jews and Moslem, Buddhist and Hindu, agnostic and atheist? Does it separate us from men and women of science, from all those who have no faith in Jesus and his risen presence?

Again, this is a challenge we Christians have not yet adequately faced. Ideally, the eucharistic community is a sign of the unity of all men and women. Ideally, it should point to, should lead to, unity and peace among all peoples and nations. That we have not yet succeeded in living the Eucharist in this powerfully unifying way is all too clear. This is yet another challenge for tomorrow.

NOTE
1. *Sacrosanctum Concilium* C.1, 5; *The Documents of Vatican II*, ed. Walter M. Abbot (New York: American Press, 1966), 113).

11

Eucharistic mysticism (2)

I

I once heard a Zen Master lecture on Buddhist and Christian symbolism. He spoke of the Buddha on the lotus as the central Buddhist symbol and of Jesus nailed to the cross as the central Christian symbol. Afterwards, having occasion to speak with him, I said that while the cross is undoubtedly a great Christian symbol, Christianity has a more important symbol, namely, the Eucharist. For while the cross speaks of the death of Jesus, the Eucharist speaks not only of his death but also of his resurrection and second coming: *Christ has died; Christ has risen; Christ will come again.*

The point is important. Every student of religion knows that symbols are of the very essence of religion and of mysticism. Symbols, and symbols alone, can carry us to mystical levels of awareness and to states of consciousness which are completely unknown to dry, discursive theology. I used to think naively that Zen Buddhism was without symbols because of its stress on emptiness and nothingness and "no dependence on words and letters." Now I realize that the very emptiness and nothingness are symbols as also are the lotus posture and the rhythmic breathing. Now I know that Zen is full of symbols.

One of the characteristics of the Judeo-Christian tradition is that the most important symbols are also historical events or historical persons. The Eucharist is a symbol and it is also the reality: the body of Christ. It is the true bread, the true manna which came down from heaven and gives life to the world.

Bread is indeed a powerful symbol. Alas, those who live in the first world do not appreciate bread because they have it in abundance and have never experienced hunger. Let them go to the third world. Let them see people undernourished, people starving, people desperate because they have no bread for their children, then they will realize that every scrap of bread is precious. Then they will appreciate the delicate command of Jesus: "Gather up the fragments left over, that nothing may be lost" (John 6:12). The children of Israel, starving in Sinai, appreciated the gift of bread; and the gospel tells us that what they, and we, really desire is the true bread which gives eternal life. This is Jesus who makes the extraordinary claim that "he who comes to me shall not hunger, and he who believes in me shall never thirst" (John 6:35).

II

Now there is a way of prayer which consists in being present to the symbol. To be present to the symbol does not mean thinking about the symbol or forming a picture of the symbol or even staring at the symbol. In Asia, where the art of presence is highly developed, one can learn to sit cross-legged, to breathe from the abdomen, to still the mind, to fix one's attention on a single object or a single point – and in this way to be totally present to the symbol. This is presence of mind and body and spirit; this is presence of conscious and unconscious mind. What a wonderful art!

But even without this art one can be totally present through love. For love engages the whole person drawing all the faculties, conscious and unconscious, to the one we love.

And in a Christian context one can learn to be totally present, lovingly present, to a crucifix or to an ikon or to a text of Scripture or to the greatest symbol: the Eucharist. Now we are present not to an object but to a person, to a loving person who has died for us. He engages not only our mind but also our heart – our affective life, our love, our all. United with this person and with the drama in which he is the chief actor we are transformed (forgive me for saying it again) and cry out with Paul: "It is no longer I who live, but Christ who lives in me" (Galatians 2:20).

Such is the symbolism of bread. But I find another richly symbolic aspect to the Eucharist. Before speaking about it, permit me by way of a digression to say something about the *mandala* in Asian thought.

III

The word *mandala* means circle. Sometimes the circle is empty: at other times it contains all kinds of buddhas and bodhisattvas. Hindus and Buddhists regard it as a source of great psychic energy. Indeed, there is a saying attributed to the Buddha: "When you fix your heart on one point, then nothing is impossible for you." When one fixes one's heart on the mandala then one becomes very, very powerful.

The mandala can be used in many ways. One can be totally present to the mandala, thus using it as an aid to meditation. Or one can draw one's mandala daily, watching it change and develop. Or one can dance the mandala. or one can form the mandala with one's body, as happens when one adopts the Lotus posture forming the "cosmic mudra" with thumbs lightly touching while the arms form a beautiful circle. Again, prayer beads are a mandala as also is the Asian prayer wheel. In all these cases the symbolism of the circle is of the greatest significance.

I said the mandala is a source of great psychic energy. Now let me say that this energy flows chiefly in two areas.

First, the circle is a symbol of integration, of wholeness, of perfection, and finally of enlightenment. Underlying this is the realization that human nature, inwardly torn and divided, is in great need of healing. We are all wounded because of the imbalance between the *yin* and the *yang*, between the unconscious and the conscious, between the feminine and the masculine. By being present to the mandala, by interiorizing it, by *becoming* it, we attain to psychic wholeness and to enlightenment.

Zen masters claim that they can gauge the degree of a person's enlightenment from the circle he or she draws. Conversely Jung, who sometimes got his patients to draw mandalas, claimed that he could gauge the degree of sickness or health from a person's mandala. I might add in passing that for some years Jung drew his own mandala each day and saw reflected therein the picture of his own psychic development. He also claimed that as the Buddha is the centre of the Buddhist mandala, so Christ is the centre of the Christian mandala. And Christians who like to draw the mandala sometimes confirm Jung's intuition.

Second, the mandala is a cosmic symbol. By interiorizing the symbol I break out of my narrow individuality, becoming one with the circle and one with the universe. In India the mandala is sometimes a symbol of God.

When I became interested in the Asian mandala and then looked at my Christian heritage I began to see mandalas every where. It was as though Christian artists and theologians had stumbled on this powerful symbol without being explicitly aware of its inner psychological dynamics. And so I saw mandalas in the stained glass windows of the great cathedrals as well as in the rosary beads. Theologically I saw a mandala in the Thomistic doctrine that through contemplation we who are wounded and divided in *the state of fallen nature* return by a cyclic process to *the state of integrity* or *the state of innocence* – the state of our first parents who, in paradise, were naked and unashamed. Here, too, the circle is a symbol of healing, of wholeness, of integrity.

However, through this apparent digression, I am leading to something highly significant. I believe that the Eucharist, particularly when circular bread was used and placed in the monstrance before the people, became the great Christian mandala.

Do not misunderstand me. I realize that the shape of the bread is not of central importance. What matters is the body of the Lord, the true bread which came down from heaven. Nevertheless, granted that faith is the central thing, it is also interesting to reflect that the ordinary laws of psychology are at work. If it is true (and I believe it is) that the circle is a source of psychic power to integrate and to make cosmic, then the use of the monstrance and the circular eucharistic bread was a great insight and a great step forward in the history of Christian religious experience. Let me say more about this.

IV

In primitive Christianity, as I have already said, the Eucharist was primarily a liturgical act by which the community remembered-and-made-present the sacrificial meal of Jesus with his disciples.

"Dying you destroyed our death; rising you restored our life; Lord Jesus, come in glory."

In the thirteenth and fourteenth centuries, however, there arose new forms of eucharistic piety which were to exercise the most profound influence on Catholic prayer and worship from that time until this very day. It all began with the desire of the people, the masses of the people, to gaze on the body of the Lord with faith and love and devotion. Put in modern terms, *they wanted to fix their eyes on the symbol.* And the bishops, partly because they saw this as a response to certain Christological and eucharistic errors and partly because they saw it as the work of the Spirit in the people, encouraged the celebrant to raise the Sacred Host after the consecration.

This custom spread rapidly throughout Europe; and we hear of pious people running enthusiastically from church to church to be present at the elevation of the host and to gaze lovingly at the body of the Lord. Nor was this devotion confined to the common people. In 1210 the bishop of Paris had ordered the Sacred Host to be elevated; and in the same year this custom was adopted in all Cistercian monasteries. And in 1222 it was prescribed for the Carthusians. In England and France there arose the custom of hanging a black curtain behind the altar so that the white host would stand out clearly against the dark backdrop. Later came the custom of making the prayer, "My Lord and my God" as one gazed on the elevated host – and this custom has survived until our day.

In 1215 the doctrine of transubstantiation, formulated by Peter of Lombard in the twelfth century was defined by the Fourth Lateran Council. And in 1264 the feast of *Corpus Christi,* which had been celebrated locally, was extended to the universal church. With it came processions and prolonged eucharistic prayer.

In the fourteenth century the monstrance or *ostensorium* in which is enthroned the Blessed Sacrament, first appeared in France and Germany; and again this eucharistic devotion was greeted with enthusiasm and spread throughout Europe like wildfire. The making of the monstrance became a fine art. Some were made as statues of Jesus; others of Mary holding the host in upraised arms. Some were very ornate and elaborate; others were so large that they were carried through the streets in carts. Today the custom of prayer and meditation before the monstrance is deeply rooted in the Latin Church and in those countries influenced by the Latin Church. From Manila to New York and from Dublin to São Paolo this eucharistic prayer is a devotion of the masses of the people.

And the Eucharist enthroned in the monstrance has all the properties of the mandala. One is present to it, totally present. One interiorizes it by eating or (if this is not possible) by a spiritual communion in which by ardent desire one receives the body of the Lord into the depths of one's being. As one assimilates the Eucharist one is filled with the most tremendous energy – for the bread is food not only for the body but also for the spirit: "Truly, truly, I say to you, unless you eat the flesh of the Son of man and drink his blood, you have no life in you" (John 6:53). And this bread of life is medicinal, healing, leading to integration of the personality, pointing beyond *the state of integrity* to the resurrection, which is *the state of glory.*

Again, the Eucharist is a cosmic symbol. Through reception of this sacrament we are united not only with the individual Jesus but with the whole Christ. We are united with those who have gone before us, with those in the state of purification, with the poor and the sick and the oppressed; for all are his members. Indeed we are united with the whole human family each of whom is related to the risen Lord in a way that surpasses human understanding.

V

Now let me come to a practical point.

Everyone knows that throughout the Christian world there is a longing for deep meditation – not for discursive meditation – but for the quiet contemplative prayer that leads to deeper states of consciousness. Put more clearly, there is a longing for mysticism.

Now I submit the thesis that the answer to this yearning is the Eucharist. Moreover, I submit the thesis that the monstrance is of central importance. In the past the faithful have prayed vocally:

now they can be encouraged to pray silently. For our time I believe it is good to have a very simple circular monstrance in which the Blessed Sacrament is exposed. It can be placed on a low table; and people who like to sit cross-legged or in the lotus posture or on a low prayer stool, regulating their breath and stilling their mind, can do so. In any case they can learn to be totally present to the symbol – just being – remembering that in this case *being* equals *being-in-love*. When this is proposed, my experience and the experience of others is that ordinary people glide into deeper states of consciousness with the utmost ease.

Needless to say, we must recall that the eucharistic presence is a prolongation of the liturgical drama: "Christ has died; Christ has risen; Christ will come again." "It is no longer I who live but Christ who lives in me." "Abba, Father!" We can remain without words in a total and loving presence.

VI

I have spoken of total presence to the symbol, of interiorizing the symbol, of becoming one with the symbol; and all this means total presence to the Lord, interiorizing the Lord, becoming one with the Lord. Now following on this one can make a prayer of offering, a prayer whereby, united with Jesus, one offers oneself to the Father in the Spirit. I spell it out in words but the offering can be made in wordless silence.

Here let me say that prayer of offering is eminently eucharistic. This is because the Last Supper was a sacrifice in which Jesus offered himself to the Father for the salvation of the world. The church stressed this point and spoke of the Eucharist as the fulfillment of all the sacrifices of the Old Testament beginning with that of Abraham, who was willing to sacrifice his son, Isaac.

During the eucharistic liturgy the faithful have always been encouraged to offer themselves with Jesus. As a sign of this they sometimes carry in procession to the altar the bread and wine which will be offered during the sacrifice, as well as other gifts symbolizing the offering of their hears and their lives. In this way they are encouraged to offer their whole selves to the Father.

Now this offering, made briefly during the eucharistic celebration, needs to be prolonged. And I might say in passing that this is one more reason for reserving the Eucharist in the tabernacle or in the monstrance: simply that the time of liturgy is short and mystical experience takes time. Sometimes for one flash of loving insight one must spend fifty minutes of boredom. Consequently the time of liturgy alone will not ordinarily suffice for mysticism. But let me return to the prayer of offering.

As I have said, this offering can be made while one sits before the monstrance interiorizing the Eucharist so that the mystery of Christ is not just "out there" but also "in here." And now, one with Jesus or clothed with Jesus, I offer myself to the Father for the salvation of the world. Such prayer is very traditional. Take, for instance, the well-known prayer of Ignatius *Sume et suscipe* ("Take and Receive"), a prayer which I myself now take in a eucharistic context. This is an act of total offering and it can be an act of mystical offering. Let me explain.

Early in the *Spiritual Exercises* Ignatius speaks of a discursive prayer wherein one freely uses one's memory, understanding, and will. But now, at the end, he proposes something different. Now he says in effect: "Lord, take my memory – *I will not remember*. Take my understanding – *I will not think*. Take my will – *I will make no colloquy*." And in this way I am brought into silence, into mystical silence, without words or reasoning or petition. Now I enter a new state of awareness where words are no longer necessary. Yet I do not reject words and phrases. Rather do I say: "If you want me to remember, make me remember. If you want me to think, make me think. If you want me to petition, make the petition within me." This is the summit of *wu-wei* or nonaction, the summit of letting God act. This is the true void. Here is mysticism at its height.

And so again we have in the presence of the Eucharist a prayer of total silence – but now of silent or blind offering. It is a silence which is Trinitarian, since one with Jesus I offer myself to the Father in the Spirit. If words do escape my lips they will likely be: "Abba, Father!"

In a similar vein there developed over the past few centuries the pious custom of daily offering one's total self – prayers, works, actions, sufferings – to the Father in union with the eucharistic sacrifice of Jesus. This was known as the morning offering. Followed through in a radical way it could lead to high mysticism. It is furthermore interesting to recall that the Council, speaking of the universal vocation to holiness, points to martyrdom as the supreme offering and the supreme testimony of love:

> From the earliest time, then, some Christians have been called upon – and some will always be called upon – to give this supreme testimony of love to all men and women, but especially to persecutors. The Church, therefore, considers martyrdom as an exceptional gift and as the highest proof of love . . . By martyrdom a disciple is transformed into an image of his Master . . .[1]

Since these lines were written many Christians have offered their lives not only in the traditional style of martyrdom but also as martyrs for social justice. Surely this total holocaust is the apex of eucharistic mysticism: the offering of one's all to the Father in union with Jesus.

VII

For the bread is broken. Jesus took bread and blessed and broke and gave to his disciples. This is no mere convention. The eucharistic bread is broken because Jesus was broken when he died on the cross and the martyrs were broken when their blood flowed out on the parched earth. And we also are broken in order to be healed and remade.

As the eucharistic mandala is broken, it points towards an even more mysterious mandala: the Trinity. The old theologians spoke of the circle of *circumincessio*, the circle of the indwelling of the Son in the Father and the Father in the Son and of both in the Spirit. We also enter into this cyclic process in accordance with those words of Jesus in the fourth gospel: "In that day you will know that I am in my Father, and you in me, and I in you" (John 14:20). And it is through the Eucharist that we enter into the Trinity – identified with the Son we live in the Father and in the

Spirit. In this way the Eucharist leads to the ultimate and eschatological mandala which is the Trinity.

NOTE
1. *Lumen Gentium* C.5, 42; *The Documents of Vatican II*, ed. Walter M. Abbot (New York: American Press, 1966), p. 71).

12

Mysticism and life

I

One of the great religious problems of our day is the cleavage between prayer and life. We all know of pious people who patronize the church on Sunday; who swindle, cheat, and exploit the poor from Monday till Saturday; and who kneel piously in the pews on the following Sunday. Nor are the mystics exempt from such aberrations. Here we must be honest. Look at history and you will see clerics, mystical people, who were cruel, unjust, ruthless, and unscrupulous in daily life – and then they went devoutly to their morning *prie-dieu*, blotted the whole thing out and piously entered the cloud of unknowing. Alas and alack for the weakness of human nature! In varying degrees we all do this. We blot out of consciousness the things we don't want to see.

Jung speaks of *the shadow*. This is not just our evil side. It includes *everything we do not want to see*. We love the darkness, "And this is the judgement, that the light has come into the world, and men loved darkness rather than light because their deeds were evil" (John 3:19). Even the most consummate mystic has his or her shadow, his or her blind spots, his or her unregenerate areas. To have a shadow is part of the human condition: it is a consequence of what we call original sin.

This, then, is a problem we must confront in the life of prayer and the life of mysticism. And what I want to suggest in this chapter is eminently practical. I say: *Let life flow into your prayer and let prayer flow into your life*. Be open in prayer. Face your shadow. Do not blot things out. Take them in and be present to life when you are present to God. Learn the great art of being present to God, to yourself, and to life.

II

As an example of one who was present to God, to herself, and to life, I propose the Virgin Mary as she appears in the pages of the third gospel. Here we read that Mary and Joseph came down from Nazareth to Bethlehem, where Jesus was born. And Luke writes: "But Mary kept all these things, pondering them in her heart" (Luke 2:19). What was Mary pondering in her heart? No doubt the journey from Nazareth, the rejection of Jesus at the inn, the birth of the child, the visit of the shepherds. Her life was flowing into her prayers. She was turning over in her heart the happenings of these days. This is not discursive prayer: it is a savouring, a tasting, a relishing, a wondering, a contemplative presence to God, to self, and to life.

And at the end of the same chapter a similar sentence occurs. Jesus had been lost. Mary and Joseph, after a three-day search, found him in the temple. And his mother (was she angry? or just bewildered?) complained: "Son, why have you treated us so?" (Luke 2:48). And Jesus answered: "How is it that you sought me? Did you not know that I must be in my Father's house?" (Luke 2:49). And Luke ends the chapter by telling us that "his mother kept all these things in her heart" (Luke 2:51).

They did not understand. Nor were they the first parents who could not understand their child. "How is it that you sought me?" This was like a zen *koan*. How could they not seek him?

Mary kept these things in her heart. Her life was flowing into her prayer; and she lived in silent wonder.

And was the whole life of Mary a similar prayer? When Simeon said that a sword would pierce her soul, when she followed Jesus in his public life, when she stood at the foot of the cross – was she constantly pondering these things in her heart? The Lukan portrait of Mary, the mystic, would suggest that this indeed was so.

For the prayer of Mary was penetrated with yet another mystical word: *Fiat*. "Behold I am the handmaid of the Lord; let it be to me according to your word" (Luke 1:38). It was as though she said: "Let God act; I will not put obstacles in His way; I welcome His action; I will cooperate." And this word *fiat* echoed in her heart as she pondered the events of life.

With this *fiat* something momentous happened not only in Mary's womb but also in her mind and heart. An inner revolution took place as she accepted her vocation and her destiny. And her greatness is precisely here. Remember how, much later, a woman raised her shrill voice in the crowd and shouted to Jesus: "Blessed is the womb that bore you and the breasts that you sucked!" But he said, "Blessed rather are those who hear the word of God and keep it" (Luke 11:27). He was saying that the sanctity of Mary was not just in her physical maternity but in her total acceptance of the word of God. *Fiat.*

I believe that the *fiat* is the key to mysticism. It is the Christian version of the Taoist wu-wei or noninterference. "Let life flow at its deepest level. Let the forces of the universe act. Let God act. I will not fight against His will."

And the *fiat* came swiftly and spontaneously to the lips of Mary because of a prior enlightenment: "Hail O favoured one, the Lord is with you" (Luke 1:28). Hearing these words Mary knows that she is loved, uniquely loved and lovable. She is without sin. And with the realization of God's love for her came the loving and trusting response of love for God. *Fiat.* Let it be done.

III

We are all invited to imitate the prayer of Mary. We can all ponder in our hearts the happenings of daily life and utter our fiat. Such prayer can be a modification of the prayer of quiet. It is as though there were two levels of psychic life or two states of consciousness existing at the same time. At one level we enjoy the obscure sense of presence and union – this is the level of the true self. And at another level the events of life are flowing in and out in an unstructured way.

Now it is all-important to remain attentive to God's presence at the deepest level. Do not *cling* to the events of life. Let them come and let them go, while you remain with God.

Literally anything can come into this kind of prayer; our joys, our sorrows, our anxieties, our successes – our temptations however sordid, our failures however humiliating, our hopes however sublime. Sooner or later our shadow will painfully surface; and if we face it squarely in God's presence we will come to the joy of self-acceptance and enlightenment.

Into this prayer come our neuroses, fears, hang-ups. Sometimes in this psychological age one hears: "Solve your psychological problems first and pray afterwards!" As if the gospel were for the psychologically healthy! In fact the gospel (and consequently Christian prayer) is for the neurotic, the psychotic, as well as for the sinner. Anything can come into the prayer and anything can be healed.

Again, the life of the senses can flow into this prayer. By this I mean the sound of the wind, the heat of the sun, the roar of the waves, the rustle of the leaves. I can walk through the forest aware of every sound, present to life, present to myself, present to God.

Or again, some people take their dreams into this prayer of pondering. It is not a question of interpreting the dream or understanding it, but rather of being present to it while, at a deeper level, I am present to God.

Now this kind of contemplation may sound very simple; and simple it is. But it can also be demanding. For if with Mary I am uttering my *fiat*, if I am surrendering to the deeper forces within me, if I am surrendering to God, then I am losing control. I am handing over to another. "It is no longer I who live but Christ who lives in me." And, of course, we all like to be in control; we all like to run our own ship. Where am I going? Where is this prayer leading me? What a risk! Now I am like Peter, to whom the Lord said: "Truly, truly I say to you, when you were young, you girded yourself and walked where you would; but when you are old, you will stretch out your hands, and another will gird you and carry you where you do not wish to go" (John 21:18).

We can be sure that as the *fiat* effected a profound revolution in Mary, so it will effect a profound revolution in us. This revolution is nothing less than metanoia or conversion of heart.

IV

This Marian contemplation is valuable for decision making. Again, one enters the state of consciousness where God is present; and into this void one brings the matter for discernment. It is not a question of searching for an answer but of being present and allowing the decision to be made (perhaps over a period of weeks or months) at the depths of one's being, at the level of one's true self.

And let me here pause to say that such contemplation is eminently suitable for the laity. We live in an age when Christians have to make decisions, sometimes agonizing decisions, in areas of economic, political, social life – decisions which may affect the lives of millions of people. Now there was a time when devout Christians asked the institutional church to make their decisions and the institutional church felt obliged to do so. But those days are gone. The Council speaks clearly of "the autonomy of earthly affairs" saying that the temporal order has its own laws in which the church is not competent. Concretely it advises the lay person:

> Let not lay people imagine that their pastors are always such experts, that to every problem which arises, however complicated, they can readily give them a concrete solution, or even that such is their mission. Rather, enlightened by Christian wisdom and giving close attention to the teaching authority of the Church, let lay people take on their own distinctive role.[1]

This short passage is in fact revolutionary. It indicates that we are moving out of the age when the institutional church could lay down the law on every subject, telling people what to do. We are now in an age of conscience. We are now in an age when people must make their own decisions. In this age the role of the institutional church is to teach the gospel and *to teach the people to pray and to discern*. Nor is ordinary prayer enough. Only through mystical prayer can people attain to the inner freedom whereby they will see what is right and have the courage to do it.

V

Again, this Marian contemplation can be of immense value for those who work in situations of extreme poverty and oppression. We all know that those who see exploitation, oppression, and injustice before their very eyes undergo great struggles. If you see innocent people beaten, humiliated, tortured, degraded by police and military; if you see them misrepresented by the press and calumniated by the establishment, what do you do? Some people get wild with anger; they cooperate with terrorism and join a campaign of bombing. Others get depressed and discouraged: they lose all hope. Others are paralyzed by fear. Others are attracted to a false ideology which perverts or twists the gospel. Others pray and let this painful situation flow into their prayer. What agonizing prayer! Now it is almost intolerable to sit still.

In these circumstances, let us remember that Mary pondered things in her heart as she saw her son unjustly condemned and crucified. What agonizing prayer! How difficult it was to utter that *fiat*! And we, too, if we ponder these things in our hearts, if we can be quiet when all hell breaks loose inside us, then the *fiat* will come; and it will bring new energy, new hope, new strength – not the energy and hope and strength which come from human nature but the energy and hope and strength which come from God. For the *fiat* is dynamic. It would be an abysmal understanding to think that *fiat* means: "Let the injustice and the oppression and the murder continue." It does not mean that. It means, "Let God act. Let God act within me at the deep, mystical level. Let the universe act. I will cooperate with the immense power deep in me and in the universe." What revolutionary energy is here!

VI

"But," you say, "is this mystical prayer? Can there be a mystical prayer wherein the content is the humdrum events of life or economics or civil war or oppression or the work in which I am engaged? Surely one forgets all this in authentic mystical experience."

Some mystics forget everything. But others do not. Take, for example, St Ignatius. Towards the end of his life he was writing *The Constitutions of the Society of Jesus*. If you or I were writing such a book we might say to ourselves: "When I go to pray I'll speak to God and forget about my book. I'll bury it beneath a cloud of forgetting. To think about it would be a distraction. Let me put it out of my mind and talk to God."

But Ignatius did not do this. Those constitutions were the warp and woof of his prayer, day after day. And while discerning about what he should write or not write he had abundant tears, visions of the Trinity, visions of Mary. Read his *Spiritual Diary*. It is a remarkable document showing the most profound coexistence of earth and heaven, of practical action and sublime mysticism.

But why speak of Ignatius when the same thing can be found in St Paul? Read the introduction of his epistles and you find that love for his flock and anxiety about his churches was the core of Paul's mysticism. "And so, from the day we heard of it, we have not ceased to pray for you, asking that you may be filled with the knowledge of his will . . ." (Colossians 1:19). In Paul there was no schizophrenic cleavage between his relationship with God and his relationship with people. It was all one. Life was flowing into his prayer as his prayer flowed into life.

VII

I have spoken about how the happenings of daily life can flow into our prayers as they flowed into the prayer of Mary. Now let me add another aspect of this Marian contemplation, an aspect that is peculiar to our day.

We know that in this century the human race has undergone a change of consciousness: we now share in what I might call a universal or global consciousness. By this I mean that we become increasingly aware of the joys and sufferings of the whole of humanity in a way which was impossible for St Ignatius or St John of the Cross or even for St Paul.

Now the Council encourages Christians to develop in themselves this consciousness of the world and this concern for the whole human family. The magnificent opening sentence of the document. *The Church Today*, runs as follows:

> The joys and the hopes, the griefs and the anxieties of the men and women of this age, especially those who are poor or in any way afflicted, these too are the joys and hopes, the griefs and anxieties of the followers of Christ.[2]

Here and elsewhere the Council asks us to resonate with the world while fostering in our hearts a sensitivity and a compassion for the poor and afflicted everywhere.

Now this affects prayer. It means that as prayer develops and as consciousness expands, we come to ponder in our hearts not only our own personal joys and sufferings but also the joys and sufferings of the whole world. Concretely, the oppression of the poor, the torture of the innocent, the agony of the third world, the injustice of the first world, the danger of nuclear war, the pollution of the atmosphere — all or any of these may enter into our prayer. The true follower of Christ has a heart that is open to the whole world. "Mary kept all these things pondering them in her heart."

But let me be realistic. The suffering of the world is immense; and each one of us cannot take responsibility for all that pain. Perhaps what is asked of us is a certain openness whereby we allow the Spirit to bring to our awareness those problems about which we should pray at any given time.

I hear you say: "That sounds fine. But what can I do about it? Little me? I am helpless in the face of such misery. Why should I worry my head off and make myself sick?"

And yet, even if you cannot do anything practical you can *suffer with* (this is the root meaning of compassion) and this is a value in itself. This was the prayer of Mary: a suffering with her son. And in our day such compassion does in fact achieve much. What we need is a conversion to justice and compassion on the part of a significant number of people. We need ten just men and women who will influence the collective unconscious, ten just men and women who will influence the Teilhardian *nousphere*. This is more important than the frenetic activity of thousands of others.

VIII

I hear you say: "But what about the cloud of forgetting? Does not the author of *The Cloud*, a writer you love and admire and about whom you have written profusely – does he not tell the contemplative to bury every single creature beneath a cloud of forgetting and go to God in naked silence?"

Quite frankly, I am not so enthusiastic about the cloud of forgetting as I once was. Yet I believe it is justifiable for several reasons.

First of all, forgetting everything is a transitional stage of purification. It is a time when one is liberated from clinging in order to remember with detachment and serenity.

Again, if while you are prayerfully pondering things in your mind and heart – if at this time you are swept into a cloud of unknowing, forgetting everything and present only to God, by all means follow that call. In a certain sense you forget everything, but in another sense you are present to the world in a new way. Some people, solitaries or hermits, are called precisely in this way. True, they forget the social suffering of the world, but they come up against the very source of evil in the dark night. This vocation I respect. I have written about it already in this book. I believe it is the sublime vocation of few people.

Finally, as life flows into prayer, so prayer must flow into life. The loving presence of God experienced in mystical prayer can be experienced also in the hurly-burly of life. The anguishing absence of God experienced in mystical prayer can be experienced in the hurly-burly of life. This is the ideal of contemplation in action.

NOTES
1. *Gaudium et Spes* C.4, 43; *The Documents of Vatican II*, ed. Walter M. Abbot (New York: America Press, 1966), p. 244.
2. ibid. p.199.

13

Mysticism and poverty

I

"Blessed are the poor . . ." These words welled up from the depths of his being. They were the very core of his message. "How happy are the poor! How really blessed are the poor!"

Exegetes have asked about the meaning of this gospel poverty. Some have said that the poor were the masses of the people in the Roman Empire who had to work in order to live. Others say that Jesus spoke of the *anawim,* those who, feeling their utter helplessness, relied only on God. *I myself believe that Jesus spoke primarily about himself.* And for this reason his words have power. If a bloated capitalist were to pull on his cigar and say that the poor are blessed, we would smile. But Jesus said it. He was talking out of his own experience of poverty and ecstatic joy. "How happy are the poor . . . !" This is the Jesus who was born in poverty, the Jesus for whom there was no room in the inn, the Jesus who had nowhere to lay his head. Above all, this is the Jesus who emptied himself, taking the form of a slave, who cried out, "Eloi, Eloi, lama sabacthani." And this same Jesus, out of the depths of lived experience, cries: "How happy, how blessed, how blissful are those who are poor!"

Such was the great mystical experience of Jesus. It was utterly radical in nature. It was a process which began in Bethlehem and reached a great climax on the cross when he emptied himself in a total kenosis. And he experienced the joy and the bliss of resurrection when God highly exalted him and bestowed on him the name which is above every name, "that at the name of Jesus every knee should bow in heaven and on earth and under the earth, and every tongue confess that Jesus Christ is Lord, to the glory of God the Father" (Philippians 2:10).

And the followers of Jesus share in his experience. They too become poor, radically poor; they too are exalted. Think of the

Virgin Mary who in the third gospel can speak of her kenosis saying that "he has regarded the low estate of his handmaid" only to add:

> For behold, henceforth, all generations will call me blessed. (Luke 1:48)

And the same pattern is found in Abraham who is willing to lose everything, even his son Isaac, and is exalted so that by his descendants all the nations of the earth shall bless themselves. Again, it is found in Peter who has left everything but will receive the hundredfold. Yes, the person who sells everything and gives to the poor in order to follow Jesus has blissful joy, has the most profound mystical experience. Such is the gospel promise.

And subsequent history confirms this. Think of Francis of Assisi who stripped himself naked, handed his clothes to his father, and said that his true Father was in heaven. How Francis loved the Lady Poverty! What joy he found in her sweet company! The mystical joy of radical poverty is a fact of experience. How often we hear people say that their time in prison – when they were oppressed and deprived of everything – was the happiest time of their life. In the very moment of total loss they experienced the exhilarating joy of resurrection. In losing their lives they found their lives.

Nor is there anything inhuman in this total loss. The fact is that as life goes on we must all lose everything. We grow old; we are stripped; we die. And if we accept this loss of all we find the joy of resurrection, not just after death but also here and now. Such is the pattern of human life. How happy are those who are poor!

II

In this book I planned to write little about Buddhism. Nevertheless I would like here to say a word about that great religion which has helped me understand more richly my Christian heritage.

Buddhist poverty is radical. One way of meditation is to sit cross-legged and recite the word *mu* with the exhalation of the breath. *Mu* means *nothing*; and as I breathe, I empty myself of clinging to all things. (Please note that I do not empty myself of all things but of clinging to all things.) And so I let go of clinging to material things such as money and possessions, of clinging to thinking and reasoning and rationalization, of clinging to my desire for revenge, to my pride, covetousness, lust, gluttony, envy, anger, and sloth. And now there comes a great liberation and a great enlightenment. Such is the joy of possessing nothing.

It should be noted that the great enemy is not money and possessions but covetousness, which can be a vice of rich and poor alike. As long as we covet things and cling to them we cannot be happy, as long as we multiply our needs we cannot be at rest, because these needs become so many burdens, so many chains keeping us in bondage. The gospel constantly warns us not to hoard – not to be like the man who builds bigger and bigger barns and then dies in his sleep. "Fool! This night your soul is required of you . . ." (Luke 12:20). This story makes sense to Buddhists. They understand well how Paul, once liberated, can call himself "poor yet making many rich, as having nothing yet possessing everything" (2 Corinthians 6:10).

The Christian, like the Buddhist, can pray with *mu*. His or her prayer can be a total self-emptying while awaiting the joyful enlightenment of resurrection. Christian prayer, however, will differ from that of the Buddist in that it is Christocentric. I empty myself in imitation of Jesus, in the company of Jesus, in love for Jesus. This emptying is a putting on of the mind of Christ Jesus who emptied himself taking the form of a slave and was exalted, so that every knee bows at the mention of his name. Indeed this is the process outlined by St John of the Cross who speaks graphically about *all and nothing (todo y nada)*. This is a living out of the gospel truth that in losing our life we find our life.

And there is another prayer of poverty suitable for Christians. One can simply sit cross-legged, empty, and naked before God. One is without words, without possessions, without thoughts, just being. Now one recognizes one's total poverty. Now one can cry from the heart: "Blessed are those who know that they are poor!" In the existential recognition of my own poverty I find enlightenment and strength. With Paul I exclaim: "When I am weak then I am strong" (2 Corinthians 12:10).

III

From all this it will be clear that the poverty of the gospel is not just economic poverty but a total emptiness, a total liberation from clinging. The first beatitude is all-embracing. The oppressed, the captives, the persecuted, the blind, the handicapped, the underprivileged, all are poor.

Now sometimes theologians have tried to rationalize evangelical poverty and to show that the teaching of Jesus makes sense. Futile endeavour! This is like trying to explain the cross which, Paul tells us, is supreme foolishness. One will come to an understanding of evangelical poverty not by rationalization but by treating it as a Zen koan.

Concretely, entering into a deep state of consciousness, I take the words "Blessed are the poor" into the very depths of my being. I become present to them. This is not a question of rationalization but of presence. And as I turn them over in contemplative fashion I begin to feel the wonder of it all: I even experience shock. Until now my unconscious belief was, "Blessed are the rich," but here is a totally different story. I remain with the words until I finally identify with them, become one with them, live them. Now in a flash I feel convinced that the poor are blessed because I am poor and I am blessed. Now I realize that Jesus was poor and Jesus was happy; Mary was poor and Mary was happy. Now I know beyond all doubt that this saying is true. Now I grasp the text not because I understand it rationally but because I live it. Or, more correctly, *I understand the text through life.*

And let me refer to one more Buddhist insight.

Buddhists have a saying that emptiness equals compassion. This means that poverty equals compassion. I empty myself totally in order to receive the whole universe into my heart (Eastern Buddhists say into my *hara* or belly) with an immense compassion. And this Buddhist saying can also be Christian. Jesus emptied himself, taking the form of a slave in order to save sinful men and women. The salvation of the human race is rooted in the compassionate poverty of the Son of God.

Likewise evangelical poverty leads to compassion or *is* compassion. If we want a norm for the authenticity of our poverty here it is: Does my Christian poverty lead to compassion for suffering people everywhere?

IV

When we see the centrality of poverty in the gospel story we understand how thousands upon thousands of dedicated men and women through the centuries have vowed themselves to a life of total poverty. Imitating the kenosis of Jesus they make a vow to live this most radical mystical life with its suffering and its immense joy.

"Beautiful theory," you say. "But the facts are different. Already in my short life I have met lots of discontented monks and religious who don't understand their vows of poverty. They say they are not poor by any standards. They feel guilty. They want to exchange their vow of poverty for a vow of simplicity. Besides, the church is scandalously rich. Even in third world countries, the church and religious orders own lots of property and land. Sometimes they remind me of multinational companies; and, worst of all, they have a reputation for paying low wages to their employees. All you say about mysticism is fine, beautiful, wonderful; but it just doesn't fit the facts."

I hear you. And it is not easy for me to respond. But let me try.

First, about the monks and religious who are ill-at-ease with regard to their vow of poverty. Alas, it is true that the mystical dimension of poverty was lost. I believe that much responsibility lies with the canon lawyers and moral theologians. They wanted to delineate clearly the meaning of poverty. *They wanted rules.* They wanted to tell the religious what he or she could or could not do. They wanted to tell us what was sinful and what was lawful. They were uncomfortable with mystery and they had little understanding of mysticism. The notion of process was absent from their laws. I cannot recall that they said anything about the link between poverty and compassion.

And so, observation of the vow of poverty degenerated into fidelity to the rule of poverty. "Keep the rule and the rule will keep you" was the great slogan. And the rule told people to turn in their earnings faithfully to the treasurer, to ask scrupulously for permissions, not to have superfluities. Wonderful rules! But what about the mystical joy of kenosis? What about compassion? Small wonder that many modern religious do not know what poverty is about. And the answer?

The answer is a renewed and authentic understanding of the New Testament. We find the answer when we identify with that man who found the treasure in the field and who *with great joy sold everything to buy the field*. That man was a mystic. Again, the answer is to see the life of poverty as a process whereby one becomes more and more poor as Jesus became more and more poor. It is a gradual losing of all things reaching a great climax in death and resurrection.

Your second comment about the wealth and power of the church is even more painful. It reminds me of the fact that we are all weak and sinful and that the followers of Christ commit the same sins as other people in our day. Let me first say a word about how we got into this mess.

The spirituality of the Bible is eminently communitarian. Religious experience is experience of the people; love of God is the love of the people; the Eucharist is the sacrament of the community; sin is the sin of the people. What counts is the community.

As Christianity developed in the West, however, the individual or personal dimension of religious experience was more and more stressed; and it was particularly stressed in the field of mysticism. Whereas the bride of the Song of Songs represented originally the people, the community, the church, she came to represent the individual soul searching lovingly for her bridegroom. In itself this was not a bad thing. But the sad truth is that the community dimension of spirituality and particularly of mysticism was obscured and even lost.

And all this had great repercussions on the approach to poverty. In religious orders the poverty of the individual was legalistically stressed, but the poverty of the institution was forgotten. We forgot that the community, the institution, the church, no less than the individual, have a mystical vocation to imitate the Jesus who emptied himself, taking the form of a slave.

Only in the last two decades have we become acutely aware of the need for communal poverty in the modern world. Only now do we become aware of the value of institutional virtue and the evil of institutional sin.

Here the Latin American bishops give courageous examples to the universal church. They see that recognition of our sinfulness is the necessary basis for change:

> The Latin American bishops cannot remain indifferent in the face of the tremendous social injustices existent in Latin America, which keep the majority of our peoples in dismal poverty, which in many cases become inhuman wretchedness . . . and complaints that the hierarchy, the clergy, the religious are rich and allied with the rich also come to us . . . Many causes have contributed to create this impression of a rich hierarchical church. The great buildings, the rectories and religious houses that are better than those of the neighbours, the often luxurious vehicles, the attire inherited from other eras, have been some of those causes.[1]

The bishops go on to say that a very great number of parishes and dioceses are in fact extremely poor and that many of the clergy live in complete deprivation. Yet they confess:

> Within the context of the poverty and even of the wretchedness in which the great majority of the Latin American people live, we, bishops, priests and religious, have the necessities of life and a certain security, while the poor lack that which is indispensable and struggle between anguish and uncertainty.[2]

They then ask for a conversion of heart, a new commitment to the poverty of Jesus, a commitment to the poverty of compassion whereby the person with two coats shares with the person who has none. Nor is it sufficient that this be a conversion of the individual. It must be communal. We must become the church of the poor as Jesus was the friend of the poor. Interesting too is their appeal to the masses of the people:

>A sincere conversion has to change the individualistic mentality into another one of social awareness and concern for the common good. The education of children and youth, at all levels, beginning in the home, ought to include this fundamental aspect of the Christian life.[3]

This conversion from an individualistic mentality to a mentality of social awareness is surely one of the greatest challenges not only to Christians but to all men and women interested in the survival of the human family.

And obviously this appeal of the bishops is particularly relevant for people living in the first world. For it is no secret that the affluent countries are exploiting the third world with harsh brutality. They are, as the Council observed, "hypnotized by economics;" and only a conversion to the poor will save us from global disaster.

In the first world a step in the right direction is the growing "exposure to the poor." Opportunities are given for people to see the grinding poverty and misery of the oppressed masses; opportunities are given for people to see the frightening consequences of nuclear war; statistics are available showing the billions of dollars spent on arms while millions die of hunger. If all this information flows into the prayer of Christians, bringing about a profound conversion of heart, we can have hope for the future.

V

I hear you say: "You talk about conversion of the heart. You talk about mystical emptiness in imitation of Jesus who emptied himself, taking the form of a slave. And you ask this not only from the individual but also from the community. You ask for conversion not only of the businessmen in Wall Street but even of the clerics in the Vatican. Surely this is not realistic. Surely this is a romantic dream."

If this is a romantic dream, then Christianity is a romantic dream. For this is the core of the Christian message. I realize that we are weak. I realize that we are particularly weak in all that concerns money. I realize that we all have our lapses and always will. But if we lose sight of "Blessed are the poor . . ." then we betray the gospel of Jesus Christ. Christianity is a radical religion, a mystical religion. Let us not water it down.

Realistically I see that the whole world will not be converted nor will all Christians. But if a significant number of people change their hearts and dedicate themselves to the poor, they can change the world. Remember the ten just men who could have saved Sodom. "Then he said, 'Oh let not the Lord be angry, and I will speak again but this once. Suppose ten are found there.' He answered, 'For the sake of ten I will not destroy it' " (Genesis 18:32).

Let us pray that ten just men and women will be found in the first world lest it succumb to the fate of Sodom.

NOTES

1. Joseph Gremillion, *The Gospel of Justice and Peace* (New York: Orbis Books, 1975), p. 471.
2. ibid.
3. ibid. See also the 1968 Medellín Conference Documents in *The Church in the Present-Day Transformation of Latin America in the Light of the Council* (Washington, D.C.: United States Catholic Conference).

14

Mysticism and peace

I

On the slopes of the Mount of Olives a small Franciscan chapel marks the spot where Jesus wept over the city he loved. "And when he drew near and saw the city he wept over it, saying, 'Would that even today you knew the things that make for peace' " (Luke 19:41).

I loved to come to this hallowed place to enjoy the panoramic view of Jerusalem and to cast my mind back over those centuries pregnant with history. At the centre of all stands the resplendent Dome of the Rock built magnificently by seventh-century Moslems on the very spot where Solomon constructed his beautiful Temple of cedarwood and gold. Here also stood the second Temple, the wonderful stones and the wonderful buildings towards which Jesus and his disciples turned their prayerful gaze. "Do you see these great buildings? There will not be left here one stone upon another that will not be thrown down" (Mark 13:2). Then the El Aqsa Mosque, the Antonia Fortress, the Tower of David. Further back the church of the Holy Sepulchre which commemorates Golgotha and the heartrending *Lama sabachani*. What vibrations from the past! What history! "O Jerusalem, Jerusalem ... How often would I have gathered your children together as a hen gathers her brood under her wings, and you would not!" (Luke 13:34).

I reflected on Jerusalem's bloody history of four millennia. City of David, city of peace, the holy city, the city away from which a prophet cannot perish! Jerusalem was besieged more than fifty times, conquered thirty-six times and destroyed ten times. It was conquered by Egyptians, Assyrians, Babylonians, Persians, Seleucids, Romans, Moslem Arabs, Seljuks, Crusaders, Saracens, Mameluks, and Ottomans. But two events stood out in my mind.

The first was in 587 B.C. when the Babylonians destroyed

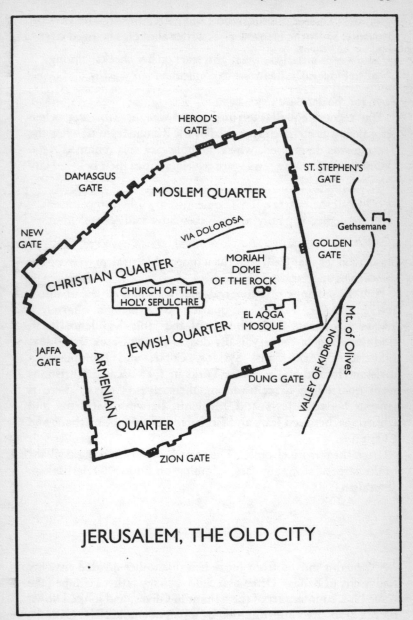

HEROD'S GATE

DAMASGUS GATE

ST. STEPHEN'S GATE

MOSLEM QUARTER

NEW GATE

VIA DOLOROSA

Gethsemane

GOLDEN GATE

CHRISTIAN QUARTER

MORIAH DOME OF THE ROCK

CHURCH OF THE HOLY SEPULCHRE

EL AQGA MOSQUE

JEWISH QUARTER

Mt. of Olives

JAFFA GATE

ARMENIAN

DUNG GATE

VALLEY OF KIDRON

QUARTER

ZION GATE

JERUSALEM, THE OLD CITY

Solomon's Temple of cedarwood and gold, dragging the Jews off into exile. Sadly the Hebrew poet writes about his beloved city:

> She weeps bitterly in the night, tears on her cheeks; among all her lovers she has none to comfort her. (Lamentations 1:2)

Alas, for the desolate city!

The second equally terrible event was in A.D. 135 when Jerusalem was mercilessly sacked by the Roman legions, when the Temple was desecrated, when the holy city was renamed *Aelia Capitolina,* when the Jews were banished from their beloved city forever:

> O God, the heathen have come into thy inheritance; they have defiled thy holy temple; they have laid Jerusalem in ruins. (Psalms 79:1)

Small wonder that Jesus told the women of Jerusalem to weep for themselves and for their children.

And the unhappy situation today! Jerusalem is carved up into a Jewish quarter, a Moslem quarter, an Armenian quarter, a Christian quarter. The Church of the Holy Sepulchre itself, traditional site of Calvary, is divided up among Greek Orthodox, Franciscans, Armenians, Syrians, Copts, and Ethiopians, a division effected by the ruling Turks in 1757 because Christians were quarrelling fiercely among themselves. And so there is tension between Jews and Moslems, between Moslems and Christians, between Jews and Christians, between Christians and Christians.

Then the terrorist bombs. The armed soldiers frisking civilians in the streets, stopping cars, climbing on buses. "O Jerusalem, Jerusalem . . . !"

II

My thoughts moved from Jerusalem to another divided city: my native city of Belfast. Often as a child with my father I climbed the Cave Hill, counterpart of the Mount of Olives, and looked down on the drab city almost hidden by a pall of smoke. The Catholic

Falls and the Protestant Shankhill. The Union Jack and the Tricolor. "No Pope here." "Remember 1690." "Join the IRA."

Even at that time Northern Ireland was a vicious police state, and I knew that I belonged to a repressed and underprivileged minority. But today! The inhuman atrocities of the army and the police: the equally inhuman response of the terrorists. The bombs, the snipers, the booby traps, the maimed, the blind, the armless, the legless. The soldiers smashing down doors and ripping the insides out of televisions in their search for guns. The lethal rubber bullets leaving children wounded and dying in the streets. The explosions in pubs and dancehalls. The senseless sectarian killings. The assassination squads of the British army. The secret interrogation centres. The horrendous prison conditions, the sophisticated and brutal torture. The men on the blanket. The dirty protest. The agonizing hunger strike. The intransigence of Margaret Thatcher. The cruel death of Bobby Sands. And on top of all, the massive unemployment, the grinding poverty, the institutionalized contempt for human rights. "And when he drew near and saw the city he wept over it saying, 'Would that even today you knew the things that make for peace' " (Luke 19:41).

But why do I speak of Jerusalem and Belfast? Think of the division from Berlin to Tehran, from Kampuchea to South Africa, from Warsaw to Kabul. Think of the violence in the streets of Chicago and New York. Think of the racial riots in London. And then you will realize that Jerusalem is a symbol of a world divided. Yes, the whole world is a Jerusalem, a global city where superpowers have created a fear of nuclear destruction, a global city cruelly divided between the wealthy north and the impoverished south, the starving many and the affluent few. "And when he drew near and saw the city he wept over it . . ." (Luke 19:41).

I have heard it said that the situation in Jerusalem is hopeless. No solution! I have heard it said that the situation in Belfast is hopeless. No solution! I do not believe this. If the situation in Belfast and in Jerusalem is hopeless, then the situation in the whole world is hopeless. For the problem is everywhere the same.

III

We all know that the basic problem is neither Jerusalem nor Belfast nor Moscow nor Washington. The basic problem is the human heart. "For from within, out of the heart . . . come evil thoughts, fornication, theft, murder, adultery, coveting, wickedness, deceit, licentiousness, envy, slander, pride, foolishness" (Mark 7:21). Wise old Jung reflecting on the awful happenings of the 1940s spoke of an unconscious psychic epidemic, vicious and brutal, stalking Europe like the black death of the dark ages; and one wonders if we are still in the throes of a psychic epidemic infinitely more pernicious than the black death. The Preamble of the Constitution of UNESCO clearly recognizes the psychic dimension of our predicament: "Since wars begin in the minds of men and women, it is in the minds of men and women that the defence of peace must be constructed."

All this is obvious and recognized by everyone. But how are we to heal the human mind and heart? We can heal broken legs and we can rebuild cities. But what about the mind?

The gospel tells us that the human mind and heart are healed only through metanoia. And the gospel is clear about the reasons for the destruction of Jerusalem. It says nothing about the economic, political, and military background. It says nothing about the awesome and ruthless power of the Roman legions against which the fanatical zealots could not stand. It says nothing about the arrogance of Vespasian and the cruelty of Titus. For underlying all this was a more fundamental problem:

You were not faithful to the covenant

or

You did not change your hearts

or

"You did not know the time of your visitation" (Luke 19:44)

Yes, the central problem was metanoia or change of heart.

This is the message of the gospel and, indeed, of the whole Bible. Jesus was following an Old Testament tradition when he said that infidelity to the covenant brings destruction. "Woe to you, Chorazin! woe to you, Bethsaida! for if the mighty works done in you had been done in Tyre and Sidon, they would have repented long ago, sitting in sackcloth and ashes" (Luke 10:13). They would have repented; they would have changed their hearts.

The problem then, the root problem, is conversion of heart. And vis-à-vis the modern world the gospel throws out the same challenge: "Do you want to avoid a nuclear holocaust? Do you really want peace? If so, change your hearts."

Divided city. Strumpet city. The harlot. The faithless one. Sodom and Gomorrah, Belfast, Jerusalem, Moscow, Dublin, Washington, Tokyo, London, Beijing, Cairo. The message is the same. "Unless you repent you will all likewise perish" (Luke 13:3).

IV

On the Mount of Olives I discovered a Zen temple. It was constructed by Nakagawa Soen whom I met at Mishima where he lives in an exquisite little temple called *Ryutakuji*. The Master felt that the holy city should have a Buddhist presence to complement the teachings of Jews, Moslems, and Christians. Modest and unassuming, the tiny temple is situated on the top of the hill. On one side, the Mount of Olives sweeps down to Jerusalem; on the other side, the Judaean wilderness sweeps down to the Dead Sea. The Master said with wry humour that his temple was close to the Dead Sea but atop the mountain of "O Live!"

But the panoramic view was not apparent from the dimly lit meditation hall where I sat for several hours with four Israelis and the Japanese teacher.

At first I was surprised to find a Buddhist temple there. I was even shocked. It seemed out of place. What was a Zen temple doing in the city of David, the city of Jesus, the city whence Mohammed ascended to heaven? But the longer I sat the more I realized that Zen has an important message for the monotheistic religions.

For the fact is that Zen abhors all divisions, abhors all use of the discriminating intellect, abhors all words (*no dependence on words and letters* is the great slogan) whereas the divisions and wars and quarrels among the monotheistic religions have been caused primarily by our clinging to words, to letters, to dogmas, to formulas, to structures, to doctrines. If only we could soar above all these formulations to meet the living God, Yahweh, who is our common Father. If only we could meet the God to whom the formulations point. If only we could move towards a mystical state of consciousness where all is one. Alas, instead of that, we have fallen into an idolatry of doctrines; we have judged people's orthodoxy by whether or not they subscribe to the correct formula; we have burned people at the stake because they did not use the right words. How much better if we judged orthodoxy by love of God and neighbour!

And Zen goes not only beyond words and letters but beyond fear, anxiety, greed, pride, lust, envy, anger. It goes to the serene atmosphere of unity, to the reconciliation of opposites, to the oneness of being. It has its change of heart, its metanoia, its *satori*.

Now what I say of Zen is true also of Christian mysticism. It also leads to an altered state of consciousness where all is one in God. If we are faithful to the gospel we will come to see that words and letters (even the most sacred words of the Bible) are no more than a finger pointing to the moon. Let us look at the moon which is God and let us join hands with Jews and Moslems whose eyes are fixed on the same God – the God of Abraham, of Isaac, of Jacob. Let us rise above that evil sectarianism which has wrought such havoc in Jerusalem, in Belfast, in Rome, and in Geneva.

Lest there by any misunderstanding, let me here add that I am not against words. They have their place. Without the finger we cannot see the moon. My point is that we have divinized words; we have made the relative absolute. Only by passing from a discursive, wordy Christianity to a mystical and supraconceptual Christianity can we authentically find God and authentically love our non-Christian brothers and sisters in a world that is fast becoming one.

V

About Christian conversion of heart I have already spoken at length. I have said that it consists in fidelity to the covenant, whereby we accent God's love and love in return. "We love because he first loved us" (1 John 4:19). I have said that fidelity to the covenant includes fidelity to the gospel teaching that the poor are blessed. Practically, I asked you to take the koan "Blessed are the poor," to become present to the words, to turn them over in your mind, to relish them, to be baffled by them, to live them until (perhaps after weeks or months or years) a tremendous inner revolution takes place whereby you become poor, you identify with Jesus poor, you experience the ecstatic joy of kenosis. Only then can you say that you understand the text.

Now in the same way I propose the koan "Blessed are the peacemakers for they shall be called the children of God" (Matthew 5:9). Read what the exegetes say (God bless them!) and learn all you can. But do not stop there. Become present to the words, turn them over in your mind, relish them, be baffled by them, live them until (perhaps after weeks or months or years) a tremendous inner revolution takes place whereby *you become a peacemaker, you identify with Jesus the peacemaker, you experience the ecstatic joy of being a peacemaker*. Now you understand the text at a new level of consciousness, at a mystical level of consciousness where all is one in Jesus.

You say: "But I need no great conversion in this area. I long for peace as do millions of others. What is this great revolution you talk about?"

You say you long for peace. And I believe you. But are you willing to pay the price? Pope John wrote an encyclical letter called *Peace on Earth* (*Pacem in Terris*) and, lo and behold, he said almost nothing about war and peace: the whole letter was about justice, about respect for the human dignity of every person and every group of persons in the whole world. We all say we want peace (and we certainly do fear nuclear war) but, if we are serious, we must make the sacrifices so that fewer people die of hunger, fewer people live in subhuman conditions, fewer people have their human dignity flaunted and trampled into the ground.

A conversion to peace includes a conversion to justice, to poverty, to the whole Sermon on the Mount, so that we turn the other cheek, love our enemy, do not resist the evil one, give away our cloak as well as our coat. Ay, there's the rub! What a revolution in consciousness! You and I have still a long way to go.

"All right," you say. "I have a long way to go. But I still have problems. If this is the real meaning of 'Blessed are the peacemakers' how come Christians took so long to understand the text? How come the Church preached the crusades, encouraged wars, threw holy water on guns and battleships? And there is the scandalous fact that Christians have been fighting among themselves for centuries."

Yes. Some things in our history make me blush. Christians have sinned like everyone else. But let me say a word about the background.

The early Christians loved peace and were troubled in conscience about serving in the Roman Imperial army. St Maximilian was martyred because he refused military service. St Martin of Tours remained in the army until called upon to kill in battle and then refused to do so. Tertullian (155–240) declared that in taking Peter's sword Jesus disarmed every soldier. Listen to Origen (185–254):

> No longer do we take the sword against any nation nor do we learn war any more since we have become the sons of peace through Jesus ... [1]

For Origen, Christians help the Emperor not by the sword but by their prayers. In short, in primitive Christianity there was a mystical and eschatological approach to peace, a belief that peace is God's gift as it was the farewell gift of Jesus: "Peace I leave with you, my peace I give to you ..." (John 15:27).

The problem began with the conversion of Constantine after the Battle of the Milvian Bridge in 312. How deeply Christian the Emperor was is a disputed and controversial point which need not occupy us here. Enough to say that Christianity became part of the establishment (a doubtful blessing indeed) with a growing sense of its duty to defend the Empire. We find Augustine (354–430) urging the soldier Boniface not to retire to a monastery but to take up arms in defence of the North African cities menaced by barbarian hordes. The same Augustine elaborated the "just war" theory which dominated Catholic moral theology until the Second Vatican Council. In fairness to Augustine we must remember that he wrote at a time when Rome was on the verge of collapse (it fell ignominiously in 411 before the onslaught of Alaric the Goth) and the barbarians were at the gates of Hippo where he was bishop.

I need not here trace the history of the just war theory. Only let me say that the mystical approach of the fathers gave way to the casuistic, legalistic approach of moral theologians with their endless distinctions and quibbles about when one may or may not kill. In the last chapter I said that love for the Lady Poverty was replaced by a collection of rules about poverty. Now let me add that love for the Prince of Peace was replaced by a collection of casuistic rules about when it was licit to make war, to kill, and to destroy. It is one more example of the awful wound inflicted on Christianity by the weakening of its mystical life.

VI

Yet the Holy Spirit is always at work; and I see developing in our poor world a new spirituality, a vibrant and beautiful spirituality of peace. It has been germinating for decades; it will bring forth more luxuriant fruit as time goes on. Ecumenical in nature, this spirituality is associated with the names of Mahatma Gandhi, Martin Luther King, Jr, Thomas Merton, Dorothy Day, Mother Teresa, Helder Camara, Daniel Berrigan, and a host of others. It takes its inspiration from the gospel but is open to the influence of non-Christian religions. It is greatly inspired by *Pacem in Terris* of Pope John, by *Populorum Progressio* of Pope Paul, by numerous statements of the World Council of Churches, by statements of the Latin American bishops. This spiritual current influenced the whole Jesuit order which in 1975 made a radical commitment to justice and peace as well as to solidarity with the poor.

This is a real mysticism for our time. I call it mysticism because it demands a total commitment to justice and nonviolence far beyond anything that reason could ask for. It is for people who are so much in love with peace and the Prince of Peace that they are willing to sell everything for the field in which the treasure lies buried. It is for people who glory in the cross of Our Lord Jesus Christ, Gandhi said powerfully that the violent person knows how to kill but the nonviolent person knows how to die. Indeed, anyone who makes a commitment to this way must be prepared to suffer and to die as did Gandhi, as did Martin Luther King, Jr, as did Anwar Sadat, as did Archbishop Romero. For the path to peace is drenched in blood: it is a path of martyrdom. Hence the shocking paradox that Jesus does not bring peace but the sword.

Let me outline some of the characteristics of this mystical movement, remembering that the process is still in its infancy and will grow to maturity as the years pass by.

1. It is a spirituality of total dedication to the poor. Not to the poor in a merely humanitarian sense but to the poor in whom one finds God. Listen to Gandhi:

> I count no sacrifice too great for the sake of seeing God face to face. The whole of my activity whether it may be called social, political, humanitarian or ethical is directed to that end. And as I know that God is found more often in the lowliest of His creatures than in the high and mighty I am struggling to reach the status of these. I cannot do so without their service. Hence my passion for the service of the suppressed classes.

In these words we find not only great compassion but also great faith. Gandhi himself said that he embraced nonviolence not because it was a successful way of liberating India from British rule but because it was the right thing to do. Its aim was not just freedom for the people but also the conversion of the oppressor. Gandhi had great faith in God, great faith in the power of truth.

2. It is a spirituality of radical nonviolence which refuses to tolerate killing of any kind even as a last resort, even in defensive action. It believes that there is no alternative to peace and that violence is no longer a way of solving problems. Hence it opposes both institutionalized violence and terrorist violence, leaving its adherents in a position of total vulnerability. It is a spirituality of

forgiveness of one's enemy, of turning the other cheek, of giving one's coat as well as one's cloak.

But here let me be clear. It is not a spirituality of ignominious surrender. Rather does it explore just anger, channelling human energy into righteous indignation and passionate love for justice. It fights by nonfighting, by suffering, by witnessing to the truth, by defying unjust authority. It demands not only great courage but also great intelligence — lovers of peace find ingenious ways of expressing their dissent in nonviolent ways. And they are willing to dialogue with the adversary, always courteous, always simple like the dove, always wise like the serpent.

3. It is a way of life. For it is one thing to undergo a conversion: it is another thing to live out this conversion in daily life. This spirituality demands a change of life-style whereby a love for peace and for the poor pervade one's every action and operate in all one's relationships. It is not enough to demonstrate against nuclear weapons (good and laudable though this is), we must also change our way of thinking and our way of living.

4. It believes that one best helps the poor by education — by raising their consciousness, by giving them a sense of their human dignity. Pope Paul said well that "the new name for peace is development." He spoke of "integral human development" meaning education of the whole person, including that person's religious and spiritual qualities.

"Wonderful," you say. "But you are talking activism, not mysticism. Where is the mystical element in all this frenetic work for peace and social justice?"

I'm glad you mentioned that. The task confronting us today is to unite activism with mysticism. And the spiritual movement I here describe tries to do just that. You ask for the mystical element?

First, all mysticism is summed up in the *Fiat* of Mary. Let it be done. Let God act. Let the forces of the universe work. *Wu-wei*. And this spirituality leaves everything to God. It believes in the power of truth, the power of the cross, the power of suffering, the power of death, the power of all those seemingly negative things which make way for the action of God and are finally the most positive of all. What could be more mystical than this?

Again, looked at rationally this spirituality is crazy, as the cross is crazy. The more reasonable policy might be to build up nuclear weapons, to defend oneself, to liquidate the enemy. Many stolid Christians take this position. They talk as though Jesus Christ was the great proponent of common sense. How little they understand the gospel! How little they understand the cross! "We preach Christ crucified, a stumbling block to Jews and folly to Gentiles, but to those who are called, both Jews and Greeks, Christ the power of God and the wisdom of God" (1 Corinthians 1:23–24). The foolishness of the cross is at the centre of the Christian mystical experience.

Can we dare hope that people of goodwill throughout the world will unite in this spirituality of peace? Can we hope that mystical and prophetic leaders will give us the guidance we need? Can we hope that the great religions, transcending sectarianism, will teach their disciples to love and to work for peace and justice? Listen to one great prophet of peace. Speaking to young people in France in 1981 Archbishop Helder Camara said:

> Shake the world . . . You young people, bursting with intelligence and creative imagination, prepare exhibitions and shows to demonstrate the folly of the arms race and to show what could be done with this money if it were to be spent otherwise . . . Political and military forces spend a million dollars per minute, $640 billion per year, to prepare for war and to manufacture nuclear arms . . . We know today that a nuclear submarine can carry 20 missiles which can destroy 800 cities like Hiroshima and Nagasaki . . . Is it not frightening? This could provoke a nuclear war capable of destroying all life on earth . . . Bread should be shared among all. Last year 50 million people died of hunger and the United Nations says that two-thirds of the world's population lives in subhuman conditions . . . We must go to the root of the problem, we must go to justice . . . Avoid the scandal of a small group of countries always richer because they crush the others, crush nearly all humanity . . . Be people determined to create a more livable world.

The power of the masses is immense. Public opinion can stop wars and halt the arms race. Tyrannical governments fear nonviolence much more than terrorism. Religion, an updated religion, can be an irresistible force in our modern world.

VII

"Beautiful!" you say. "But I have one more problem. You started this book with a promise to show me the unique and distinctive dimension of Christian mysticism, and you end up with Gandhi, with a Buddhist temple on the Mount of Olives – just as earlier you glorified Buddhist poverty, quoted Albert Einstein and spoke about the koan and the mandala. How come?"

I hear you. Let me be frank. I did not foresee that I would end this way. But as I wrote, the conviction grew within me that Christians can no longer stand alone. If we are to be faithful to Jesus of Nazareth, if we are to be faithful to the gospel in the modern world, if we are to be faithful to the Holy Spirit acting in the Council and in the masses of the people, in short if we are to be faithful to our vocation as Christians, we must join hands with people of other faiths. We must humbly learn from their theological insights and their age-old wisdom. We must learn from them while sharing our own treasures. Together with them we must work for a world peace which we alone cannot construct.

So if we want mysticism, let us first get beyond narrow sectarianism to authentic Christianity. Our challenge is to cooperate with others while retaining our identity and allowing them to retain theirs. Concretely, this means cooperating with others while growing in love for Jesus Christ and the gospel. This is the way of the future.

NOTE
1. *Contra Celsum* C.5, 33.

15

The woman

I

This book has been an exploration into the roots of Christian mysticism, an attempt to see what is unique, special, and distinctive in the Christian mystical path. Such an effort, however, would be woefully incomplete without a chapter on the role of the Virgin Mary. For she is the star of the sea, enlightening weary travellers, guiding them sweetly through turbulent waters to the gate of heaven.

Before speaking about mysticism proper, however, let me say a word about the role of Mary in the ordinary Christian life.

II

Mary plays a central role in the Christian story, particularly in the story of redemption. It all begins with Genesis which is a man-woman story, a deeply human drama wherein Eve has a principal role, playing opposite Adam and cooperating in his sin. Where would Genesis be without Eve?

And as the Fall is a man-woman story, so the Redemption, in the interpretation of the church fathers, is also a man-woman story. It is the story of Jesus and Mary. Remember how Paul speaks of Jesus as the second Adam: "The first man was from the earth, a man of dust; the second man is from heaven" (1 Corinthians 15:47). And the church fathers, commenting on Paul, speak of Mary as the second Eve. "Comparing Mary with Eve, they call her 'the mother of the living,' and still more often they say: 'death through Eve, life through Mary.' "[1] Again, the fourth gospel sees Mary as "the woman" to whom Jesus entrusts the beloved disciple and the whole human family. And Christian tradition sees this beautiful woman looking across the centuries to the first woman with whom the human race began. In short, as Eve cooperated with Adam in the sin of the world, so Mary cooperates with Jesus in giving life to the same world.

In all this, however, the Council warns against exaggerations. "We have but one Mediator, as we know from the words of the Apostle . . . For all the saving influences of the Blessed Virgin on men originate, not from some inner necessity, but from the divine pleasure."[2] And even more directly the Council states:

> The Church does not hesitate to profess this subordinate role of Mary. She experiences it continuously and commends it to the hearts of the faithful, so that encouraged by this maternal help they may more closely adhere to the Mediator and Redeemer.[3]

The subordinate role of Mary is something the Christian consciousness accepts quite naturally. It never seems that Mary is, so to speak, downgraded. For there is another kind of equality: an equality arising from love. Of this equality Jesus spoke when he called his disciples "friends." "No longer do I call you servants . . . but I have called you friends . . ." (John 15:14, 15). Here Jesus lovingly raises the disciples to the status of equals and his words were later concretized in the doctrine that, as Jesus was son by nature, we are sons and daughters by grace. Now my point is that what is true of the disciples is preeminently true of Mary to whom Scripture and tradition ascribe a unique role in the drama of salvation. Some theologians have even spoken of her as coredemptrix.

About Mary's privileges I need not speak in detail. Scripture scholars find more and more wealth in the early chapters of the third gospel. Archaeologists find ample inscriptions witnessing to a primitive church praying fervently to Mary. The apocryphal writings of the second and third centuries show us Christians fascinated by the person of Mary. After the Council of Ephesus (431), love for Mary grows both in the cultured monastic life and in the hearts of illiterate masses. In short, the whole church, people and shepherds alike, pour forth prayers to the Mother of God.

But to understand the Catholic approach to Mary, one must understand the Catholic approach to scriptural interpretation, a point with which I have struggled throughout this book. The Council, speaking of the role of Mary in the Old Testament, writes: "These earliest documents, *as they are read in the Church and are understood in the light of a further and full revelation*, bring the figure of the woman, Mother of the Redeemer, into a gradually sharper focus."[4] I italicize these words to emphasize that the Council goes beyond the historical-critical approach to the fuller sense of *sensus plenoir*. It finds references to Mary in Genesis, in Isaiah, in Micah, just as the Christian tradition has always found her in the wisdom literature.

What I am saying is that the praying church (the *ecclesia orans*) throughout the ages has well understood this equality stemming from love and from unique privilege. The praying people have well understood the love of Jesus for Mary and of Mary for Jesus. Forms of the Jesus prayer illustrates this well. There is, for example, the formula: "Jesus, Mary" or "Jesus, Mary and Joseph" or again (a formula which brings out the paradox of subordination and equality) "Jesus mercy: Mary help." I need not speak here of the *Memorare* of Bernard of Clairvaux, of the *Salve Regina* chanted hauntingly each evening in the hushed atmosphere of Cistercian monasteries, of the rosary recited by millions throughout the world. Enough to say that in Catholic spirituality of the last few centuries intimacy with Jesus and Mary has found a special place, expressing itself symbolically in the Sacred Heart of Jesus and the Immaculate Heart of Mary. The two hearts are one. Love for Jesus and love for Mary are not two things, but one thing.

Coming to mysticism, let me recall my earlier thesis that Christian mysticism consists in loving the Christian mystery and being transformed by it. Now I say that if we really live the mystery of Christ we will discover that we are also living the mystery of Mary. For she shares preeminently in the mystery of her Son. We will find that we are living the mystery of Jesus and Mary; we will find that we are transformed not only in the image of Jesus but also in the image of Mary.

III

I hear you say: "I resonate with what you say and it sounds theologically palatable. But I still have questions. The Protestant reformers were part of the *ecclesia orans*; yet they rebelled against the special cult of Mary. Moreover, some modern Christians protest that devotion to Mary detracts from that commitment to Jesus which is the very centre of the Christian life. What do you say to that?"

It is true that some modern Christians are not enthusiastic about devotion to Mary. But were the reformers like that? A Lutheran scholar, writing in *America* about the Virgin Mary, speaks of "the extraordinarily similar sentiments of the Father of the Reformation, Martin Luther, and of the Fathers of the Second Vatican Council."[5] In fact Luther had great devotion to Mary. He wrote copiously about her. He defended her perpetual virginity. He kept an image of the Virgin on the wall of his study. Listen to his prayer in his beautifully moving meditation on the *Magnificat*:

> O Blessed Virgin, Mother of God, you were nothing and all despised; yet God in His grace regarded you and worked such great things in you. You are worthy of none of them, but the rich and abundant grace of God was upon you, far above any merits of yours. Hail to you! Blessed are you, from henceforth and forever, in finding such a God.[6]

Nor was Luther alone. In Zurich the iconoclastic Zwingli (1484–1531) retained the *Hail Mary* in public worship. In some Lutheran orders the feast of the Immaculate Conception and the Assumption were retained well into the latter part of the sixteenth century. I need not here speak of the profound cult of Mary in the Greek and Russian churches and throughout the Middle East. All points to the consistency with which the *ecclesia orans* has honoured the mother of God.

I believe that the notion of a Mary usurping the place of Jesus comes later than the Reformation and coincides with the loss of a truly mystical mentality in the West. The mania for dividing things in an either-or way is sometimes (rightly or wrongly) attributed to Descartes. "You can have this or that; but you cannot have both: Jesus *or* Mary but not Jesus *and* Mary." What a disastrous dualism! Whereas primitive and medieval Christianity could see *the mystery of Christ* as a single entity including many mysteries – the Trinity, the Incarnation, the Redemption, the mystery of Jesus, the mystery of Mary – post-Cartesian theological thought began to chop everything up. And so we find a split not only between Jesus and Mary but even between God and His creation.

I myself reacted against this either-or mentality when I came East and met Zen. As you probably know, Zen abhors the divisions of the discriminating intellect and stresses the unity of being. I believe that dialogue with Zen helps us regain that mystical sense of oneness whereby we have no difficulty in accepting both Jesus and Mary.

Let me add that from the earliest times Mary was invoked as ark of the covenant and tabernacle of the Most High. She is filled with the presence of God. She is filled with the Holy Spirit. In her womb dwells the Word made flesh. All these symbols point clearly to the union of Mary with the Trinity and especially with her Son who is the Word. The thought of a Mary separated from the Trinity and from Jesus was totally foreign to the early Christian mentality, as it is foreign to any mystical mentality.

IV

Let me now describe how Marian devotion develops in the hearts of the faithful. These may begin with vocal prayer to Mary – reciting the rosary, or the litany of Loreto, or consecrating self to the Virgin Mary. And through this they may arrive at a certain intimacy with Mary whereby they speak spontaneously to her in times of trouble, asking for her help and protection. In an interview with *Time*, Lech Walesa, talking about his struggle with the authorities in Poland, speaks of his relationship with Mary. "When things got tragic or critical, I would say, 'Mother Mary, I'm losing, now what are you going to do about it?' Then I would take some time for myself. And I would say, 'What will be, will be. OK, it's your thing. How will you solve this?' " Then he would relax with the reflection that there was a leader other than himself: the Virgin Mary. Such intimacy with Mary informs, as it has always informed, the lives of countless Christians.

As intimacy grows, words become less necessary and we may simply find ourselves in the presence of Mary – an all-pervading presence, a feminine presence, a warm and loving presence. Earlier in this book I spoke of the so-called acquired and infused contemplation. I said that a time comes when contemplation is not something I *do* but something that *happens*. Now, in the same way, the presence of Mary becomes a *given*. Not that I have a mental picture of what she looks like. I may have no image whatever. Like Gerard Manley Hopkins I may experience the presence of Mary like the air I breathe – "wild air, world-mothering air, nestling me everywhere." Turning to Mary I may cry out with the poet:

> Be thou then, O thou dear
> Mother, my atmosphere

Yes, Mary is now the atmosphere in which I walk – a feminine atmosphere, a protecting atmosphere, a guiding atmosphere, a loving atmosphere.

It may be that at this time one prays by contemplating a symbol of Mary. I have spoken already of a form of contemplation consisting of "presence to a symbol" and at that time I spoke of presence to the Eucharist. Now let me add that there is a prayer of "just being" in the presence of Mary, "just being" in the protective love of Mary. Presence to Mary. One may be present to a Marian ikon. Or one may hold the rosary in one's hand. The sense of Marian presence is an altered state of consciousness. With it we are at the gates of mysticism.

But can we authentically speak of a Marian mysticism?

Here let me be clear. Earlier in this book I have associated mysticism with the unconditional, unrestricted love that goes on and on and on. Clearly, such love can be directed to God and to God alone. Consequently we can never say that Mary is the object of mystical experience. What we can say, however, is that Mary is our mystical guide, our mystical travelling companion, our mystical protectress. She has been invoked as Our Lady of the

Way. She can be compared to the cloud by day and the pillar of fire by night that guided the children of Israel through that great and terrible wilderness to the promised land. In short, Mary leads us beyond herself into the cloud of unknowing which is the mystery of her Son, as it is the mystery of the Father and the Holy Spirit. Entering this mystery and united with Jesus, we cry out: "Abba, Father!"

At this point, as we enter the night, Mary seems to disappear from consciousness. Of course she is present. But her presence is no longer tangible. We know that she is present not because we sense that all-pervasive closeness – "Be thou . . . my atmosphere" – but because of dark faith.

Through Jesus to the Father, with Mary as mystical companion. It is a beautiful path and a secure path. But it is not a rose garden. It may even be full of conflict and temptation. But Mary is the health of the sick, the refuge of sinners, the comfort of the afflicted, the help of Christians. She is at once most powerful and most faithful. When she is present, all is well.

Yet I do not say that his Marian path is the way of all Christians. On the journey to God there are many charisms, many gifts. In the lives of some Christian mystics, Mary remains in the background, imperceptibly present, not tangibly so. In the lives of others, her presence manifests itself forcibly at one period in their lives and then falls into the background. But she is always there – because she shares preeminently in the mystery of Christ into which the Christian mystic is necessarily drawn.

But can we speak of a certain pattern in this Marian mystical experience?

V

Earlier I tried to say that all Christian mystical experience is modelled on the covenant. God loves me with an everlasting love. His fidelity reaches to the skies and His love will never fail. I open my heart to accept this love and, having accepted it, I love Him in return – with that unconditional, unrestricted love that goes on and on and on. Through this love I enter into altered states of consciousness as I relish that all-embracing and enveloping presence. Presence leads to union. I become one with God. Yet I am not God.

Looking at Marian mysticism in the light of this model, we see that the first step consists not in loving Mary, but in accepting her love. As in all mysticism the initiative comes from God Who gives consolation without previous cause, so in this Marian path the initiative comes from Mary who enters our lives in a gratuitous way. As the wounded stag appears on the hill, so also on the hill appears one of whom it was said, "And a sword will pierce through your own soul also" (Luke 2:35). As Jesus was wounded with love, so Mary also is wounded with love for us.

The second step consists in loving her in return. While relishing her presence, fragrant like the air we breathe and warm as the atmosphere around us, we enter into altered states of consciousness whereby with her we recite our *Fiat*, with her we recite our *Magnificat*, with her we ponder in our hearts the mysteries of Jesus. With her we go through Jesus to the Father: "Abba, Father!" And in this way we undergo a profound metanoia and are transformed.

This love for Mary terminates at the Father. But it is authentic love for Mary, just as when we love people for God, we authentically love those people. Let me mention some characteristics of this Marian mystical love.

Traditionally love for Mary is associated with chastity. But chastity in the earliest tradition was not primarily centred on sexuality as it is today. The author of *The Cloud* calls a woman unchaste when she loves her husband for his money and not for himself. Chaste and perfect love, the great ideal of St Bernard and the galaxy of mystics who surrounded him, was "disinterested love." It was the love of which Jesus spoke when he said: "If you loved me, you would have rejoiced, because I go to the Father" (John 14:28). Such love is totally centred on the beloved; yet paradoxically it brings true happiness and leads to the discovery of the true self.

Chastity or chaste love is mystical experience. St Ignatius tells us that shortly after his conversion he had a mystical vision of Mary which brought a total liberation. Ignatius was slow to accept the authenticity of his own visions; but this one brought such remarkable fruits of liberation that he felt confident that it was the work of the Virgin herself. So powerful is the love of Mary for us and so powerful is the love she calls forth in our hearts.

Here let me pause to make a comment on chastity. It will be remembered that I said that love for poverty is a mystical experience, but that we obscured this mystical dimension with rules and regulations and guilt trips of all kinds. Similarly I said that love for peace is originally a mystical experience, but we obscured it with casuistic rules about just wars and the legitimacy of killing people in certain circumstances. Now let me say that chastity also was originally a mystical experience, an experience of mystical love. But we obscured it with all kinds of *do's* and *don'ts* about sexuality which obscured the mystical dimension of chaste love, and often caused anguishing scrupulousity and guilt to the most innocent people. Alas for legalism! Alas for pharisaism!

Chaste love is modelled on the love of Mary herself. While we poor human beings lost the image of God in which humanity was originally created, Mary never lost this God-like image. Her love was disinterested from the beginning. She was immaculate.

Again, love for Mary is love for the whole church of which she is the model. It is not an exclusive Mary-and-I love, but a love stretching out to baptized Christians, to Jews, to Moslems, to Hindus, to Buddhists, and to all men and women of goodwill. The universal or social dimension of Marian love appears in the sayings of the great mystical visionaries of our times. These speak of Mary's concern for a world moving towards nuclear war and total destruction. The keynote of their message is that peace will only come through prayer and conversion of heart: "Pray! Pray! Pray!"

VI

But let me speak about the doctrine of the Assumption, defined by Pius XII in the apostolic constitution *Munificentissimus Deus* in 1950. This constitution speaks of Mary as the new Eve who "although subject to the new Adam is most intimately associated with him in the struggle against the infernal foe." It goes on to say that just as the resurrection of Jesus was an essential part and the final sign of his victory, so it was fitting that "the struggle which was common to the Blessed Virgin and her divine Son should be brought to a close by the glorification of her virginal body."

As can be readily seen, the constitution associates Mary with the redemptive work of Jesus and claims that just as the body of Jesus rose, so the body of Mary was assumed into heaven. Karl Rahner explains the doctrine by calling Mary "the perfectly redeemed and the representative of perfect redemption." He writes that Mary "has entered into that perfect fulfilment which every Christian hopes for from the grace of God, as the outcome and fruit of human life."[8]

Remember that when Paul speaks of the resurrection of Jesus, he speaks in the same breath of the resurrection of the human family. "For if the dead are not raised, then Christ has not been raised" (1 Corinthians 15:16). As Jesus rose, we also will rise. And the apostolic constitution tells us that Mary "even now" has achieved this state of glorification.

Now all this is important for understanding the sense of Marian presence about which I have spoken. Just as the Risen Jesus is present with us in his glorified body, just as he walks with us through life on our way to Emmaus, so Mary assumed into heaven is "even now" present with us in her glorified body. That is why we can compare her to the air we breathe. That is why we can believe that she guides us through life like the cloud by day and the pillar of fire by night. She is the perfectly redeemed.

Having said all this, however, let me confess that the doctrine of the Assumption has been the subject of controversy, a cruel bone of contention. Among its enthusiastic supporters, however, we find no less a person than Carl Jung who speaks of the 1950 definition as "the most important religious event since the Reformation."[9] Jung's theology is often unorthodox (how could it be otherwise?), but underlying the unorthodox theology are jewels of psychological and theological insight.

Jung was fascinated by the way in which the doctrine came to be defined. Pius XII claimed that he received petitions from the whole Catholic world begging for definition of a doctrine that had been in the hearts of the people for more than a millenium and that was part of their living faith. The Pope saw here the action of the Holy Spirit speaking through the masses of the people in union with their shepherds. Once again it was a question of the *sensus fidelium*, the *ecclesia orans*. Once again it was *vox populi: vox Dei*.

Now Jung saw this *sensus fidelium* as the collective unconscious of the church. It was perfectly obvious, he wrote, that for some time there has been a deep longing in the masses for the glorification of the feminine, a longing to recognize Mary as Queen of Heaven. "Anyone who has followed with attention the visions of Mary which have been increasing in numbers over the past few decades, and has taken their psychological significance into account, might have known what was brewing. The fact especially that it was largely children who had the visions might have given pause for thought, for in such cases the collective unconscious is always at work."[10] In defining the doctrine, he claims, the Catholic church was obviously listening to the people.

As can be seen, the historical-critical approach, which was later to hold the field in scriptural and patristic studies, played a minimal part in the definition. This delighted Jung. "The dogma of the Assumption is a slap in the face for the historical and rationalistic view of the world, and would remain so for all time if one were to insist obstinately on the arguments of reason and history."[11]

He goes on to say that in accepting living tradition as a theological source and in remaining in touch with the movements of the Holy Spirit, Catholicism manifests her material spirit, whereas the Protestant emphasis on reason manifests a paternal spirit. And he concludes with an ecumenical and almost humorous plea for union and cooperation between sister and brother.

Let me add, however, that Jung wrote in the 1950s and that the tables have turned since then. Now Catholic scholars immersed in the historical-critical approach are in danger of losing their sense of archetype and symbol, whereas Protestant scholars move towards the sense of mystery. Perhaps Jung's brother-and-sister prophecy is becoming a reality.

VII

Since Jung wrote confidently about the unconscious longing in the masses for the exaltation of the Mother of God, psychologists and theologians everywhere have come to recognize the importance of the feminine dimension in religious experience. Just as in our affective lives we need masculine and feminine influence in order to grow, so in our religious lives we need this dual influence. Chinese philosophy reminds us of this. It insists that there must be balance between the *yin* and the *yang* in the human body, in the human psyche, in culture, in politics, in economics – and, we might add, in the approach to God. Without this balance, men and women can become sick. Without this balance, the whole culture can become sick.

Now the fact is that Christian symbols, as we now use them, are largely masculine. Realizing that this could cause imbalance, psychologists and theologians are studying the feminine in God. They speak of God not only as father but also as mother. They see the Holy Spirit, *Sophia*, as a feminine principle. These studies are only beginning. I believe they are of crucial importance for the future of theology and for the future of world culture.

And yet the feminine dimension in God is not enough. We need a feminine dimension in redemption. If our prayer is to be fully human we need not only a man of flesh and blood who was like us in all things except sin – who was weary, tempted, and rejected; we also need a woman of flesh and blood to whom we can turn in time of need. Traditionally this woman has been Mary. She has been "our life, our sweetness and our hope." She has been the health of the sick, the refuge of sinners, the comfort of the afflicted, the help of Christians.

And in all this she plays a role that Jesus cannot play. This may sound offensive to pious ears which rightly stress the unique mediatorship of Jesus. But I ask you to reflect that, in becoming flesh, the Word took on the limitations of flesh. He was a Jew, born in a certain country, speaking a certain language, educated in a certain culture, and thinking according to certain cultural patterns. And included in these limitations is the fact that he was a man, not a woman. And so the Catholic tradition has held that he entrusted the feminine role to Mary, not because she was equal to him as mediator, but because he loved her and he loves us.

And so the masses of the people have always prayed to Mary. If one goes to the great shrines of Mary throughout the world; if one goes to Guadalupe or Lourdes or Fatima; if one goes to Quiapo or Baclaran here in Manila; if one watches the prayer of the people, it is difficult to deny that the Holy Spirit is present and that Mary is present. She is indeed our life, our sweetness, and our hope.

NOTES

1. *Lumen Gentium* C.8, 56; *The Documents of Vatican II*, ed. Walter M. Abbot (New York: American Press, 1966), p. 88.
2. ibid, p. 90.
3. ibid, p. 92.
4. ibid, p. 87.
5. John J. Elliott, "The Image of Mary: A Lutheran View". *America*, New York, 27 March 1982.
6. ibid.
7. "An Interview with Lech Walesa". *Time*, New York, 4 January 1982.
8. See Karl Rahner, *Theological Investigations: Vol.I God, Christ, Mary, and Grace.* (New York: Seabury; London: Darton, Longman and Todd, 1961), pp. 224ff.
9. C. G. Jung, *Answer to Job* (Princeton; Princeton Univ. Press, 1969), p. 464.
10. ibid., p. 461.
11. ibid., p. 467.

Epilogue

The stag appears on the hill, wounded and thirsty and longing for cool waters. He is wounded with compassion; he is wounded with love.

Jesus is the wounded stag. And Christian mysticism begins and ends with the mystery of his cross and the mystery of his great love. This is the love which reveals the Father. This is the love which impels him to lay down his life for his friends. This is the love from which neither death, nor life, nor angels, nor principalities, nor things present, nor things to come can separate us.

And the love of God in Christ Jesus creates something new in us. It makes us cry out in ecstasy: "Jesus is Lord!" It makes us identify with Jesus in the intimate call: "Abba, Father!" It effects a change of heart and a revolution in consciousness whereby we are totally and radically and foolishly committed to the gospel. In the modern world it effects a change of heart and a revolution in consciousness whereby we are totally and radically committed to peace. As today there is no living Christianity without a living commitment to peace, so there is no mystical Christianity without a mystical commitment to peace.

In this book I have written about the social implications of Christian mysticism, stressing the need for conversion to peace. For everywhere we need conversion. Everywhere we need total commitment to peace. It is a question of survival. And this total conversion and radical commitment will not come from an enlightened assessment of the military potential of the super-powers. It will not come from studying the just war theories of the old moralists. It will not come from wild panic at the awful consequences of nuclear conflagration. All this might help. But the crucial thing is a radical, foolish, and mystical love for the gospel.

I concluded this book with a chapter on one whose eyes are fixed on the wounded stag. She asks for a radical commitment to the gospel when she says quite simply: "Do whatever he tells you" (John 2:5). With these words she describes the path of Christian mysticism and shows us the way to peace.

INDEX

Aaron, 263
Abraham, 217, 322, 336
Absence of God, 251–7
Acquired contemplation, 248
Acquired presence, 248
Adam, 269, 344–5
Alaric the Goth, 339
Ambrose, St, 218
Anger, handling, 260–2
Anxiety, 263–4
Aquinas, Thomas, 234, 235, 298–9
Aristotle, 267
Assumption: doctrine of, 352–4;
    feast of, 347
Augustine, St, 213, 235, 230–40, 271,
    290, 338–9

Baptism, 281
Begin, Menachem, 213
Belfast, 332–4
Benedict XII, Pope, 256
Benedictus Deus (1336), 256
Bernard of Clairvaux, St, 346, 351
Berrigan, Daniel, 339
Bible, see Scriptures
Boniface, 338–39
Bouyer, Louis, 225, 228, 230
Bread, as symbol, 302–3
Butler, Edward Cuthbert, 239–40

Camara, Archbishop Helder, 339,
    342
Centre of soul, doctrine of, 267
Chastity, 351–2
Children: as sensing God's presence,
    244; visions of, 354
Christ, see Jesus Christ
Church, scandal of richness, 325–
    8
The Church Today, 319

The Cloud of Unknowing, 213, 224,
    235, 249, 290, 320, 351
"The Community liturgy", 298
Community of God, importance of,
    219–21; in Eucharist, 298–301
Connaturality, knowledge of, 234–5
Constantine, 338
The Constitutions of the Society of
    Jesus, 318
Contemplation: acquired, 248;
    infused, 248–9; of Virgin Mary,
    313–20
Conversion, need for, 270, 282–5,
    327–8, 335, 337, 357
Corpus Christi, feast of, 299, 306
Council of Ephesus (431), 345
Covenant, 274–85; new, 279, 282
Covetousness, as enemy, 323

Darkness: Moses as seeing God in,
    240–1; in mysticism, 251–7
Day, Dorothy, 262, 339
Death, experience upon approach-
    ing, 245–6
Decision making, through con-
    templation, 316
Descartes, 347
Desert: as place of God's revelation,
    213–19; as place to meet the Devil,
    258–65
Desolation, in mysticism, 251–7
Devil: conflict with, in desert, 258–
    65; temptation of Jesus, 266, 268–
    9
Dionysius, 228, 229, 234, 241

Eating, mysticism of, 296–7
Ecclesia orans, 220, 347, 354
Eckhart, Meister, 213
Einstein, Albert, 284–5, 343

Elias, 239
Elizabeth, 268
Essence, God's presence by, 247
Essenes, 215, 297
Eucharist: community dimension, 298–301; importance of, 219, 279; Jesus' presence in, 293–7, 307–8; mysticism in, 293–311; raising of Sacred Host in, 306–7; as sacrifice and offering, 308–10; as symbol, 302–3, 305, 307
Eve, 271, 344–5, 352
Evil, problem of, 270–1. *See also* Sin

Fabri, Felix, 215
Faith, 223
False mysticism, 229
Feminine dimension, in God, 355–6
Fiat, as prayer of Mary, 313–17, 341
Francis de Sales, St, 264
Francis of Assisi, St, 292, 322
Friendship with Jesus, 287–8

Gandhi, Mahatma, 262, 339, 340, 343
Global consciousness, 318–20
God; absence of, 251–7; the feminine in, 355–6; presence of, 243–50
Grace, God's presence by, 247
Gregory of Nyssa, St, 213, 228, 234, 240, 241

Helena, Empress, 274
Historical-critical approach to Scriptures, inadequacy of, 234
Homilies on the Exodus, 228
Hopkins, Gerard Manley, 349

Ignatius of Loyola, St, 242, 249, 269, 271, 272, 290, 291, 292, 309, 318, 351–2
Immaculate Conception, feast of, 347
Immaculate Heart of Mary, 346
Infused contemplation, 248–9
Infused presence, 248
Injustice, contemplation to deal with, 317

The Inner Eye of Love, 223
Ireland, political situation in, 332–4
Isaac, 217, 322, 336

Jacob, 217, 259, 336
Jaspers, Karl, 282
Jerusalem: history of, 230–2; map, 331; as symbol of divided world, 334
Jesus Christ: friendship with, 287–8; mystery of, 225–9; mystical relationship with, 286–92; as one of poor, 321, 324; temptation of, 213, 266, 268–9; as wounded stag, 227
Jesus prayer, 346
John, 242, 276, 292, 298
John, Pope, 337, 339
John of the Cross, St, 213, 227, 229, 236, 241, 247, 248, 256, 267–8, 278, 318, 323
John the Baptist, 213
Joseph, 313
Jung, C. G., 259, 304, 312, 334, 353–4, 355
"Just war" theory, 339

King Jr, Martin Luther, 262, 339
Knowledge of connaturality, 234

Lateran Council, Fourth, 306
Lawrence, Brother, 243
Lex orandi: lex credendi, 220, 301
Life of Moses, 228, 240
Love, 223, 227, 234, 237, 247–8, 251, 275–82, 287
Luke, 268, 269, 313
Luther, Martin, 347

Malachi, 299
Mandala, 304–5, 307, 310, 311
Martin of Tours, St, 338
Martyrdom, 310, 340
Mary, Virgin, 268, 273, 284, 292, 322; devotion to, 348–9; doctrine of Assumption, 352–4; as feminine in God, 355–6; love of church for, 345–6, 351–2; mystery of, 346, 348; as mystic, 313–20; as our

Mary, Virgin, [*cont'd*]
mystical guide, 349–50; and Protestant reformers, 347; role in Christian story, 344–5
Mary Magdalen, 268
Mary of Bethany, 290
Maximilian, St, 338
Meaning, loss of, 252–3, 254
Memorare, 346
Merton, Thomas, 262, 339
Metanoia, Christian, 245, 279–85
Michaelangelo, 241
Milvian Bridge (312), Battle of the, 338
Monstrance, 306–7
Moses, 216, 217, 218, 228, 243, 245, 253, 255, 263, 274, 275, 290; friendship with God, 237–8; knowledge of presence of God, 235–7; as lawgiver, 241; as leader, 241–2; as mystic, 233–42; as prophet, 241; as seeing or not seeing God, 238–41
Munificentissimus Deus, 352
Mystery of iniquity, 270–1
Mystery, mysticism as, 225–6
Mysticism, Christian: challenge to renew, 231–2; compared to Buddhist and Hindu, 217; defined, 223–32; false, 229; with Jesus, 286–92; misunderstandings of, 230; objective dimension to, 224; origin of word, 225–6; states of consciousness, 229; symbols of, 226–7; universal vocation to, 246–7

Nilus, St, 228
Nuclear war, 335

Oedipus, 252
Oppression, contemplation to deal with, 317
Origen, 228, 235, 290, 338
Original sin, 269–70

Paul, St, 215–16, 221, 225, 228–9, 235, 239, 242, 251, 261, 262, 271,
275, 280, 281, 283, 284, 285, 287, 288, 291–2, 295–6, 297, 298, 303, 318, 323, 324, 344, 353
Paul, Pope, 285, 339, 341
Peace, mystical movement of, 330–43
Peace on Earth (Pacem in Terris), 337, 339
Peter, 271, 287, 315, 322, 338
Peter of Lombard, 306
Pius XII, Pope, 352, 353–4
Plato, 267
Poor, exposure to, 328–9. *See also* Poverty
Populorum Progressio, 339
Poverty: Buddhist, 322–3, 324; as compassion, 324; contemplation to deal with, 317; mystical joy of, 321–9
Prayer, 238, 288–9, 299–301; life flowing into, 312–20; of offering Eucharist as, 307–10; of quiet, 244–5
Presence, God's: acquired, 248; by essence, 247; by grace, 247; infused, 248; by love, 247–8
Psychotherapy, 252

Queen of Heaven, Mary as, 354
Qumran, 215, 297

Rahner, Karl, 246
Romero, Archbishop, 340

Sacrament, importance of, 217–19, 220–1, 228
Sacred Heart of Jesus, 226–7, 346
Sadat, Anwar, 213, 340
Sands, Bobby, 333
Salva Regina, 346
Satan, *see* Devil
Scriptures: importance of, 217–19, 220–1, 228; inadequacy of historical-critical approach, 234
Sensus fidelium, 220, 354
Simeon, 313
Sin, 269·71; original, 270, 312
Sinai, map, 214

AAO-0545

Soen, Nakagawa, 335
Solomon, 330
Soul, centre of, doctrine of, 267
"The Spiritual Canticle " 227, 256
Spiritual Diary, 318
Spiritual Exercises, 269, 309
Symbol: being present to, 303; Eucharist as, 302–3, 305–6, 307

Temptations, 258–65; of Jesus, 213, 266, 268–9
Teresa, Mother, 339
Teresa of Avila, St, 213, 229, 238, 245, 282, 289, 290, 292
Tertullian, 338
Thatcher, Margaret, 333
Theodoret, 228
Theologia Mystica, 228
Thérèse of Lisieux, 253–5
Thomas, St, 239–40, 247, 255
Time, 348
Titus, 334
Transubstantiation, doctrine of, 306–7
Trinity, as mandala, 310–11

Universal consciousness, 318–19
Universal vocation to mysticism, 246–7

Vatican Council (1963–65), Second, 218, 231–2, 234, 246, 280, 283, 288, 293, 294, 310, 316, 318–19, 328, 339, 345, 346, 347
Vespasian, 334
Viaticum, 299
Vision, as goal of mysticism, 255–6
Void, 289
Vox populi: vox Dei, 220, 354

Walesa, Lech, 262, 348
Western Mysticism, 239
Word, *see* Scriptures
World Council of Churches, 283, 339
Wounded stag, Jesus as, 227

Yin/yang balance, 355

Zwingli, Ulrich, 347